COLLECTOR'S VALUE GUIDE TO

ORIENTAL DECORATIVE ARTS

Sandra Andacht

Antique Trader Books

A division of Landmark Specialty Publications

ISBN: 0-930625-80-3
Library of Congress Catalog Card Number: 97-74597

Editor: *Kyle Husfloen*

Book Designer: *Virginia Hill*

Design Assistants: *Lynn Bradshaw, Aaron Wilbers, Barb
Brown, Donna Bruun, Karen Curler*

Cover Design: *Jaro Sebek*

Please note: Though listings have been double-checked and every
effort has been made to insure accuracy, neither the author,
editor nor the publisher can assume responsibility for any losses
that might be incurred as a result of consulting this guide, or of
errors, typographical or otherwise.

Printed in the United States of America

To order additional copies of this
book or a catalog please contact:

 Antique Trader Books
P.O. Box 1050
Dubuque, Iowa 52004
1-800-334-7165

CONTENTS

●

ACKNOWLEDGEMENTS

The author extends her sincere appreciation to the following for their contributions and support: Jeffrey Andacht, Stuart Andacht, Debbie Andin, Marvin Baer, Robert Benedict, Philip Cadeaux, David Camisa, Enes Carnesseca, Dennis Carroll, Alicia Celli, Arlene and Jim Constantine, Vera Curapic, Dorothy Egan, John Emmerson/The Emmerson Collection, Stephen Feldman/Asian Rare Books, Stephen Golden, Lisa Field, Mark Fogel, Carolyn Goodin, Florence C. Holmes, Kyle Husfloen, Teddy Ioannou, Harold Jaffe, Mike Kaye/ The Mike Kaye Collection, Shelly Kaye, Spyros Konitsiotis, Virginia and Frederick Korz/ The Korz Collection/Wing Antiques, Bernard McManus, Robert Miller/ A Step Behind, Miracle Ventures Inc. Oriental Art, Joan Molen, Cindy Pagan, NADA, Jack Pavlick/The Pavlick Collection, Michael Pearce, Louie Pharr and David Greenbaum/The Pharr/Greenbaum Collection, Peter Piacentini/The Piacentini Collection, Arlene Rabin, Linda and Jaime Ramirez, Tomoko and Philip Rosenfeld, Theresa & Richard Schirripa, Mrs. Phyllis Signoriello, James Signoriello, Florence Simon, Roni Simon, Elizabeth Soum, Irene Stella, Joan Stigliano, The Orientalia Journal, Judy and George Voll, Donna and Harvey Weinreb, Don Wisser, Mike Zadrow, Hess Zunk.

Photography:
Arthur Field, Field Studio, Little Neck, New York

FOREWORD

I am honored to write this foreword. I have been Sandra Andacht's friend and associate for more than 15 years and I am always amazed at her depth of knowledge and her extraordinary enthusiasm. Whenever she has been stymied by some object, she has persisted until she was able to find the information needed. She has the good fortune to have the gift of observation and even the smallest details of various objects are stored in her mental computer as well as her electronic computer. In addition, she is surrounded with devoted associates and friends, who, when called upon by Sandra, always do their utmost to help in her quest for information. Her reference library is extensive, and she often lends materials as well as her services. She is a superb teacher because of the humanistic impulse to bring all the details into line with the arts, the passions and the fears of people who experience and use Oriental decorative arts in daily life as well as making these objects parts of their collections.

Determining values for Oriental decorative arts and antiques is quite difficult because values are subject to the variances of the market. Realized prices obtained from well known auction houses are only one part of the overwhelming task of obtaining values. One must allow for economic variables, political variables (e.g.: Hong Kong), as well as psychological variables when making judgments about items which are being acquired for a collection.

Another one of Sandra's many gifts is the ability to make "fair" judgments. She is able to detach herself from her personal preferences when evaluating an object. I have worked with her and know this to be true.

The amount of time and energy that went into the preparation of this book is mind boggling. I know of no one more capable and competent to have completed such a monumental task. I am sure that the *Collector's Value Guide to Oriental Decorative Arts* will become and remain the No. 1 reference book for collectors and aficionados for many years to come.

—*Harold Jaffe*

(Harold Jaffe is President of the Louis Comfort Tiffany Society and Founder of the Appraisal Studies Programs at New York University, George Washington University and Long Island University. He is the Director of the Institute of Appraisal Arts and Sciences and Senior Member of the American Society of Appraisers.)

Chapter 1
ARMOR, ACCOUTREMENTS AND WEAPONRY

——————————●——————————

ARMOR

————●————

Domaru parade armor, 17th c., the black lacquered zunari-kobuto with short fukugaeshi pierced with crests and decorated with gold leaf, and with five stage shikoro laced with purple and white silk thread, the large maedate decorated with gold leaf, the wakidate formed as a Buddhist ken; the iron mempo black lacquered and formed as a grimacing face, the four lame shikoro laced with white silk thread; the nine stage gold lacquered okegawa-do laced in white and red silk thread with a rising sun motif, mounted with a deerskin pouch; with matching sode, kusari-gote, kote hidate and suneate; with fur shoes; with wood storage box (Color Illus. page 27) **$50,000-70,000**

Composite Nimai-do (suit of armor), 18th or 19th c., eight plate russet iron hoshi-kabuto (helmet bowl), the black lacquered fukigayeshi with gilt mon, black lacquered-style mempo of iron with throat guard of black lacquered iron; the Yokohagi-style nimai-do of two piece horizontal plate form engraved with Bashiko standing on the back of a dragon amid clouds, the kusazuri (hip guards) and haidate (thigh guards) of black lacquered leather, the Bishamon gote (armored sleeves) and integral sode (shoulder guards) with black lacquered iron plates, black lacquered leather suneate (shinguards), the whole laced in blue **6,000-8,000**

Nimai-do, do of koane with gold leaf and laced orange and set with eight kasazuri of five plates of kozane each, all gilded and laced, suji-kabuto of sixty-two plates lacquered black and with four lame gilt shikoro, unsigned; mempo with russet lacquer and four lame yodare-kake, o-sode and haidate gilded and laced; Shino-gote with gilt-iron plates; o-tateage-suneate of six integral gilt-iron plates; together with a gusoku-bitsu............**12,000-16,000**

ACCOUTREMENTS

————●————

Abumi (stirrups), inlaid iron, Kaga Province, 18th c., conventional shape, each decorated with large peony blossoms, foliage and scrolls in silver hirazogan (inlay), the interior red lacquer, 11" long, losses to lacquer **$2,500-3,500**

Abumi, lacquered iron, 18th c., the gold ground decorated with silver flowerbeads, conventional shape, the interior nashiji, cracked, chips, 12" l. **1,500-2,000**

Sword stand, lacquered, 19th c., for three swords, decorated on the nashiji ground with fowl in gold and colored takamaki, 20½" h., worn **1,200-1,800**

Sword stand, lacquered iron, 19th c., for five swords, conventional form, standing on large feet with roiro-mura-nashiji ground, the cross piece with dragon and waves with Mt. Fuji in the background, losses to lacquer, 20¼" h. **900-1,200**

Swordcase (Katana Zutsu), 17th c., decorated with gohei mon in gold hiramakie on a crushed raden ground, interior in roiro, copper fittings, losses to raden, 43½" l **1,500-2,500**

WEAPONRY

●

Arrows, bow and quiver, 19th c., the quiver of tan leather containing two removable inner containers held by a spacer, lacquered in brown on the inside, twenty arrows, black-lacquered bow bound with red-lacquered rattan, the quiver and arrows approximately 35" l., the bow approximately 87" l., some arrow tips missing, lacquer cracked, the set **$3,000-5,000**

Matchlock gun, early 19th c., Yonezawa-style, cylindrical barrel slightly flared toward the muzzle, decorated with silver, wood stock, brass plate with internal spring mechanism, iron hammer arm, trigger guard and ramrod decorated in silver and brass inlay with foliate decorations, the barrel approximately 12" l. **1,000-1,500**

Quiver, carved bamboo with black lacquer interior containing bamboo practice arrows with metal tips, early 20th c., 42" l., (Color Illus. pg. 28) ....the set **300-500**

SWORDS

Aikuchi, 18th c., blade in morohazukuri (completely straight), 5¼", itamehada with najare: nakago: two mekugiana, maru-kurijiri; koiguichi made of copper **1,000-2,000**

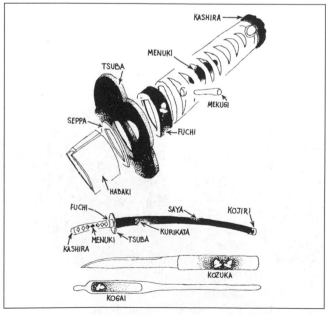

Japanese Sword Furniture

Katana blade, signed "Kuni...," of shinogi-zukuri and shallow koshiziro with o-kissaki, notareba of nie and nioi with o-maru boshi, indistinct itame-hada, the suriage nakago with two mekugi-ana and kiri-yasuri; mei Kuni (the second character missing), 25" **2,000-3,000**

Koto Katana blade attributed to Shinto no kami Minamoto Nobuyoshi, perhaps 17th c., of shinogi-zukuri and shallow koshizori with chu-kissaki, medium suguba of nie and nioi, itame-hada, slightly worn in places, kaaeri-fukai boshi, the ubu-nakago with two mekugi-ana and katte-sagari yasuri; mei Shinano no kami, Minamoto Nobuyoshi, 25" l. **3,000-4,000**

Koto Katana blade, attributed to Kyetsugu, 16th c., blade of shallow torri-zori, shinogi-zukuri, ko-kissaki, narrow suguba with some ko-midare hamon, very narrow ko-maru boshi, itame-masame-hada, suriage-nakago, mei Iyetsugu, 29" l. **800-1,200**

ShinShinto Wakizashi blade (after Normitsu), 19th c., blade of koshi-zori, shinogi-zukuri with chu-kissai, deep chouji-notare hamon of nie and nioi and sunagashi, notare-komi boshi, mokume-hada, nakago with one mekugiana, mei Ko-me Bishu Osafune Norimitsu, dated 7th yr. of Bunmeii (1745), 23¼" l., in shirasaya **1,500-2,200**

Showato blade, by Yoshiro, 20th c., blade of koshi-zori, shinogi-zukuri with chu-kissaki, suguba of nie, ko maru boshi, itame-masame-hada, ubu-nakago with two mekugi-ana, mei Seki ju Ito Yoshiro, 25½" l. **800-1,200**

Tanto, Muromachi Period, ca. 14th to 16th c., blade hiraukiri, iorimune, muzori, itame (mokume)-hada, chikei, nagare on the back, hamon-forms, suguha ko-midare, ko-ashi; abarea (midare) up to the boshi with kinsuji and sunagashi nakago-tang: ubu, kiri-uasurime, huriji-end, Kozuka: signed Kobayashi Ise Mori (kuni), fuchi-kashira made of copper with silver inlays, 12½" l. **1,600-2,800**

Wakizashi, 19th c., blade of shallow torii-zori, shinogi-zukuri with chu-kissaki, midare hamon, ubu-nakago, dull mei, 15", saya of ribbed black lacquer, iron tsuba with dragons and clouds embellished in gilt, silvered metal Omori-style fittings, tiger menuki **2,500-3,500**

SWORD FURNITURE

Fuchi-Kashira, Mitsuyuki, 19th c., Edo period, carved in relief and inlaid with Bishamon and oni, details in gold, silver, copper and shakudo......................................**300-500**

Fuchi-Kashira, Masayoshi, 19th c., Jurojin in relief details in gold, silver, shakudo and copper **275-400**

Fuchi-Kashira, Nomura Masayoshi, 19th c., Edo period, nanako ground and inlaid with rice and foliage in gold and shakudo takazogan, signed with kao **800-1,200**

Fuchi-Kashira, early 19th c., carved and inlaid with peacock and hen details in copper and gold **400-600**

Kozuka and Kogai, Nagamasa, 19th c., Edo period, iron with gilt-rimmed panel, low-relief with waves and inlaid with Hosokawa-mon in gold takazogan, the Kogai blade of silver and the reverse of the Kozuka of diagonally divided iron and silver signed with kao **2,500-3,500**

Kozuka, 19th c., shibuichi, the ground stippled with clouds, and flying bird with silver takazogan moon, the reverse with an inlaid gold panel engraved with poem **1,200-1,800**

Kozuka, early 19th c., shakudo with ishime ground inlaid with arrows, details in gold, silver and shibuichi **300-400**

Kozuka, early 19th c., shakudo, with gold, silver and copper inlay with decoration of carp **500-700**

Tsuba, brass, ca. 1900, carved in the form of Kintaro seated on a rock, the reverse with waterfall, decorated, inscribed "Mototaka," 3¼" **175-225**

Tsuba, iron, 18th c., mokko-form, two hitsu, sculptural depiction of a dragon on the front, gilt rubbed, part of dragon's tail on back, worn **200-350**

Tsuba, early 19th c., round with inlaid brass depicting flowers, finely chased, losses, dark patina..**225-375**

Tsuba, iron, late 18th-early 19th c., with pierced decoration, signed "Soheishi Soten sei" and "Goshu Hikone," silver, gold and copper overlays and inlays depicting figures from mythology, good condition **600-900**

Tsuba, Kaga school, early 19th c., shakudo, circular form, carved and pierced within the broad rim with large aoi leaf, its veins detailed in gold honzogan, the reverse of gold takazogan, 3" **1,500-2,000**

Tsuba, Nara school, 18th c., rounded rectangular form, carved with Shoki, the other side with Oni, 2⅞" **300-500**

Tsuba, iron with gilt decoration, decorated with flowers and waves, Bishu Ito School, Toshimasa saku, 19th c. (ILLUS. below, right) **2,500-3,500**

Tsuba, iron with gold and silver relief design of fisherman, birds and grasses, 19th c. (ILLUS. below, center) **900-1,200**

Tsuba, shibuichi, shakudo, gold and silver high-relief design of water buffalo with rider playing flute, 19th c. (ILLUS. below, left) **1,500-2,000**

Tsuba, Soten school, late 18th c., shakudo of oval form, carved all over on both sides within the raised rim with chrysanthemums and foliage, gilt embellishment, 3" **1,000-1,500**

Group of Japanese Tsuba

Chapter 2
CARPETS AND RUGS

●━━━━━━━━━━━━━━━━━━━━━━━━━━━

CHINESE
●━━━━━━━━━━━━━

The weaving of carpets is a very ancient art. In the monasteries of Tibet, prayer carpets were made by priests from hand-spun wool yarn from sheep, but the hair of camels and yaks was also employed and very fine rugs were made of silk. It is said that during the Han Dynasty a large carpet of elaborate design was presented to the Chinese Emperor, who gave it to a famous Chief Priest of the Tung Yuan Monastery at Peking. The carpet industry, however, was actually developed towards the end of the Yuan Dynasty and the beginning of the Ming Dynasty and occurred in the following way. A priest visiting Peking realized the opportunity and opened a small school of seven pupils in the Wu Kwok Monastery south of Peking and there he taught the whole art and craft of carpet making, spinning and dyeing wool, weaving and designing colors and patterns.

Another version of the carpet story states that the rug weaving of Kansu was introduced to Peking by two brothers under the reign of Emperor Qianlong (Ch'ien Lung). They visited Ninghsia in Kansu, brought back rug weavers and set up looms near the Temple of Heaven. The brothers disagreed and their works were divided, one group entering the factory by the East gate (Tung Men), the other by the West gate (Hsi Men). A third group of workmen, the best, were those who were taught, at the beginning of this century, the cutting out of designs by Mongolian weavers who made the fine saddle rugs so much admired and sought after.

There were fine rugs in the Imperial Palace most of which were either collected by or presented to the Emperor Qianlong. After his reign the carpet industry developed rapidly. Since the world's fair in St. Louis in 1904, Peking carpets have gained worldwide importance and since that time have been exported to the United States and Europe in great quantities.

Chinese looms were the simplest in construction. On a long plank seat the Chinese weaver worked, ate, sang and slept twenty-four hours a day. His colored balls of woolen yarns swung merrily before him keeping time to the movement of his dexterous nimble fingers as he tied the knots of wool into the warp. He clipped them off with his razor-edged knife and pounded them down into place with his crude iron-tined fork. The cotton warp was stretched on heavy beams whose weight kept it taut. For large carpets several workers worked at the same time. The method was as follows: The woolen yarns were fastened to two threads of the warp in either a Senna knot or a Giordes knot. After being securely fastened, the thread was cut to the depth of pile required. The longer the pile the softer the carpet and therefore the length would vary between 3/8" and 5/8".

The closeness of the warp gives the number of threads to the square foot, which varied from 60 to 120, 90 being the usual number for this market.

The frame of the loom was made of some hardwood, and comprised two vertical posts with horizontal beams, the lower of which was adjusted according to the height in order to give the cotton the necessary tension. Very stout beams were used, in order to avoid variations in the tension of the warp which was wound upon the upper beam, the carpet being fixed on the lower beam. The warp ran vertically from the upper beam to the lower. The weaver sat in front of the carpet and the hanks of woolen yarn for the pile were suspended behind them.

Before starting work the design of the rug was outlined on paper to the actual size of the rug. The design was then outlined upon the warp thread and the sketch of the pattern was enlarged to the size of the carpet to be made. The various colors in the rug were indicated on the paper design by means of figures. The working paper design was attached to the loom behind the warp thread and every detail of the design was marked on the warp, except for the color numbers which could easily be read off the design through the warp while weaving was in progress.

The loops for the pile were knotted as follows: The pile yarn was laid beneath the first thread, then over the second warp thread, then back beneath the first one, between the first and second upwards. The weaver cut the finished loop from the yarn and at the same time cut the second end the same as the first one. Two picks were entered after each of the loops. The fineness of the carpet was indicated by the number of rows of loops per foot and varied from 60 to 120. Carpets were made up to a width of 22 feet and any desired length.

The ancient vegetable dyes were almost a thing of the past except for the blue for which indigo was still used.

Silk rugs were also made in Peking (Beijing) but required more experienced and deft weavers. They required a finer warp and had many more threads to the square foot and took a longer time to produce. Chinese silk rugs do not compare in fineness with the Persian products, where hundreds of threads could go into a square inch. (Reprinted with permission of The Orientalia Journal).

ORIENTAL
(non-Chinese)

━━━━━━━━━━━●━━━━━━━━━━━

PATTERN NAMES

The problem for most people in learning the pattern names of Oriental carpets and rugs is looking for some structured organization to the names. Unfortunately, there are as many exceptions as there are rules. For the most part, the pattern names in Persia derived from the village where the carpet or rug was originally woven. Hamadans are a good example. The term "Persian" defines a style of design that developed in the 16th century (the political borders have changed but generally that area is modern Iran). The names used represent political borders as they were. Some people can associate the 2,500 design variations with the 1,500 villages in which they were woven so pattern names can be a convenient means of classifying design traditions.

Village and tribal rugs tend to be small. Women dyed wool in small amounts for home production. The large, older carpets with uniformly dyed ground were commercially dyed by an establishment capable of dyeing 100 pounds of wool or more at one time. That quantity required a very large stationary vat.

Successful patterns tended to be copied. One village would develop a pattern or color combination. If it sold well the surrounding villages would try to adapt or copy the pattern.

There are basically two types of pattern: carpets with repetitive patterns (which can be any size); and patterns designed within the border (a later development). The relationship between the pattern to the space within the border is important.

With repetitive patterns the repeating design element can be as small as one or two inches or as large as one or two feet. The repetitive pattern extends in all directions according to the old design traditions and the border merely defines the size of the particular space it will fill.

In designs within a border, the most common variety has a central medallion as the focus of the decoration. There can be, however, a number of designs that run throughout the ground without a large medallion.

COLOR

Traditional colors are, for the most part, reds and blues. They are the colors for which dyestuffs have been traded widely for hundreds of years. Within the reds and blues there are enormous variations of shades, all of which are affected by the design.

One of the reasons that the traditional colors were dark was that white wool was not commonly available. Red and blue covered up the color variations within the wool. Semi-antique and modern wools are, for the most part, white and so softer pastels can be used.

The introduction of pastel hues in carpets and rugs has meant that similar examples from all over the world have been woven. Between modern pastel hues and traditional colorations, there is also a modern variation combining jewel and pastel colors.

QUALITY

All wool is not the same. Different varieties of sheep produce different types of wool. It is usually the lowest grade wool that is found in lesser quality carpets. It is important to become familiar with the feel of the wool.

Each knot in a carpet and rug was tied by hand. A single weaver may have worked eight hours per day, seven days a week. It might have taken up to six months to weave a carpet of moderate value. A more valuable piece could take up to twelve months to weave. This is one of the reasons for the high prices in today's market.

With regard to semi-antique and modern pieces, knots per square inch are really knots per day. A weaver would tie between 6,000 and 8,000 knots per day with wages based upon the these numbers. A more difficult design, with many color changes, also determined pay scales. In addition, the height of the pile also changes the numbers of knots per square inch. The more knots per square inch, the more complex the pattern.

There can be as many as 50 different color changes

in a horizontal row of knots. If, in a particular size rug, there are less than 50 warps available the pattern could not be executed. Since rug weaving is an ancient art the details of construction have evolved over the years so that a pattern may be produced to meet current market demands and costs. One of the reasons that the number of knots is used for a basis in evaluating quality is that this shows how the design was executed.

The interaction of the wool yarn, the height of the pile, the complexity of the decoration, as well as the number of knots per square inch determine the quality of construction. Keep in mind that a piece with fine yarn, low pile, complex decoration and fine weave can have the same quality as another example using heavy yarn, high pile, less complex decoration and simple weave.

CONDITION

Good original condition is always most desirable, but remember that carpets and rugs can be repaired! Missing border fringes can be replaced and careful shampooing will remove years of dirt. Some stains can be removed and burns can be invisibly repaired.

GLOSSARY OF ORIENTAL RUG TERMS

Abradj—color change within an area caused by use of a different dye lot.

Arabesque—an ornament having interlacing tendrils to form an eight-pointed medallion.

Ashkali—a border having a row of octagons with a line between them and line connecting them (Kashaki carpets).

Band—a narrow strip of woven or knotted materials used for tents (Turkomen).

Barber's Pole—an English term for a pattern of oblique varied colored stripes in the medallion or border.

Bird—an Anatole rug having a leaf form design that resembles a bird.

Border—the running edges that enclose the central field. The border can contain both wider and narrower stripes also termed *guards*.

Boteh—a design resembling a leaf, the tip bent sideways.

Chess Board—the field is divided into squares.

Chinatamani—a design of three balls in a triangular arrangement.

Cloudband—a wavy pattern.

Corner—the pattern in each corner of the field.

Elephant's Foot—the octagon found in the main design.

Engsi—a rug made for hanging over the entrance of a tent.

Farsibaff—a Meshed carpet knotted with Persian knots.

Feraghan—another name for the Herati pattern.

Field—the central area of a carpet which is enclosed by a border.

Figural—a design having figures.

Fringe—the warp threads at the top and bottom that hang loose, not woven with the weft.

Garden Design—represents a Persian garden(flower beds, pathways, streams, etc.).

Giordes—the Turkish knot.

Goblet Border—a border design having stylized goblets between serrated leaves.

Gul—the basic design of Oriental carpets, especially Turkomen and Afghans. It is an octagon but can have various forms.

Haji Hanum—a design with a central vase and flower (a prayer decoration).

Hashang—design with crab-like shapes.

Hasti Badomi—a carpet having a field divided into four segments by a cross decoration.

Herati—a pattern with a central rosette surrounded by a lozenge or diamond shape. Along the sides there are palmettes and four hanging lanceolate leaves which curve outward.

Joshaghan—a pattern with diamond shapes (looks like snowflakes).

Karaja—a geometric ground and border with approximately three medallions, one large and two smaller ones on a ground covered overall with designs.

Knots—The Giordes or Turkish knot is made by looping the yarn around two warp threads and drawing it up between them. This is also termed a "closed knot" and was used in Turkey, parts of Persia, Afghanistan, and the Caucasus. Carpets with this knot have warp threads which lie side by side. From the back one should feel two bumps for each knot. The Persian or Sine knot is also made by winding the yarn around two warp threads, however, only one end of the yarn is drawn up between them. The other end is drawn up outside on either the right or left. This knot is also called the "open knot." The back should show only one warp thread for each knot. Jufti knots are woven over three or four warp threads. This knot results in a lesser quality piece.

Lantern—a hanging lamp design.

Leaf—a common decoration (Lanceolate leaves area spear-headed and curved outward.)

Maj Nun—a weeping willow.

Meander—a line of design(s) arranged to form a border pattern.

Madachye—a dogtooth pattern.

Medallion—a central design (floral, circular, square, rectangular, or geometric). It can be used as a repetitive decoration.

Mehrab—the niche in a Prayer Rug. It has a pointed arch and can be supported by pillars.

Millefleurs—small floral ornaments symmetrically placed.

Mina Khani—repetitive rosettes surrounded by lozenge shaped petals.

Mir—the palm leaf sideways.

Miriboteh—repetitive botehs overall.

Numdal—a carpet made of felt.

Open Ground—a carpet with a medallion which may have corners, the ground void of designs.

Palmette—the section of a flower.

Piece—a term used to describe any carpet or rug (also mats and runners).

Pomegranate—a design common to Samarkand carpets.

Prayer Rug—the design has a Mehrab at one end.

Ram's Horn—a pattern found on Shirvan rugs and Turkomen prayer rugs.

Running Dog—the design evolved from the Greek Key pattern.

"S" Border—found on Caucasian pieces.

Serabend—a pattern of small palm leaves tilted sideways.

Skirt—an additional border differing from the other borders.

Soumak—similar to the kilim because there is no pile. It has weft threads left hanging giving it a shaggy appearance.

Sutural Border—a border containing zigzag lines forming adjacent triangles.

"T" Border—common to pieces from Chinese Turkestan.

Tarantula—a design resembling a stylized spider.

Tree of Life—a stylized tree trunk and branches in a pictorial or geometric form.

Warp—threads running from top to bottom on any woven material.

Weft—threads running from side to side on any woven material.

Zille—a kilim of Russian origin similar to a Soumak with a design of a stylized dragon.

PATTERN NAMES

Abade(Persia)—village south of Ispahan. The most common pattern found on carpets from this area is a diamond shape in the center of the field, surrounded by small geometric shapes. The warp and weft are cotton.

Afghan (Afghanistan)—a name for all the carpets and rugs made in Afghanistan. The most common design contains rows of octagonal shapes (guls) separated by stylized branches. Most common is deep red and deep blue. Pieces having yellow come from the Beshar region.

Afghan Bokara (Afghanistan)—a Bokara decoration on an Afghan piece.

Ahar (Persia)—production of carpets similar to Heriz with curvilinear designs.

Anatole (Turkey)—the term for all rugs from Turkey including Giordes, Ladik, Melas, etc.

Arasbaran (Persia)—a nomadic tribe that settled near Kirman. The rugs are generally bright blue, red and ivory. The decorations include large lozenges, boteh, geometric patterns, three or more large diamond shapes filled with and surrounded by other decorations. The warp threads are thicker than the weft threads. The backs of such pieces look ribbed.

Baktyar (Persia)—this tribe comes from an area that consists of hundreds of villages. The common decoration contains rows of squares filling in the entire field in a repetitive manner.

Begardeh (Persia)—a type of Hamadan, usually good quality, thick, the medallion and corners serrated or wavy.

Beloudj (Afghanistan, Persia)—produced by nomadic tribes. The rugs include prayer rugs with the main colors being very dark blue and red. The Persian rugs are called Meshed-Beloudj. Modern Meshed-Beloudj are made with cotton warps and wefts having small geometric overall designs. The Afghan pieces are called "Herat-Beloudj" and were and continue to be produced with wool warp and weft (including a mixture of camel or goat hair).

Beloudj Bokara (Persia)—a Beloudj with a Bokara decoration.

Bergamo (Turkey)—pieces have geometric decorations with one or more medallions surrounded by small designs.

Beshire (Afghanistan)—a tribe that settled in the areas where Turkmenistan, Uzbekistan and Afghanistan meet. The decorations include florals with red and blue predominating.

Bibibaff (Persia)—a type of Baktyar named for a Princess.

Bidjar (Persia)—very heavy and stiff carpets with thick pile (due to the large number of weft threads beaten down with a thick iron comb). The patterns include Herati with borders that can be filled with rose decorations.

Birjand (Persia)—a fine quality Meshed.

Bokara (Russia)—the name for rugs made by the Turkomen tribes (and the decorations). A typical design contains rows of guls linked by lines running from top to bottom and side to side. The lines intersect in the center of each gul thus creating two pairs of alternate segments. The spaces between the rows are filled with cross-shaped designs. Sometimes the pieces have a skirt.

Borchalou (Persia)—a rug with fine knots from the Hamadan area. The designs can be floral with medallions on a cream or red ground.

Caucasus (Russia)—rugs produced along the border between Persia and Russia. This class of rugs includes: Erivan, Kazak, Derbend, Karabagh, and Shirvan. Caucasian carpets should have geometric decorations except for the Armenian carpets which have floral designs (Karabagh and Erivan).

Chelosotor (Persia)—a very fine Baktyar with a medallion surrounded by colored rosettes.

Chi-chi (Russia)—a kind of Shirvan.

Devlet-Abad (Afghanistan)—in today's market it applies to a lesser quality piece which can have a pink appearance on the reverse.

Dorosch (Persia)—the weft should be a single thread of yarn with every eight or nine rows having three threads.

Erdebil (Persia)—similar to a Shirvan and known for runners.

Erivan (Russia)—capital of Armenia. The pieces have a brown tint in the red.

Feraghan (Persia)—carpets and rugs with variations of the Herati pattern.

Giordes (Turkey)—rugs with a plain ground and prayer design. Also the name of a knot.

Gorovan (Persia)—an inexpensive Heriz.

Hamadan (Persia)—a city in Kurdistan. The wool is the longest lived. A variety of designs both overall and in medallions, the Sine being one of the most common decorations. The main colors are red and blue. Among the most important Hamadan pieces are those which come from Arasbaran, Borchalou, Feraghan, Husseinabad, Jozan, Karaja, Kurd, Mahal, Melayir, Saveh, Sharibaff, Tafrish, Tuserkhan, and Weisz (all of which are villages and not decorations.)

Haroun (Persia)—a carpet similar to a Keshan but of lesser quality. The weft threads are irregular and the design does not show on the reverse as distinctly as the Keshan.

Hereke (Turkey)—a piece having Persian decorations executed in wool as well as silk with silver and gold threads.

Heriz (Persia)—a center of carpet manufacture. Motifs can have a central medallion with prominent corners executed in soft colors. Lesser quality pieces include Mehraban and Gorovan.

Hinikhan (Persia)—a lesser quality Baktyar that is thin and coarse.

Ispahan (Persia)—the most common decoration is a central medallion surrounded by interlacing tendrils covering the entire field.

Joshaghan (Persia)—common are diamond shape decorations; corner pieces may have the Greek Key edged with white.

Kansu (China)—similar to Samarkand with Chinese stylized designs.

Kaputrenk (Persia)—a mid-range Hamadan.

Karabagh (Russia)—carpets with a wide range of decorations and rich colors, including herati, boteh and medallions.

Karaja (Persia)—decorations similar to those of the Caucasus with a much coarser wool.

Kashgar (China)—similar to Samarkand but from Chinese Turkestan.

Kashkai (Persia)—carpets similar to Shiraz but having very fine knotting and wool. Motifs include diamond-shaped lozenges with a field filled with floral designs.

Kayseri (Turkey)—known for prayer designs as well as Persian designs; most family prayer rugs come from Kayseri.

Kazak (Russia)—the rugs from this area in the southern Caucasus have deep pile; the top and bottom area sometimes finished with kilims.

Keshan (Persia)—town famous for producing silk carpets with hunting scenes. Metal brocading was sometimes woven into the carpets. Production was halted due to the Afghan invasions of 1722 and revived in the 19th century. Known for fine knotting and pictorial decorations which include a large central medallion and corner pieces with similar designs.

Kherkin (Afghanistan)—a carpet made by Turkomen nomads; the wool is lustrous but the stitches are coarse.

Kirman (Persia)—elaborate floral decorations having, for the most part, a central medallion(s) sometimes with intricate patterns overall. Some carpets have a Korani pattern which resembles the gilt bookbinding designs found on the Koran. Modern pieces are similar in designs to French Aubussons. Older pieces have short pile, modern pieces have thicker pile. Pieces with plain ground have fewer stitches than the borders.

Kirscheyir (Turkey)—these rugs can have an additional border at the top and bottom; the field is generally geometric with a central medallion.

Kizil Ayak (Afghanistan, Russia)—a form of Pendik rug.

Konya (Turkey)—geometric decoration, coarse with poor quality wool.

Koum (Persia)—carpet production began in this city in the early 1930s. No original designs.

Kuba (Russia)—in the Shirvan district, famous for the 'Dragon' carpets.

Kum-Kapu (Turkey)—semi-antique reproductions of antique carpets.

Kurd (Persia)—carpets produced by nomadic tribes in Kurdistan. The decorations are geometric with a coarse weave.

Ladik (Turkey)—prayer design rugs with three or more tulips at the top of the mehrab.

Leylahan (Persia)—a light red or pink ground with groups of flowers overall; sometimes there can be a small center medallion (Hamadan-style).

Luristan (Persia)—similar to Kurds, the Luri rugs have bright colors and geometric decorations.

Mahal (Persia)—a Meshed carpet of good quality.

Mazlagan (Persia)—from an area near Hamadan, the decoration is generally a serrated leaf central medallion having an edge of zigzag lines. There are generally three border bands.

Mecca Shiraz (Persia)—among the finest carpets from the area of Shiraz.

Melas (Turkey)—prayer rugs similar to Giordes and Ladik; they commonly have a gold border and a light brown ground.

Melayir (Persia)—a large carpet district. Carpets can have the Persian knot or the Turkish knot, with similar patterns of florals rendered in bright hues (mauve-like red and/or orange).

Mir (Persia)—a carpet having small botehs in the decoration.

Moud (Persia)—a very fine Meshed carpet.

Nayin (Persia)—carpets similar to Ispahan with pale hues including green or blue with ivory or beige.

Oushak (Turkey)—semi-antique carpets that are coarse with overall designs in green, deep blue and red.

Pendik (Afghanistan, Russia)—produced by the Turkomen tribes. There are two types: 1.) Kizil-Zyak is known for the contrast of the reddish-brown coloring and the white which comes from the hue of cotton rather than wool for some of the white knots; and 2.) A type generally executed in red and blue with fine knots. Modern pieces have longer pile and a darker reddish brown hue.

Russia Bokara (Russia)—Bokara carpets produced by the Tekke tribe around Merv.

Saff (Turkey)—a prayer rug made in Kayseri. It should have 6 to 10 mehrabs down the length of the rug so that people can kneel side by side. It can be made of silk.

Samarkand (China)—a Russian trading center for the sale of carpets from Chinese Turkestan.

Samarkand is the term for carpets produced by the nomadic tribes in western China. Although the wool is not good quality the design of a flowering pomegranate tree grown from a vase at each end with flowering branches over the field is attractive. Borders are geometric and sometimes have the Greek Key.

Sarouk (Persia)—carpets from this village have a large central medallion formed with floral decorations, simple borders with one wide border and a narrow one on each side. Sarouks which are post-World War I have a thicker longer pile than those produced before the war.

Serabend (Persia)—an area producing carpets with feature rows of small botehs.

Seyhur (Russia)—a rug with a Saint Andrew-type cross, the borders blue and white.

Sharibaff (Persia)—a trading center for nomadic rugs. Most of this type of rug have wool colored with vegetable dyes. Diamond-shaped patterns (lozenges) are common together with a narrow border of diagonal stripes.

Shirvan (Russia)—an area in the Caucasus known for carpets that can have the ends of the warp threads, at the bottom, left as loops (Southern Caucasus). Northern Caucasus carpets can have the ends of the warp threads cut and knotted at both top and bottom

Sine (Persia)—known for rugs which are finely knotted. The back of such a piece should feel rough. Motifs can be overall and include boteh and herati. Also known for kilims.

Sivas (Turkey)—carpets and rugs that look Persian; the back will show a Turkish knot and many of the hues have a bluish tint.

Soumak (Persia, Russia, Turkey)—a place in the Caucasus. The carpets have geometric decorations including diamond-shaped lozenges in blue on a red ground.

Tabriz (Persia)—carpets produced in this city have classic designs mixed with central medallions surrounded by floral decorations.

Tekke (Afghanistan)—a Bokara-style rug produced by a Turkomen tribe.

Tuzerkhan (Persia)—from the Hamadan area, these rugs can have a medallion in red and green on a camel-colored ground.

Weisz (Persia)—from the Hamadan area, similar to a Bidjar. Common decorations include medallions on a pink or red ground. These rugs have a very tight weave.

Yezd (Persia)—near Ispahan, production is similar to Kirman. A lesser quality carpet in cotton is also produced.

PRICE LISTINGS
for Carpets & Rugs

Afshar rug, South Persia, late 19th c., overall lattice with stars in dark and medium blue, red, ivory, bluish green, reddish brown, apricot, with meander border in apricot, stains, worn areas, 5' 4" x 4' $2,000-3,000

Bahktiari carpet, West Persia, second quarter 19th c., large central oval medallion and blossoming vines in midnight and navy blue, ivory, rose, red, gold and bluish green on a reddish brown field, midnight-blue spandrels, ivory palmette border, worn areas, minor repairs, 14' x 11' 6" 5,500-7,500

Baluch prayer rug, Northeast Persia, late 19th c., "tree of life" decoration in dark blue, brown and reddish brown on a tan field, stained and worn, especially at corners, 3' 5" x 2' 5" 500-900

Bidjar rug, Northwest Persia, first quarter 20th c., Herati decoration in red, sky blue, rose, reddish brown, blue and bluish green on a deep blue field, the border with blue rosette and leaves, minor repairs, worn spots, 7' 4" x 4' 10" 1,800-2,400

Bidjar rug, Northwest Persia, ca. 1900, palmettes and quartrefoil boteh decorations in light blue, red, rose, bluish green and brown on a dark blue field, red "turtle" border, worn, 6' 11" x 4' 450-700

Chi-Chi rug, Northeast Caucasus, late 19th c., alternating rows of octagons and polygons in blue, gold, deep bluish green, rust and red, diagonal bar border, worn, 6' x 4' 3" 1,600-2,200

Chinese carpet, 19th c., yellow ground with design depicting two monks blowing conch shells and flanking an incense burner on a lotus-petal stand, all surrounded by Buddhist emblems within a shaped cartouche, above stylized wave and cloud border and beneath a panel of dragons, the design in shades of brown, orange, red, blue and ivory, 70½" x 178" (ILLUS.) 5,500-7,000

Chinese carpet, ca. 1900, open circular medallion of flowers and birds in royal blue, ivory and bluish green on a dark blue field, ivory key fret border, little wear, 9' 6" x 7' 6" **3,500-4,500**

Chinese carpet, ca. 1900, tan and ivory floral medallion on a dark blue field, the corners with vines within a dark blue border, evenly worn, 15' 5" x 12' **4,500-7,500**

Chinese Kilim, ca. 1900, flying cranes, flower vases and plants in rust, tan, blue, ivory, on a light brown field, border missing, small repairs, 10' 6" x 4' 8" **500-800**

Chinese mat, early 20th c., a circular decoration of sailboat surrounded by small flowers in ivory, dark and light blue on a burgundy field, 3' x 3' **275-475**

Chinese pillar rug, late 19th c., cloudbands, lanterns and dragon above waves in dark red, tan, blue, gold and brown, repaired, discoloration, 5' 8" x 2' 6½" **1,000-1,500**

Chinese rug, ca. 1900, the light blue field covered with vases on stands, the corners with floral designs, in navy, rose, ivory, tan, and gold, the outer border (guard border) with flower and scroll, stained overall, 9' 6" x 5' 6" **900-1,300**

Fereghan rug, West Persia, ca. 1920s, palmettes, leafy vines and vases in light and dark blue, red, gold, aubergine, deep bluish green and tan on a dark blue field, ivory spandrels, red rosette and vine border, worn, small repairs, 6' 10" x 4' **1,800-2,500**

Hamadan rug, Northwest Persia, ca. 1900, diamond lattice with rosettes in dark and light blue, gold and bluish green on the abashed rose-red field, three meandering borders, plain camel outer border, worn overall, 9' x 5' **1,000-1,500**

Heriz carpet, Northwest Persia, ca. 1930, large stepped diamond medallion and serrated leaves in midnight blue, navy blue and light blue, rose, tanish gold, bluish green on a rust ground, ivory spandrels, midnight blue "turtle" border, worn corners, and worn center, 9' 6" x 9' **1,200-1,800**

Karabagh rug, South Caucasus, late 19th c., hooked diamond medallion in gold, apricot, red and bluish green on a dark

blue field, serrated leaf border, very worn, 4' x 3' **600-1,000**

Kashan carpet, West Central Persia, ca. 1920s, overall palmette, rosettes and blossoming vines in three shades of blue, rose, gold, and bluish green on a rust field, dark blue palmette border, slightly worn overall, 16' 8" x 10' **8,000-12,000**

Kerman carpet, Southeast Persia, ca. 1900, lobed circular medallions in ivory, floral sprays in rose, blue, gold, aubergine and bluish green on a pale bluish green field, ivory border with similar decoration, worn overall, 15' 6" x 8' 8".............**6,000-8,000**

Konya rug, Central Anatolia, late 19th c., six large hooked octagonal medallion in light blue, rose, aubergine, gold and bluish green on a red field, "S" decoration border, very worn overall, 5' 6" x 3' 2" **400-600**

Kuba prayer rug, Northeast Caucasus, late 19th c., rows of small palmettes, shield and diamond designs in red, medium blue, tan, aubergine and bluish green on an ivory field, red rosette and vine border, repaired, 5' x 3' 2" **3,000-5,000**

Mahal carpet, West Persia, late 19th century, evenly worn, approximately 9' 8" x 9' (Color Illus. pg. 27).............**4,500-6,500**

Mahal carpet, West Persia, early 20th c., ca. 1925, overall decorations of palmettes, rosettes, serrated leaves and flowering vines in dark blue, red, gold, bluish green and tan on an apricot field, dark blue rosette and vine border, moth damage, 15' 6" x 9' 11" **8,000-10,000**

Oushak carpet, West Anatolia, ca. 1920s, small ivory cartouche on a lemon field with pale green, cream and saffron palmettes and vinery, ivory spandrels within a pale green palmette and split leaf arabesque border, evenly worn, 13' 6" x 10' 3" **6,500-9,500**

Sarouk rug, West Persian, ca. 1920s, quatrefoil medallion and vases with flowering vines in blue, camel, green, rust and bluish green on a rose field, the border with dark blue palmette design, minor wear overall, 4' 9" x 3' 6" **1,000-1,600**

Serabend runner, Northwest Persia, ca. 1900, staggered rows of boteh in rose, ivory, red, gold and bluish green on a

navy blue field, ivory rosette border,
worn, 15' x 3' **1,200-1,600**

Senneh rug, Northwest Persia, late 19th-
early 20th, serrated hexagonal medallion,
matching spandrels and Herati design in
two shades of dark blue, red, rose, bluish
green, and gold on an ivory field, red
palmette and vine border, small repairs,
worn areas, 6' 8" x 4' 6" **1,500-2,000**

Shirvan prayer rug, East Caucasus, late
19th c., hexagonal lattice with flowering
plants in royal blue, red, ivory, reddish
brown, tan, and bluish green on a gold
field, red border, worn overall,
4' 6" x 3' 9" **600-900**

Shirvan rug, East Caucasus, late 19th c.,
light blue, tan, gold, and bluish green on a
red field, keyhole medallion pattern, ivory
crab border, repaired,
4' 10" x 6' 11" **1,000-1,500**

Tabriz carpet, Northwest Persia, late 19th
c., overall lattice with palmettes, rosettes
and cloudband decorations in dark blue,
light blue, tan, ivory and tannish gold on
a rust field, turtle border with similar
hues, moth damage, overall wear,
13' x 9' 8" **9,000-15,000**

Tabriz pictorial prayer rug, Northwest
Persia, early 20th c., camel mirab with
landscapes, animals and figures beneath a
narrow prayer arch in blue all within a
deep madder palmette border, some wear,
5' 11" x 4' 7" **3,000-4,500**

19th Century Chinese Carpet

Chapter 3
CERAMICS

───────────●───────────

GLOSSARY

Enamel—A vitreous opaque covering used on ceramics and other materials. They can be used either over or under the glaze.

Glaze—A vitreous covering used to make objects impermeable to liquid or grease.

Porcelain—Composed of kaolin, feldspar and silica. It is translucent and vitreous.

Pottery—Also termed 'earthenware,' it can be porous or semi-porous.

Slip—An opaque liquid composition made from clay.

Stoneware—An opaque pottery that is hard and vitrified.

CIIINESE CERAMICS

───────────●───────────

EXPORT PORCELAIN
(also termed Trade Porcelain)

China Trade or export porcelain was introduced in the West by Portuguese traders. They were successfully followed by the Dutch, English, and other Europeans. Trade porcelain was not exported to the United States until 1784, when the ship The China Empress landed in Macao. The following information will help identify the various patterns.

Armorial (also termed Heraldic)—These wares date from the end of the Kangxi period, ca. 1695. The East India Company processed orders in Ching te Chen and the porcelain was sent as blanks to be decorated in Canton. Armorial pieces were specially ordered. These wares can have genre designs (scenes replicated from European prints, ship decorations, figural designs, animals and birds, as well as mythological adaptations). The wares were later copied at various European factories including Vivinis and Samson.

Canton Blue and White—Canton blue and white has patterns similar to Nanking blue and white. The basic designs of each consist of a landscape with an island, bridge(s), trees, birds, mountains, rocks, figures, clouds, boats and river used together or in part. The Canton border has a blue outer border, sometimes overworked with a primitive star pattern and an inner pattern of wavy lines. This is termed "star and cloud." Another pattern found on Canton blue and white has a border containing slash lines rather than stars. This is termed the "rain and cloud" border. This pattern is still being produced. (See the later listing for this pattern taken from a 1914 catalogue published by Vantine's, NYC.) In addition, this pattern is found with the Rice Grain decoration.

Canton (Famille Rose Patterns)—Near the end of the 18th century, export wares in Famille Rose (pink palette) were produced. The various patterns include: Rose Canton, Rose Mandarin, Rose Medallion, Rose and Long Life, 100 Butterflies, Garden, Tobacco Leaf, Auspicious Figures, and Bouquet.

> **Rose Canton**—Similar to Rose Medallion but the pattern is void of figures. It can have alternating reserves of flowers and insects.
>
> **Rose Medallion**—This pattern has reserves filled with figures on a gold ground with green tendrils around a center reserve (medallion) of a pink peony blossom.
>
> **Rose and Long Life**—A pattern which as a large peony blossom with bird perched on a branch.
>
> **Garden**—A pattern which has a segment of a garden and much open space.
>
> **Bouquet**—It has a center design of a floral bouquet with much open space.
>
> **Auspicious Figures**—This is a pattern with figures taken from Daoist and Buddhist symbols

which are also seen in the 100 antiques pattern. All the figures are placed with their feet facing the center, like spokes. This pattern was introduced during the Daoguang period.

Rose Mandarin—This pattern contains figures in various poses with a border of fruits, flowers, insects.

Butterfly and Cabbage—A pretty pattern with a butterfly upon a cabbage leaf. Sometimes the leaves radiate around a central reserve which can contain initials or a Shou (longevity) symbol.

Dragon and Chrysanthemum—A pattern dating from the Guangxu period having dragons and chrysanthemums on a yellow or turquoise blue ground.

Fitzhugh—Basically Fitzhugh is a blue and white ware produced at the same time as Canton and Nanking and in the same place (Ching te Chen). The Fitzhugh pattern can have a circular center medallion or could have been produced by special order with an eagle or a monogram. In addition, the pattern can have four panels of floral designs and a wide border broken into overall areas and filled with diapers (repetitive patterns), of which some symbols can be butterfly shapes. Fitzhugh can have a trellis border with four split pomegranates showing the inside of the fruit and butterfly shapes with wings spread. In the center there can be a center medallion with groups of flowers and emblems, all surrounding a medallion or oval monogram. Generally Fitzhugh has a "post and spear" border. The pattern is found in blue and white as well as green, orange, red, yellow, sepia and black. It can have gilt trim.

Nanking Blue and White Cup and Saucer

Imari—Generally this ware features a gray or green-ish or bluish green-tinted glaze with basic coral, underglaze-blue and gilt designs. It was produced to compete with Japanese Imari. As with the large majority of Export Porcelain, shapes conform to Western designs.

Nanking Blue and White—Nanking blue and white differs from Canton blue and white. Nanking borders have a "post and spear" border. The wares can also have gilt trim. Overall designs are comparable to Canton blue and white.

Blanc de Chine—This ware has been produced for both the domestic and trade markets since the Ming Dynasty. Pieces were originally manufactured for the Buddhist monks who needed deities for the propagation of their religion (especially for those working in maritime trades). The glaze should have a dense waxy looking appearance. The color of the white can vary from stark white to ivory to white with a bluish tint.

Rice Grain—This porcelain ware has small openings in the body of the porcelain which, when filled with glaze, form a translucent design. Held to the light, this translucent pattern gives a lacy effect to the porcelain. It is termed "rice grain" because the perforations are similar in shape to a grain of rice. Among the most common patterns formed by these perforated shapes are star shaped designs or radiating flower petals. Sometimes the central decoration is taken from Canton patterned wares.

CHINESE PORCELAIN
(Traditional)

Traditional Chinese porcelain was produced in a variety of techniques, many of which have been used since the Ming Dynasty. The following are among the styles or techniques which are popular in today's market.

Doucai *(Tu ts'ai)*—First appearing in the Chenghua period (1465-1487), it combines colored enamels (red, green, yellow, aubergine), applied over the glaze with underglaze-blue outlines.

Sancai *(San ts'ai)*—The earliest pieces are associated with three-color funerary wares.

Wucai*(Wu Ts'ai)*—Associated with the reign of Wanli, the basic color range contains red, yellow, turquoise, various greens, brownish black and aubergine, sometimes used with underglaze-blue.

Three Color on Biscuit—This applies to wares that have enamel applied directly onto the biscuit (paste).

Famille Rose—Pink palette wares.

Chinese Blanc de Chine Guanyin

Famille Jaune—Yellow palette wares.

Famille Noir—Black palette wares.

Famille Verte—Green palette wares.

Monochromatic Wares:

Apple Green—The color of Granny Smith apples either with or without a crackled glaze.

Celadon—Chinese celadon wares can be olive green or pale green. It originated during the Song Dynasty. Northern wares are dark and Southern wares are light in color. Later it continued during the Qing (Ch'ing) Dynasty and into the 20th century. Celadon was used in combinations with other hues.

Clair de Lune—Pale lavender blue.

Copper Red—This applies to flambé, mule's liver, and cherry red tones.

Imperial Yellow—A clear lemony shade which reminds one of Guldens Mild Mustard. Imperial yellow with white interior was reserved for use by concubines of the first rank.

Peach Bloom—Varies from peach to gray to green; the more uniform the hue the more valuable.

Powder Blue—This hue was blown on through a tube which was likely covered with a piece of gauze, hence its name. It was also used in combination with gilt and/or Famille Verte designs.

Robin's Egg—A speckled blue which resembles the color of actual robins' eggs.

Sang de Beouf—Oxblood.

Tea Dust—This can be a shade of green or brown which resembles the color of powdered tea.

Two Color Wares:

Blue and Yellow—Used by fourth through seventh rank concubines—respectively (blue with yellow dragons).

Green and Yellow—Used by second and third rank concubines.

Fahua (Fa Hua)—Pottery, porcelain and stoneware objects which have decorations made with ridges (outlines) in relief.

Funerary wares—Wares which were buried in tombs.

Guyuexuan (Ku Yueh Hsuan)—"Ancient Moon Terrace," an opaque white porcelain resembling milk glass with designs in famille Rose.

Chinese Porcelain Elephants

Yixing *(I-Hsing)*—In today's market, the most collectible form of Yixing wares are teapots. The unglazed Yixing wares can vary in color and include buff, brown, reddish brown and similar shades. Pieces can be undecorated, decorated with enameled designs, or decorated with applied low-relief decorations. These pottery wares can also be found glazed overall.

PRICE LISTINGS
for all Chinese Wares of the Ming and Qing Dynasties and the 20th Century

ANIMALS, BIRDS AND FIGURINES
(18th, 19th and 20th c.)

Buddhist lions, late 19th or early 20th c., yellow, green and brown on rectangular bases, impressed mark "CHINA," 5" h., facing pair **$175-225**

Buddhist lions, Kangxi, each sitting on a pierced plinth, three-color glaze (aubergine, green and ochre), one with foot on pup, the other with foot on brocade ball, 8" h. (Color Illus. pg. 29) **1,500-2,000**

Cockerels, early 19th c., white and brown standing upon brown rockwork, the details of the features picked out in red, 13½" h., facing pair **2,000-3,000**

Cranes, porcelain, each on open rockwork, blue, yellow, green and aubergine feathers, white bodies picked out in black, black legs, black and green rockworks, late 19th c., 14¼" h., pr. (ILLUS.) **1,500-2,000**

Dog, 18th c., a hound seated on its hind legs with head slightly turned to left, iron-red color with bell, fur picked out in gray, the eyes black, edge of one ear restored, 7½" h. **4,500-6,500**

Elephant, early 19th c., Famille Rose palette, standing four-square with head held down to the right, carrying a saddle cloth, trunk down, 4" h............................**850-1,500**

Elephants, 19th c., flambé glaze, 8" w., pair (ILLUS.) **1,200-1,500**

Elephants, 19th c. copper red, standing four-square with raised trunks, 12" h., facing pair **1,000-1,500**

Figure of a boy, Kangxi, holding a vase with lotus, his apron decorated with a crane amid clouds in Famille Verte palette, 11" h. **1,500-2,000**

Porcelain Cranes

Figure of Guanyin (Kuan Yin), Kangxi, seated cross legged in long robes carrying a scepter, upon a lotus plinth rising from a hexagonal base, 10" h.........................**1,500-2,200**

Figures of Ladies, late 19th c., each seated on a tree trunk holding a flower, their attire in Famille Rose palette, one base repaired, one with hairlines, 6¾" h., facing pair **1,000-1,500**

Figure group of HeHe Erxian, Kangxi, standing on a pierced rockwork base, one holding a lotus, the other a fly whisk, three color on biscuit, restored................**800-1,000**

Figure group, man astride an elephant, early 19th c., 14" h. (Color Illus. pg. 28) **1,800-2,500**

Figural set of 8 Immortals, ca. 1920s, Famille Rose palette, each with his or her attribute, 6" h., the set................................**300-500**

Geese, ca. 1930, turquoise and white, impressed mark "CHINA," 2½" h., pair..........**25-40**

Mud figure, coin carrier, green robe, 5" h. **45-65**

Mud figure, man, elder with hat on back and yellow robe and staff, 7" h. **75-110**

Mud figure, man, elder with staff, yellow coat, 1" h...**20-30**

Mud figure, seated elder, with blue robe holding book, 5" h. **40-65**

Mud figure, woman, blue robe, yellow fan, 1"h. **20-30**

Mud figure, woman with teapot, blue-glazed robe, 10" h. **150-175**

Monkey, first half 19th c., iron-red and natural tones, seated with hind legs crossed, the left arm at the side, the right hand holding a peach, 3" h. **700-850**

Mythical beasts, turquoise and aubergine, early 19th c., each with head turned to one side, facing pair **3,000-5,000**

Parrots, Kangxi, each a deep turquoise standing upon aubergine rockwork, one beak restored, 8" h., facing pair...........**1,500-2,500**

Parrots, 19th c., style of Kangxi, each in shades of green standing on splashed rockwork, restoration to both, 8½" h., facing pair **500-700**

Parrots, early 20th c., ca. 1920s, style of Kangxi, in yellow and green on green rockwork, 7" h., facing pair......................**100-175**

Phoenix, early 20th, Famille Rose palette, detailed feathers, open rockwork base, impressed mark "CHINA" inside base, 16" h. **500-700**

Rabbit, 18th c., glazed turquoise on biscuit, eyes picked out in dark blue, 6" h. **3,000-5,000**

Rooster, late 18th or early 19th c., red comb, feathers in yellow, green, aubergine and white, on splashed rockwork base, 10" h. **1,000-1,500**

ARMORIAL (HERALDRY) AND EUROPEAN SUBJECTS

(Unless specified otherwise, Armorial listings are Famille Rose palette.

Bowl and cover, late 18th-early 19th c., both pieces reticulated, the cover surmounted with pod knop, the interior of bowl with the arms of Shee impaling Power, 10" d. **$1,500-2,500**

Charger, ca. 1730, coat of arms of Hamilton quartering Arran and Douglas, Duke of Hamilton, Spencer in pretense, within the ribbon of the Order of the Thistle, flanked by a pair of deer, the crest inscribed with

motto "THROUGH," chipped, frits, 15" d. **2,000-3,000**

Cup and saucer, blue and white, mid-19th c., American market, painted with eagle holding two arrows in its claw below a motto "Crescit Eundo" **800-1,200**

Meat dish, 18th c., the center with floral bouquet in red and gilt, coat of arms of the Duke of Alba below a coronet and angel crest, motto "TU IN E ET EGO PRO EA," frits, rubbed, 15" w......................**1,200-1,800**

Milk pitcher and cover, 18th c., pear-form decorated with European ladies scantily clad in bucalic landscape, finial restored, 4" h. **1,500-2,200**

Plate, late 19th c., with the arms of King Dom Luis I of Portugal (r. 1861-1889), and the motto "PALACIO DO GOVERNO DE M," rim frits, 9½" d. **800-1,200**

Plate, 18th c., two coats of arms beneath a ducal coronet and laurel wreath, stylized leave decoration on rim, rim frits............**900-1,200**

Plate, 18th c., the border with scrolls and shell designs, painted with coat of arms of Andrade of Spain, 9¼" d. **2,000-2,500**

Plate, 18th c., octagonal, decorated with the arms of Beauchamp, of Essex with Amyas quartered inpretence below spearhead borders, chipped, 8" d. **800-1,200**

Plate, ca. 1730, painted and gilded at the center with the coat of arms of Izod within a pink diaper cavetto, 8½" d......**2,000-3,000**

Plate, 18th c., decorated with two coats of arms in alliance, lotus and scroll border, 7" d. **600-900**

Plate, ca. 1775, the center with a flowering peony branch, the rim with the arms of Chambers impaling Wilton opposite the crest of a chipped boar, frits and chips, 8¾" d. **700-900**

Plate, 18th c., decorated in center with scantily clad lady, trellis border in gilt, rubbed, 7" d. **1,000-1,500**

Spoon tray, 18th c., eight-lobed with scene of European couple fishing, floral and gilt border, rubbed, 4¼" **400-650**

Tea bowl and saucer, Qianlong, Continental coat of arms beneath a coronet, rococo scrolls and leaves in border, 4¼" d. **700-900**

Tea bowls, 18th c., scalloped rim painted with European couple in a landscape, rim frits, 2 pcs. **400-600**

Tea caddy and cover, rectangular form coat of arms of Grill, the cover with lion-form finial, restored, 4" h. **400-700**

Tureen, cover and undertray, Qianlong, oblong octagonal form with hare head handles, decorated with a medallion enclosing the monogram "INS" below and anchor, the rim with flower festoon entwined with bamboo, the cover with flower-form finial, underplate 11" w., the set **10,000-15,000**

Vase, 19th c., ovoid form with tall neck and everted rim, decorated with panels of two coats of arms in alliance below a crown, flanked by lions holding banner above the motto "LOVE AND FAITH," the shoulder applied with dragons, the neck with phoenix-form handles, 21½" h. **3,000-4,000**

BLANC DE CHINE

Eight Immortals, early 20th c., each with "CHINA" impressed on base, each with attribute, 5½" h., the set **$150-225**

Figure of a European gentleman, Kangxi, wearing a hat seated on rockwork and playing a flute, restored, 6½" h. **1,500-2,200**

Figure of an elder holding a child, ca. 1920s, 6" h. (ILLUS.) **100-150**

Blanc de Chine Elder Holding a Child

Blanc de Chine Figure of Guanyin

Figure of Guanyin (Kuan Yin), 18th c., standing on a dragon amid waves, 7" h. **3,000-5,000**

Figure of Guanyin, 18th c., seated holding a scroll in the left hand, top knot with hairpin, 7" h. (ILLUS.) **3,000-4,500**

Figure of Guanyin, 18th c., standing upon swirling waves holding a scroll in the right hand, losses 18" h. (ILLUS. with Introduction) **7,000-9,000**

Figure of a Lohan, 17th c., an ascetic seated on a rock, his loose robe falling from one shoulder revealing an emaciated body, one hand holding a pearl up to tempt a dragon writhing in waves below, fingers restored, 6½" h. **1,500-2,500**

Figure of a Nobleman, tile work, Ming Dynasty, 9" h., chipped and cracked **400-500**

Figure group, boat with musicians, 19th c., 8" w. (ILLUS.) **1,500-2,000**

Joss stick holders, 19th c., inform of Buddhist lion seated on rectangular base, one paw raised and resting on a ball, 6½" h., pair **800-1,200**

Blanc de Chine Figure Group of Boat with Musicians

Blanc de Chine Buddhist Lions

Libation cup, 17th c., with relief designs of animals, birds and flowers, 2¼" h. **500-700**

Libation cup, Kangxi, the sides with low-relief tiger, deer, dragon and crane with pine trees, 4½" h. **500-750**

Model of Buddhist lions, 18th c., 3½" h., pair (ILLUS.) **1,800-2,500**

Model of a tree, gnarled prunus tree trunk with flowering branches, 18th c., losses, 19¾" h. **4,000-6,000**

Teapot and cover, 17th c., bamboo-form with curved bamboo-form handle and spout, the rim and spout mounted in gilt silver, the cover a wood replacement **600-950**

BLUE AND WHITE

Bottle, Kangxi, globular body with petal-shaped panels filled with flowers and branches, 8" h. **$1,800-2,800**

Bottle/vase, Ming-style, 19th c., globular body painted with flower and scroll, the shoulder with key fret border, flared mouth with band of waves above a ruyi head border, 12½" **600-800**

Bowl, Kangxi, painted with continuous design of The 8 Immortals with their attributes, the interior with dragon and flaming pearl, 8½" d. **1,500-2,000**

Bowl, Ming Dynasty, ca. 1600, continuous watery landscape scene with pavilions, pagoda, trees, 8" d. **600-900**

Bowl, transitional, early 17th c., Shonzui-style, made for the Japanese market, 4½" w. (ILLUS.) **900-1,200**

Bowl, ca. 1620-1640, the interior with roundel of Shou Lao on a crane, the exterior with Shou characters, the base with Chenghua six character mark, 7" d. ..**350-700**

Bowls, Hsien Feng mark and of the period, designs of eight triagrams alternating with cranes, 5¼" d., one chipped, 2 pcs. **600-800**

Bulb bowl, late 19th c., the interior decorated with fish, the exterior with wufu (bats), 7" dia., (ILLUS.) **250-350**

Cadogan teapot, early 18th c., peach-shaped, decoration of scholars and pine tree, minor restoration, 7" h. **2,000-3,000**

Candlesticks, Ming Dynasty, Wanli, in the form of a hand bell, the lower domed section decorated with emblems above ruyi and scroll borders, the tops shaped to receive metal drip pans, 9¾" h., pair ..**2,000-3,000**

Charger, Ming Dynasty, Swatow, 16th c., decoration of pheasant amid dense foliage, the well with six shaped panels filled with flowers, 18" d. **900-1,200**

Shonzui-style Chinese Porcelain Blue and White Bowl

Late 19th Century Chinese Blue and White Bulb Bowl

Charger, Ming Dynasty, Swatow, 16th c., with two deer and bird beneath overhanging tree beside a lotus pond, 16" d. **1,000-1,500**

Kangxi Chinese Porcelain Cup

Cup, Kangxi, ca. 1700, design of plants and fish below border of circular designs, 3½" h. (ILLUS.) **1,500-2,000**

Dish, Guangxu mark and of the period, shallow form with rounded sides decorated with butterflies over rockwork, 7" d. **600-800**

Dishes, late 19th c., design of dragons chasing pearl, 5" d., the set (ILLUS.) **275-375**

Export plate, 18th c., the center with floral decoration, the border with three floral designs, 8¾" d. **300-450**

Export plate, 18th c., the center decoration with "Lange Leizen" (long ladies), the border with figural and floral medallions, 9" d. **700-950**

Jar, Ming Dynasty, Wanli, ovoid form, four quarter-lobe panels with flowers and rockwork on a diaper ground between stylized lappets below and floral panels on the shoulder, frits, firing cracks, 14" h. **2,500-3,500**

Jar, 18th c., ovoid form with lappets of t'ao t'ieh masks, fitted with wood cover, 5" h. **300-500**

Jar, Transitional, ovoid from with designs of peony and bamboo growing from rockwork, fitted wood cover, 18" h. **1,500-2,200**

Chinese Blue and White 19th Century Porcelain Dishes

Jars, early 20th c., hawthorn design on cracked ice ground, with original covers, 14" h. 2 pcs. **300-450**

Jars with covers, Kangxi, baluster-form with continuous scene of mountainscape, replacement wood covers, 13¼" h., pair **3,000-5,000**

Seal paste box, 19th c. with earlier period marking (Kangxi), dragon and phoenix decoration, 3" d. **100-175**

Vase, early 20th c., celadon ground with low-relief designs of figures in blue and white, 16" h. (ILLUS.) **900-1,200**

Vase, early 20th c., Kangxi-style, baluster-form with continuous landscape, 16" h. ...**400-600**

Early 20th Century Chinese Porcelain Vase

Vase, ca. 1700, baluster-form, with landscape design and figures on the banks of a winding river, a village to one side, 18" h. **2,500-3,500**

Vase, 19th c. with early period marking (Qianlong), bulbous with elongated neck, the body decorated with passion flowers and foliage, 8½" h. **400-600**

Vase, Swatow, 16th c., ovoid-form, the shoulders applied with four loop handles, the body decorated with flowers, chips on rim, 5" d. **300-600**

Vase, Transitional, sleeve-form, cylindrical body painted with a scene from a legend showing four figures and a riverscape, 14" h. **6,500-9,500**

CANTON AND NANKING BLUE AND WHITE

Canton bidet, 18th c., kidney shaped, 20" l. **$3,000-5,000**

Canton chamber pot and cover, 18th c., globular form with domed cover, chips, 8½" d. **2,500-3,500**

Canton chamber pot and cover, early 19th c., compressed spherical shape, ribbed bracket handle with applied ruyi decoration, 8" d. **750-1,000**

Canton cup and saucer, early 19th c., cup with flanged bracket handle, 2¾" h. **100-175**

Canton dish, early 19th c., oblong octagonal form, strong blue tones, 13½" d. **1,500-2,000**

Canton ginger jars, early 19th c., ovoid shape with flat covers, 7½" h. pair..........**800-1,200**

Canton jardinieres and matching underplates, 18th c., hexagonal, 13½" d. **2,500-3,500**

Canton meat dish, oval form, 16⅜" l. ..**1,000-1,500**

Canton salts, late 18th c., oblong octagonal form with recessed top, tapered base, 3½" l., 2 pcs. **1,500-2,400**

Canton tureen and cover, late 18th c., with boar's head handles (ILLUS.) **700-900**

Canton vase, rectangular form, 18th c., 18" h. **1,500-2,200**

Nanking basket and underplate, early 19th c., both pieces reticulated, the basket with stem-form handles, 8" l., 2 pcs. ..**1,500-2,500**

Canton Blue and White Tureen and Cover

Nanking cup and saucer, early 19th c., cylindrical cup with cuspid bracket handle, conical saucer, 2½" h. **175-350**

Nanking cup and saucer, early 18th c., the design embellished with gilt in perfect condition (ILLUS.) **500-750**

Nanking dish, early 19th c., double loop handle with vine and leaf terminal, 4¾" h. **2,000-3,000**

Nanking mug, early 19th c., double loop handle with vine and leaf terminal, 4¾" h. **2,000-3,000**

Nanking soup bowl, early 19th c., 8" d. **375-550**

Nanking soup bowl, late 18th c., 9½" d. ..**400-600**

Nanking spittoon, early 19th c., broad flaring neck, spherical body, 4½" d. **2,000-2,750**

CHINESE IMARI

Bottle, early 18th c., flattened octagonal form with four vertical panels of a flowering branch growing from pierced rockwork, the sloping shoulder with flower sprays and spearhead border around the neck, 4¼" h. **$3,000-4,000**

Bowl, 18th c., pomegranate and peony blossoms radiating from a stylized flowerhead, 11" d. **800-1,200**

Charger, Kangxi, decoration of flower-filled baskets, diaper band of flowers and butterflies in reserves, minor hairlines, 16½" d. **1,500-2,500**

Chargers, Kangxi, painted with flowering sprays issuing from a chrysanthemum medallion, 16" d., 2 pcs. **4,500-6,500**

Meat dish, chamfered rectangular form, 18th c., designs of flowers and rockwork, 18" l. **1,500-2,200**

Mustard pot and cover, 18th c., ovid form on domed base, underglaze-blue, red and gilt with decorations of cockerels, the cover with a circular aperture **700-900**

Plate, 18th c., design by Cornelis Pronk, termed "Pronk" and also termed "la Dame au Parasol" a lady feeding some ducks as she stands under a parasol held by her attendant, within decorative borders, frits 9¼" d. **1,200-1,800**

Chinese Imari Rose Water Sprinkler Bottle

Rose water sprinkler bottle, Kangxi, probably for the French market, 8" h. (ILLUS.) **1,200-1,500**

Soup plate, 18th c., decorated in center with a jar of flowers, surrounded by panels of birds and flower **500-700**

Sprinkler bottle, Kangxi, pear-form with tall slender neck, 6¾" h. **1,500-2,500**

Tea caddy and cover, rectangular form with canted (rounded) corners, Kangxi, decorated with flowering branches, the cover restored, 4" h. **800-1,200**

Teapot and cover, 18th c., ribbed globular form with floral designs, chips under cover, 3¼" h. **300-500**

Tureen and cover, 18th c., pod handles, designs of birds in a lotus pond, minor restoration, 13½" l. **2,500-3,500**

Vase and cover, baluster-form, Kangxi, decorated with two pheasants perched on open rockwork issuing peony blossoms, between lappets below and cloud bands above, cover restored, 16½" h. **1,200-1800**

DOUCAI

Bowl, interior of bats and flowers and foliage, exterior Famille Rose, Guangxu mark and period, 5½" dia., (Color Illus. pg. 30) **2,000-2,500**

Bowl, Jiaqing seal, late 19th c., painted with floral bouquets surrounded by stylized floral ornaments, the interior with similar bouquet roundel, minor hairline, 5⅛" d. **2,000-3,000**

Dish, Guangxu mark, post-1917, ogee-form, decorated in the center with radiating peach decoration, the well with the attributes of The 8 Immortals, floral meander on reverse, 6¾" d. **1,200-1,800**

Dish, Daoguang, shallow rounded sides, the interior with stylized longevity symbol in red enclosed by smaller longevity symbols in red, blue, yellow and aubergine within linked foliage, the reverse with stylized longevity symbols, restoration to rim, base with Chi Ching mark, 7" d. **1,000-2,000**

Teapot and cover, late 18th or early 19th c., globular form decorated with birds in flight and prunus, the cover with bud finial, 4" h. **1,200-1,800**

FAHUA

Brush pot, late 19th c., yellow ground with blue, green and aubergine relief motif of phoenix, clouds and flames, base andinterior European green, 6"h. (ILLUS. page 43) **$300-400**

Censer, Ming-style, late 19th c., lotus and scroll pattern, 6" h. **150-250**

Jar and cover, ca. 1900, yellow ground with green and white flowers and scrolls, base impressed "CHINA," 8" h. **150-175**

Jardiniere, 17th c., circular section, decorated with herons and insects with lotus flowers and pads rising from water reserved on an aubergine ground, interior flaking, hairline cracks in base, 11¾" d. **3,000-4,000**

Illustrated right:

Japanese Domaru parade armor, 17th c. The black lacquered zunari-kobuto with short fukugaeshi pierced with crests and decorated with gold leaf, and with five stage shikoro laced with purple and white silk thread, the large maedate decorated with gold leaf, the wakidate formed as a Buddhist ken; the iron mempo black lacquered and formed as a grimacing face, the four lame shikoro laced with while silk thread; the nine stage gold lacquered okegawa-do laced in white and red silk thread with a rising sun motif, mounted with a deerskin pouch; with matching sode, kusari-gote, kote hidate and suneate; with fur shoes; with wood storage box.

$50,000-70,000

———————————— ● ————————————

Illustrated below:

A Mahal carpet, West Persia, late 19th century, evenly worn, approximately 9' 8" x 9'.

$4,500-6,500

Illustrated left:
Chinese porcelain figure astride an elephant, early 19th c., 14" h.

$1,800-2,500

Illustrated below:
Japanese quiver, carved bamboo with black lacquer interior containing bamboo practice arrows with metal tips, early 20th c., 42" l., the set.

$300-500

Illustrated above:
Chinese Buddhist Lions, Kangxi, each sitting on a pierced plinth, three-color glaze (aubergine, green and ochre), one with foot on pup, the other with foot on brocade ball, 8" h.

$1,500-2,000

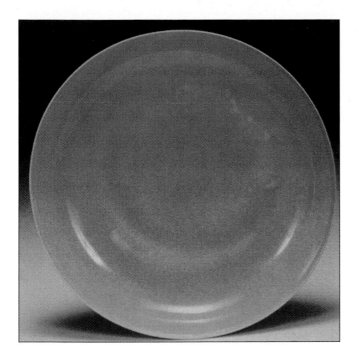

Illustrated above:
Chinese Imperial Yellow saucer dish, Hongzhi mark and period (1488-1505), well potted and covered overall with rich glaze, the base with a six-character mark, frits on rim, 8" d.
$12,000-18,000

---●---

Illustrated top, far left:
Chinese porcelain bowl, Doucai interior of bats and flowers and foliage, exterior Famille Rose, Guangxu mark and period, 5½" d.
$2,000-2,500

---●---

Illustrated top left:
Chinese porcelain bowl, Famille Rose palette, Daoguang mark and period, interior with five wufu (bats), 8" d.
$9,000-12,000

---●---

Illustrated bottom left:
Chinese porcelain footed dish, Tongzhi mark and period, scenic motif with riverscape, Famille Rose palette, 5" w.
$2,000-2,500

---●---

Illustrated top right:
Chinese porcelain brush washer, 18th c., copper red, 7" d.
$1,200-1,800

Illustrated above:
Chinese teadust glazed vase, Qianlong mark and period, globular with wide splayed foot, cylindrical neck, overall dark yew-leaf green glaze with light speckles, mark on base inciscd, 13" h.
$12,000-18,000

Illustrated above:
Chinese porcelain vase, Guangxu mark and period, blue with gilt dragons, the neck decorated with auspicious characters (long life), with gilt bands around the shoulder and below the mouth, six-character mark on base, 16" h.

$3,000-5,000

Illustrated above:
Chinese porcelain sake bottle, late 17th or early 18th c., made for the Japanese market, double-gourd form, with two panels, one with dragons and the side illustrated with a Buddhist lion, Ming palette which matches the Kutani palette, 6½" h.

$3,000-5,000

Illustrated above:
China Trade Porcelain, Tobacco Leaf pattern, tureen, cover and undertray, 18th c., Qianlong, in shape of lobed leaf, characteristic palette, tureen with lotus pod handles, the cover with floral spray knop (finial).

$15,000-18,000

Illustrated right:
Chinese porcelain covered bowl with stand, Guangxu mark and period, Dowager Empress, her studio name "Da ya zhai" in seal writing in the cartouche, base marked with characters that read "Heaven and Earth/One Family/One Spring," Famille Rose palette.

$900-1,200

Illustrated bottom left:
Chinese porcelain bowls, Daoguang mark and period, blue ground with lotus, scrolls and bats, interior and base covered with European green glaze, 5" d.

$3,500-5,000

Illustrated above:

   Japanese porcelain: Left -a porcelain vase and its original box, base of vase marked with Koransha (fragrant orchid) leaf mark in underglaze-blue, the box covered with the same trademark and label which reads "Koransha," original shipping invoice in box dates 1981, manufactured by the Koransha Co.; Right-a porcelain vase with the Fukagawa trademark on the base, Mt. Fuji in underglaze-blue; manufactured in the early 1990s. These vases cost approximately $130-150 depending upon the current value of the Japanese yen to the U.S. dollar.

———————————————●———————————————

Illustrated left:

   Chinese dish, Liao Dynasty, sancai, the floret design molded in low-relief, 7" d.

$1,200-1,800

———————————————●———————————————

Illustrated right:

   Chinese Rose Mandarin garden seats, 19th c., each hexagonal, decorated with alternating shaped panels and raised bosses, 18½" h.

$6,000-8,000

Illustrated left:
This Koransha mark (leaf spray) was used in the 19th century and can be found in red over the glaze (as illustrated here), gold over the glaze and blue under the glaze. To the best of the author's knowledge the red mark was discontinued in 1894.

Illustrated left:
This Mt. Fuji mark (Fukagawa) is over the glaze red. It appears on a vase which was manufactured for the NYK Line and dates before World War II. To the best of the author's knowledge this red mark has not been used since the end of the war.

Illustrated left:
This is the underglaze-blue Mt. Fuji mark used by the Fukagawa Co. It is still being used as their trademark. It is important to know and recognize the various patterns which have been produced and the variances within these patterns. The vase illustrated in black and white on page 63 with lappets around the neck is 19th century. However, there are new patterns similar to this (modified from the original used in the Meiji period) which will have a Mt. Fuji trademark on the base. It is not the Mt. Fuji mark which will determine age. The pattern is the determining factor.

Illustrated left:
The mark is Koransha (Fragrant Orchid-leaf spray) which is found on the modern pieces produced by the Koransha Co. The mark is just like the one used in the 19th century before the Mt. Fuji mark was used by the Fukagawa Co. This mark appears on a vase produced by the Koransha Co., ca. 1980.

Illustrated above:
   Japanese Fukagawa bowl, studio porcelain, ca.
   1910, bamboo and karako in various poses, Mt.
   Fuji mark in underglaze-blue, 6" h.
                                    $2,000-2,500

Illustrated top left:
Japanese Kakiemon dish, 18th c., the well with vase and flowers, the border with three rabbits, 8" d.

$2,000-3,000

_____●_____

Illustrated bottom left:
Japanese Kutani bottle, late 19th c., hexagonal with panels depicting carp, birds and flowers, figures, the shoulder decorated with animals of the zodiac, 12" h.

$2,000-3,000

_____●_____

Illustrated right:
Japanese Imari, 19th c., figure of Shoki and his attendant who is cleaning his ear, 12" h.

$3,000-4,500

_____●_____

Illustrated below:
Japanese Kyoto sake bottle, late 18th c., cylindrical with loops for handle, design of plum blossoms and foliage, 5½" h.

$2,500-3,000

Illustrated left:
  Japanese Kyoto ware koro (censer), last half of the 18th c., cock and hen finial, supported on three legs, 4" h.

$4,500-6,500

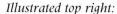

Illustrated top right:
  Japanese chawan, early 19th c., birds and camellia with foliage, signed Kenya.

$1,500-2,000

Illustrated bottom right:
  Japanese Kutani vase, late 19th c., five spouts, overall scenic design, double-gourd form with the upper portion decorated with phoenix, 10" h.

$1,800-2,500

Illustrated below:
  Japanese Kutani (AO) dish, early 19th c., ca. 1830, with attested box, the design features two of the Seven Household Gods of Good Luck, Eibsu and Daikoku, 12" x 12".

$2,500-3,500

Illustrated above:
Japanese Satsuma koro (censer), early 19th c.,
each side decorated in colors and gilt with
seasonal flowers, 4" h.

$4,500-6,500

Late 19th Century Fahua Brush Pot

Vase, 18th c., double-gourd form made in the Ming style, low-relief lotus and scroll, ruyi collar around waist, lappet border above foot, aubergine, turquoise and white, the rim restored, 19¾" h. **2,000-3,000**

Vase, early 20th c., ca. 1925, yellow ground with green and white flowers in Ming style, "CHINA" impressed on base, 14" h...**125-175**

FAMILLE JAUNE, FAMILLE NOIRE, FAMILLE ROSE, FAMILLE VERTE AND BISCUIT WARES

Biscuit bowl, Kangxi, flared sides decorated with animals amid flames and crested waves, glazed in white, yellow, aubergine on a green ground, crack partially restored **$1,500-2,000**

Biscuit libation cup, 19th c., lotus-form with applied green stalk extending to form three feet, aubergine, and yellow glaze, 3½" d. **175-225**

Biscuit parrots, 19th c., standing astride on a pierced rockwork base with slightly turned heads, green and yellow, 10" h., pair..**750-950**

Chinese Porcelain Famille Rose Bowl with Magpies

Biscuit water dropper, 19th c. Kangxi-style, modeled as finger citron covered with yellow, green and aubergine glaze, 2½" l. **200-350**

Famille Noire garden seat, 20th c., prunus decoration with gilt embellishment, 18" h. **350-500**

Famille Rose Hexagonal Cap Stand

Famille Noire vase, Kangxi, yenyen-form with high shoulder, the body tapering to a spreading foot, trumpet neck, prunus blossoms and birds glazed in green, aubergine, yellow and black on a black ground, 25" h. **15,000-25,000**

Famille Rose bowl, Qianlong, decorated with insects and flowers the border with floral design, 4" d. **300-500**

Famille Rose bowl, Guangxu mark and period, magpies and foliage with design on both interior and exterior, 5" d. (ILLUS.) **1,800-2,500**

Famille Rose bowls, nested-type, second half 19th c., flared sides, decorated with scenes of figures, the smallest 1" x 1", set of 9 ....**2,000-2,500**

Famille Rose hexagonal cap stand, late 19th c., decorated with celestial figures, gilt highlights, rim and openwork with gilt embellishment, 8"h. (ILLUS.) **375-575**

Famille Rose censer, mid-19th c., tri-lobed globular form with upright S-curved handles, painted with lotus and scroll in colors on a pink ground, the cover with a lion-form finial, restorations, 12½" h. **900-1,200**

Famille Rose dish, footed, Tongzhi mark and period, scenic motif with riverscape, 5" w., (Color Illus. pg. 30) **2,000-2,500**

Famille Rose dish, 18th c., the center with a lady on a boar, the rim with vignettes of vases on a floral ground, the base cracked, 9½" d. **600-800**

Famille Rose garniture set: three baluster-form vases and covers and two beaker-form vases: decorated in the "mandarin palette" with panels of figures in landscapes reserved on a "Y" diaper ground, one vase and cover repaired, 6" and 8" h., the set............................**2,000-3,000**

Famille Rose jars and covers, marked Qianlong but ca. 1925, elders and attendants under trees, black ruyi borders, 3½" h., pair (ILLUS.) **500-750**

Famille Rose plaque, 19th c., elder and child with ducks, 11" x 14" (ILLUS.) ..**1,000-1,500**

Famille Rose plaque, 19th c., Shoulao with deer, framed, framed size 12" x 18" (ILLUS.) **1,200-1,800**

Famille Rose plate, mid-18th c., the center with design of a merchant and his man servant, the border with floral panels on a diaper ground, 9" d. **1,500-2,000**

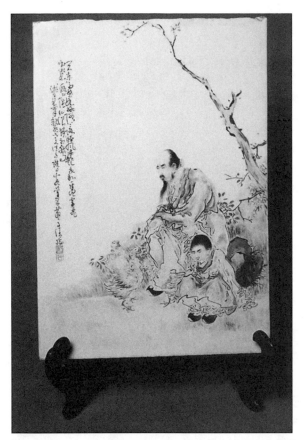

Famille Rose Plaque – Elder and Child

Famille Rose Plaque – Shoulao with Deer

Famille Rose Jars and Covers

Famille Rose plates, Yongzheng, the center with a lady playing a flute for a boy on a daybed, the rim with vignette of peach, pomegranate and finger citron on a cell patterned ground, 8" d., 2 pcs. 7,500-12,000

Famille Rose plates, Yongzheng, ruby back semi-eggshell, painted with the poet Li Taibo and an attendant, one with hairlines, 7" d., 2 pcs. **4,000-6,000**

Famille Rose plates, 18th c., the center with figures each bordered with flowers and foliage, 8" d., set of two (ILLUS.) ..**1,200-1,500**

Famille Rose tankard, ca. 1760, made for the European market, panels of figures between panels of inverted 'Y' patterns in red, blue and gilt, silver rim and handle added in Europe at a later date, 6" h. (ILLUS.) **350-500**

Famille Rose vase, the base with four-character Qianlong mark but ca. 1920s, two ladies seated beneath a tree, calligraphic poem on the reverse, the rim decorated with ruyi and jewels, 6" h. (ILLUS.) **500-700**

Famille Rose vases, square-form (cong form), completely covered in blue glaze, elephant heads and rings on each side, decorated with warriors in the Famille Rose palette, Qianlong mark but Tongzhi, 19th c., 12" h. (ILLUS.) **1,000-1,500**

Famille Rose wall vases, 18th c., lobed baluster-form applied at either side with

boys wearing green and blue tunics, 5½" h., pair **1,200-1,800**

Famille Verte charger, Kangxi, the center painted with two women and a deer pulling a cart within a double underglaze-blue circle, the base with six-character Chenghua marks **9,000-12,000**

Famille Verte tile, ca. 1700, a court scene with two seated officials and three attendants, 10" w. **2,000-3,000**

Famille Verte tile, ca. 1700, a design of blossoming branches, 10¼" w. **2,000-3,000**

Famille Rose Tankard

1920s Famille Rose Palette Porcelain Vase

Famille Rose Palette Square-Form Vases

18th Century Famille Rose Plates

Famille Verte vase, Kangxi, roleau-form with warrior on horseback and soldier in landscape, cracked, 18" h. **1,500-2,500**

Famille Verte vase, ca. 1920, Kangxi-style, baluster-form, warriors on horseback marked "MADE IN CHINA," 15½" h. **275-500**

FITZHUGH

Basket and underplate, ca. 1800, the basket pierced, underglaze-blue and gilt, gilt rubbed, 9½" d., 2 pcs....................**$1,800-2,700**

Dinner plates, early 19th c., blue and white with broad upcurling rim, 8" d., set of 6 .... **2,500-3,500**

Side plates, matching previous plates, early 19th c., 5" d., set of 6 ....**1,200-2,000**

Tureen and cover, 18th c., shaped oval section standing on a splayed foot, Fitzhugh pattern in blue and white, the cover with similar design, lotus bud top knop, 10½" l. **2,500-3,500**

MARKED AND PERIOD PORCELAIN, MING THROUGH EARLY 20TH CENTURY

Blue and gilt vase, Guangxu mark and of the period, elongated pear-form decorated in gilt with large fish among seaweed, decoration repeated on neck, gilt rubbed and worn, 12" h. **$4,000-6,500**

Blue and green bowls, Guangxu mark and period, blue ground with lotus and scroll, bats and longevity symbols in shades of white, green and gilt highlights, 3" d. (ILLUS.) **1,200-1,800**

Blue and green bowls, Daoguang mark and period, blue ground with lotus, scrolls and bats, interior and base covered with European green glaze, 5" d., (Color Illus. pg. 32) **3,500-5,000**

Blue and iron-red bowl, Guangxu and period, the sides decorated with five bats amid clouds, the interior with a roundel of bat amid clouds, 5¼" d. **2,000-3,000**

Blue and iron-red dish, Qianlong and period, dragon and flaming pearl among clouds, the reverse with two further dragons, cracked, 5½" d. **800-1,200**

Blue and white beaker vase, Gu-shape, Wanli six-character mark and of the period, squat form design of phoenix on one side, dragon on the other divided by vertical flanges, the flaring neck with peony rising from rockwork, divided by further flanges, the foot with clouds and flowerhead decorations, 8" h. **12,000-18,000**

Blue and white bowl, Kangxi mark and period, painted with lotus blossoms with stylized lappet band, the interior with a single lotus flower, rim chips restored, 5½" d. **1,500-2,000**

Blue and white cup and saucer, Kangxi mark and period, underglaze-blue designs of figures (ILLUS.) **700-900**

Blue and white "Three Friends" dish, Qianlong mark and period, the center with pine, prunus and bamboo, growing beside a pierced rock, the exterior with a lady seated on a bench watching two children playing in a garden, small restoration to rim, frits, 6" d. **3,500-4,500**

Guangxu Blue and Green Bowls

Kangxi Blue and White Cup and Saucer

Blue and white saucer dishes, Wanli six-character mark and of the period, gently flaring sides, everted rims, central roundel of dragon and phoenix within double line borders at the well and rim, the reverse similarly decorated, small rim chips, glaze fractures, 6½" d., set of 2 ....**6,000-8000**

Blue and white vase, Guangxu mark and period, blue with gilt dragons, the neck decorated with auspicious characters (long life), with gilt bands around the shoulder and below the mouth, six-character mark on base, 16" h., (Color Illus. pg. 32) **3,000-5,000**

Famille Rose palette bowl, Daoguang mark and period, interior with five wufu bats), 8" d., (Color Illus. pg. 30) **9,000-12,000**

Famille Rose palette covered bowl with stand, Guangxu mark and period, Dowager Empress, her studio name "Da ya zhai" in seal writing in the cartouche, base marked with characters that read "Heaven and Earth/One Family/One Spring" (Color Illus. pg. 33) **900-1,200**

Famille Rose vase, Hongxian mark, early 20th c., ovoid form, flared neck, decoration of scholar and attendant in a garden, 10" h. **2,000-3,000**

Famille Rose vase, Hongxian, early 20th c., decoration of Shoulao and five frolicking boys, 9" h. **4,500-6,500**

Famille Rose dragon and phoenix bowl, Guangxu mark and period, compressed globular form, inturned rim, dragon and phoenix at either side of a flaming pearl above waves, the border with key fret, 8½" d. **2,500-3,500**

Flambé vase, Qianlong mark and of the period, thickly potted, globular body, thick rich glaze of deep violet red suffused with lavender and splashes of raspberry, the base with incised mark, 15" h. **20,000-30,000**

Guan glazed vases, Guangxu mark and of the period, square form, decorated with trigrams in relief, crackled glaze, 11" h., pair..**3,000-5,000**

Imperial yellow bowl, Jiaqing mark of period, the glaze of even color, 4" d. **12,000-18,000**

Imperial yellow saucer dish, Hongzhi mark and period (1488-1505), well-potted and covered overall with rich glaze, the base with a six-character mark, frits on rim, 8" d., (Color Illus. pg. 31) **12,000-18,000**

Lime ground bowl, Daoguang mark and period, hexagonal-form, decorated with phoenix and lotus reserved on a lime green ground, the interior and base glazed turquoise, 8½" d. **1,500-2,500**

Liver red bowls, Guangxu mark and of the period, slightly rounded conical shape,

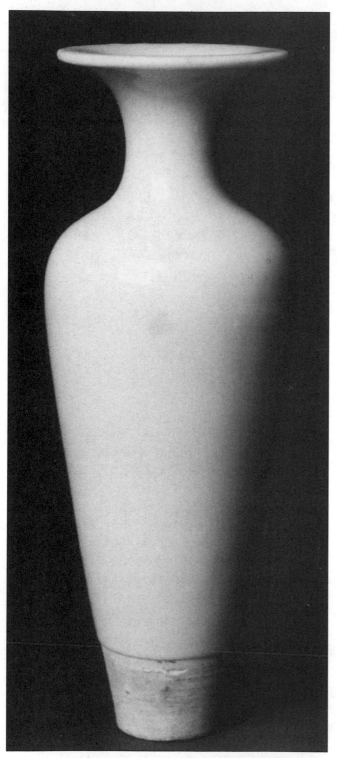

Clair de Lune Glaze Vase

each covered on exterior with liver red glaze with pinkish tones, interiors glazed white, rim chips on one, 5¼" d., pair ..**2,500-3,500**

Peach bloom seal paste box and cover, Kangxi mark and of the period, circular form, domed cover, 2⅞" d. **15,000-25,000**

Pink ground "Famille Rose" bowl, Daoguang mark and period, shallow form, decorated with phoenix and roundel of phoenix encircling a dragon medallion, the reverse with iron-red bats, 5¾" d. **1,500-2,500**

Pink ground cup, cover and stand, Guangxu mark and of the period, decorated with lotus and scrolls in colors, the stand with inturned foliate rim, 3½" h. **900-1,200**

Yellow ground Daya Zhai box and cover, Guangxu mark and of the period, circular form, the top painted *en grisaille* with insects and white flowering branches of peony, lemon yellow ground, 5½" d....**4,500-6,000**

Yellow ground Daya Zhai jardiniere, Guangxu mark and of the period, rectangular form with canted corners raised on four shaped feet, the sides with grisaille insects and white lilies on a lemon yellow ground, the interior and base turquoise, 7½" w. **3,500-4,500**

MONOCHROMES

Apple green jar, late 19th c., squat globular form, brown rim, crackled glaze, 3¼" h. **$175-300**

Blue-glazed meiping, 16th c., shouldered form tapering towards the base with lipped rim, firing cracks to body, 9" h. **3,500-5,500**

Celadon dish, Lonquan, Ming Dynasty, 14th-15th c., molded in the center with a bird amid foliage, molded cavetto and bracket rim with floral scroll, 13½" d...**1,500-2,200**

Celadon vase, 19th c. with early period marking, double-gourd form with crackled glaze, 5" h. **300-600**

Celadon tripod censer, early 19th c., ribbed body on three stylized animal form feet, even glaze, 3¼" h. **700-1,000**

Clair de lune glaze vase, 18th or 19th c., 4" h. (ILLUS.) **900-1,200**

Copper red brush washer, 18th c., 7" d., (Color Illus. pg. 31) **1,200-1,800**

Copper red vase, late 18th c., baluster-
form, rounded foot rim, minor chipping at
foot, 8" h. **1,500-2,000**

Mirror black vase, 19th c. with Kangxi
mark, baluster form with flared mouth,
12" h. **200-350**

Powder blue bowl, 19th c., flared sides
decorated in gilt with Buddhist emblems,
six-character Kangxi mark on base, 9" h. ..**600-900**

Purple dish, Qianlong mark, early 19th c.,
incised decoration of dragon and flaming
pearl on the interior, the exterior with
two dragons, 7½" d. **3,500-5,500**

Robin's egg blue bird feeder, 19th c.,
hexagonal form with two loop
adjustments, 1" **100-200**

Robin's egg blue water pot, 19th c.,
domed shape with lavender splashes,
2" h. **300-400**

Teadust-glazed vase, 19th c., globular form
with tall waisted neck, 11" h. **550-950**

Teadust-glazed vase, Qianlong mark and
period, globular with wide splayed foot,
cylindrical neck, overall dark yew-leaf
green glaze with light speckles, mark
onbase incised, 13" h. (Color Illus.
pg. 31) **12,000-18,000**

Violet-glazed surprise cup, ca. 1700, lotus
leaf form with incised veins, applied with
a stem and three short tapered feet, minor
chipping, 3" **1,000-1,500**

Yellow vase, early 19th c., pear-shaped with
slender flared neck with two tubular
applied handles, the body incised with
dragons and waves, 10" h. **1,000-1,500**

PATTERNED FAMILLE ROSE

Auspicious Figures serving dish, 19th c.,
11" l. **$350-650**

Rose Mandarin dishes, early 19th c.,
square form with slight scallop in rim,
9" d., pair **1,500-2,200**

Rose Mandarin garden seat, 19th c.,
barrel-form, the top pierced with 'cash'
symbol, 18" h. **1,500-2,500**

Rose Mandarin garden seats, 19th c., each
hexagonal, decorated with alternating
shaped panels and raised bosses, 18½" h.
(Color Illus. pg. 35) **6,000-8,000**

Rose Mandarin punch bowl, 19th c.,
rubbed, 15¾" d. **1,000-1,500**

Rose Mandarin punch bowl, early 19th c.,
rim chips restored, 18" d. **3,500-4,500**

Rose Mandarin storage jar and cover,
mid-19th c., baluster-form depicting
various courts scenes in large panels
reserved on a gilt ground, the neck and
cover bound with metal (restored),
25½" h. **3,500-4,500**

Rose Mandarin vases, 19th c., ovoid bodies
with chilong on the shoulder, trumpet
neck, one cracked, 34" h., pair **5,000-7,000**

Rose Mandarin vases, 19th c., the necks
decorated with confronting Buddhist Lions,
minor chips to one, 35" h., pair **3,500-5,500**

Rose Medallion bowl, ca. 1900, 5" d. **175-225**

Rose Medallion bowl, ca. 1900, 7" d. **250-275**

Rose Medallion bowl, ca. 1900, 9" d. **375-475**

Rose Medallion covered dish, ca. 1900,
oval, 10½" l. **400-600**

Rose Medallion covered dish, ca. 1900,
square, 9½" w. **700-850**

Rose Medallion covered dish, ca. 1840,
square, surmounted with gilt acorn finial,
interior of cover and dish decorated en
suite with exterior **1,500-2,200**

Rose Medallion cup and saucer, low, ca.
1900 ....**100-125**

Rose Medallion cup and saucer, after-
dinner, ca. 1900 ....**110-145**

Rose Medallion cuspidor, ca. 1900, low
sides **1,200-1,800**

**Rose Medallion fruit basket and
undertray,** c. 1900, 8½" l., 2 pcs...............**450-650**

Rose Medallion plate, ca. 1900, 9½" d. **125-175**

Rose Medallion salad bowl, ca. 1900 ....**375-500**

Rose Medallion sauce tureen, cover and
undertray, ca. 1900, the set **275-400**

Rose Medallion soup tureen, cover and
undertray, ca. 1900, the set **500-700**

Rose Medallion teapot and cover, bell-
form, ca. 1900 ....**400-600**

Rose Medallion teapot and cover,
ca. 1900, cylindrical form, woven
bail handle **400-700**

Rose Medallion tea set: covered teapot,
covered sugar and helmet-form creamer;
late 19th c., rubbed, the set **500-750**

Rose Medallion vases, 19th c., baluster-
form, trumpet neck, 22" h., 2 pcs. **4,000-6,000**

Two Color Wares

Blue and green dragon dish, Qianlong mark and of the period, the center with a dragon chasing the flaming pearl amid clouds and flames below two further dragons, the reverse with a similar border, rim frits, 8½" d. **$1,800-2,500**

Copper red and underglaze-blue jar, Qianlong, globular shape, two four-toed dragons amid clouds and flame scrolls, the neck with underglaze borders, the base with star crack, 4" h. **3,500-5,500**

Copper red and celadon bowl, Yongzheng mark and of the period, the exterior with five wufu (bats) in copper red on a pale celadon ground, 6" d. **8,500-12,500**

Egg and spinach (yellow and green) bowl, ca. 1900, 7" d. **200-275**

Kutani palette sake bottle, late 17th or early 18th c., made for the Japanese market, double-gourd form, with two panels, one with dragons and the side illustrated with a Buddhist lion, Ming palette which matches the Kutani palette, 6½" h., (Color Illus. pg. 32)..................**3,000-5,000**

Tobacco Leaf

Dish, 18th c., rectangular chamfered form, decorated in traditional palette with flowers and foliage, 13¼" d. **$1,500-2,500**

Platter, 18th c., characteristic palette with foliage and flowers, scalloped rim, 15½" d. **4,500-6,500**

Tureen and cover, 18th c., traditional palette with flowers and foliage, lotus handles and finial, gilt highlights rubbed, restoration to finial, 11½" d. **8,000-12,000**

Tureen, cover and undertray, 18th c., Qianlong, in shape of lobed leaf, characteristic palette, tureen with lotus pod handles, the cover with floral spray knop (finial) (Color Illus. pg. 33) **15,000-18,000**

Wucai

Bowl, Qianlong mark and of the period, the sides decorated with two five-clawed dragons chasing the flaming pearl, the interior with similar design, cracked and chipped, 4½" d. **$600-900**

Bowl, early 20th c., rounded sides decorated on exterior with stylized floral decorations

divided by C-shaped scrolls all below a garland-like border below the rim, the interior with similar designs, 4½" d. **500-700**

Bowl, Daoguang seal and of the period, dragon and phoenix design, 5" d. **5,000-7,000**

Yixing

Teapot and cover, late 18th or early 19th c., globular form with flowering branches applied in low-relief, minor rim chips to underside of cover and around spout **$1,750-2,200**

Teapot and cover, first half 19th c., rectangular-form, uniformly glazed overall in blue (ILLUS.) **750-950**

Teapot and cover, 19th c., light brown with flowers and foliage (ILLUS.) **600-900**

Teapot and cover, 20th c., pear-form with bamboo-form spout and handle, applied prunus blossoms in low-relief, 4¾" h. **100-175**

Teapot and cover, early 20th c., compressed globular form, 3¼" h. **100-175**

Vase, trumpet-form, dark brown with lighter brown branches and beige plum blossoms in low-relief, ca. 1900, 7¼" h. **500-700**

Vase, cylindrical with slightly flared rim, painted flowers and foliage in pastel shades, late 19th c., 6" h. **400-600**

Wine pot, cylindrical bamboo-form, late 19th or early 20th c. **275-400**

Yixing Blue Teapot and Cover

Yixing Teapot and Cover

NEOLITHIC THROUGH YUAN DYNASTY

Han Dynasty figure of a chicken, raised head and tail, incised feathers, traces of red pigment, 14" h. $1,000-1,800

Han Dynasty grain jar, cylindrical body supported on three animal form feet, green glaze (slight oxidation) 1,500-2,500

Han Dynasty pottery vase, green with iridescence, baluster-form with anomalistic designs in a band around the broad body, 14" h. 2,500-3,500

Liao Dynasty dish, sancai, the floret design molded in low-relief, 7" d. (Color Illus. pg. 34) 1,200-1,800

Neolithic pottery jar, Yang Sao culture, thinly potted ovoid body tapered to flat base and set with loop handles, top half painted with brownish-red pigment, designs of lines and cross hatches, 5¼" h. 300-500

Neolithic pottery jar with loop handles, 8" d. 200-450

Chinese Tang Dynasty Horse

Song Dynasty Dingyao foliate bowl, each petal lightly delineated, the glaze an even shade of ivory, 7¼" d. **3,500-5,500**

Song Dynasty Henan black-glazed jar, ovoid body, cylindrical neck, two ribbed strap handles, even black glaze stopping short of the foot, the interior partially glazed translucent brown, hairlines, 5"h. **800-1,200**

Song Dynasty Junyao jar, broad ovoid form with short upright rim, two small loop handles, the glaze an even shade of lavender stopping short of the foot, 5" h. **3,500-5,500**

Song Dynasty Cizhou globular jar, painted in dark brown on cream slip with foliage sprays, foot rim chips, 4¼" h. ..**1,000-1,500**

Song Dynasty Yingqing jarlet, ovoid, carved with two foliate medallions enclosing phoenix and clouds, tall neck with lipped rim, overall translucent pale blue glaze, 3½" h. **1,500-2,000**

Tang Dynasty figure of a camel, standing four-square on a rectangular base, curved neck, raised head, the humps inclined in different directions, all covered under a straw and amber glaze, restorations, dating consistent with a thermo-luminescence test, Oxford, 15½" h. **6,500-9,500**

Tang Dynasty figure of a dog, glazed green, head raised, restored, oxidized, 8" h. **700-900**

Tang Dynasty figure of a guardian wearing armor, 15" h. **900-1,500**

Tang Dynasty figure of a horse, pottery with chestnut glaze, bridle and harness with sancai-glazed trappings, unglazed saddle, 20" h. (ILLUS.) **20,000-25,000**

Tang Dynasty figure of a horse, well modeled with right front leg raised, mouth open, tail and mane missing, traces of pigment, restored, 21" h. **15,000-25,000**

Tang Dynasty figure of a female musician, wearing long shawl and dress with low bodice, seated on base, playing a pipa, traces of reddish orange and black pigment, some restoration, 8" h. **7,500-12,000**

Tang Dynasty figure of a warrior, traces of pigment, 14" h. **500-800**

Yuan Dynasty jar, green glaze, ovoid form with flared neck and lipped rim, the shoulders with five loop handles, the glaze with amber patches, 12" h. **1,200-1,800**

Yuan Dynasty stem cup, the bowl with flared sides supported on a tapered stem, the interior molded with a lotus head below a horizontal line, the glaze a deep celadon, 2¾" h. **1,000-1,500**

Yuan Dynasty Shufu bowl, the flat center molded with a scroll in a band interrupted by two-character shu and fu on the interior of the angled sides, the glaze a thick pale bluish white, supported on a small foot, 5" d. **2,000-3,000**

Yuan Dynasty water dropper, phoenix-form, blue and white, firing cracks, 5" l. **2,500-3,500**

JAPANESE CERAMICS

POTTERY AND PORCELAIN

Banko ware—These pottery wares are highly collectible in today's market. They come in a variety of colors including white, marbleized (brown and white), gray, brown and tapestry. Banko wares, from the late Edo period to the present, have been produced for both the domestic and foreign markets. Traditional as well as whimsical items were produced, especially teapots. Banko wares generally have impressed markings (see marks) on the base or on a handle. Motifs can be painted, incised, applied in high- or low-relief.

Japanese Banko Teapot with Cranes

Imari—The term "Imari" refers to wares which were produced in Hizen and exported from the port of Imari. Japanese Imari is sometimes mistaken for its Chinese counterpart. The Japanese products differ because they have heavier paste (porcelain body), thicker glaze, darker and runny blues, a red which is termed "brick" or "Indian" red (thickly applied). Some varieties of Japanese Imari can have lacquered designs. Gosai are Imari wares with not more than five hues; Sansai has three hues. Sometsuke is underglaze-blue and white. Brocade Imari refers to "nishikide," decorated with patterns in polychrome and gilt. The Imari wares which are marked "Arita" are referred to as Arita wares.

Imari wares include:

Fukagawa—Since about 1650, the Fukagawa family has been producing fine quality ceramic wares. Of interest, in today's market, are the ware produced in the 19th and early 20th centuries. In 1876, Fukagawa Ezaiemon established "Koransha" (fragrant orchid), an important ceramics company. The markings included an "orchid spray" (see marks) either with or without calligraphy. Some members of this company left to form new ceramic producing companies around 1880. The Fukagawa family was left with the Koransha company. About 1894, Chuji Fukagawa, the head of the company, changed the trademark (backstamp) to Mt. Fuji. The Mt. Fuji mark is still in use. The Fukagawa company produced both traditional Imari and studio ceramics.

There are several facts regarding Fukagawa porcelain which cause problems for appraisers, collectors and dealers. First, the Koransha orchid spray mark, used prior to 1894, is today being used by Koransha, manufacturers of fine porcelain. These wares are marked with an underglaze-blue orchid spray. The Fukagawa Company has continued to use the Mt. Fuji mark for more than 100 years. Both marks are found on fine porcelain wares with designs, somewhat modified, but very much like earlier designs. When in doubt, seek the advice of a specialist who is well acquainted with antique, early 20th c., and modern patterns (post-World War II). See the illustrations for further information.

Hirado—Imari wares were produced off the northwest coast of Kyushu, Japan, originally under the patronage of the Daimyo of Hirado, Matsura Shizunobu. Like many wares produced under Daimyo patronage during the Edo period, it was forbidden to sell Hirado porcelains in the domestic market.

The paste of Hirado wares is milky white, free of grit. The blue reminds one of the color of sapphires. Hirado wares can found all-white, underglaze-blue and white, underglaze-blue, white and brown, as well as in pale colors. Hirado wares are known for fine decoration and modeling.

Kakiemon–This line of potters began working at the Nangawa kiln, near Arita. The name is synonymous with the porcelain, designs and palette used by this family of potters since the 17th century.

Sakaida Kizaemon (Kakiemon I), ca. 1596-1666, was among the first ceramists to produce porcelain in Japan. He is acknowledged as having been the first to produce porcelain with overglaze polychrome enamels. Kakiemon I used Chinese recipes for his wares.

The earliest Kakiemon polychrome porcelain wares were made from the highest quality clay obtained from Izumi yama (Hizen province). The glaze was white, and the clarity of the enamels added to the richness of the wares. Kakiemon wares are decorated with simple naturalistic designs which generally cover two-thirds of an object, thus leaving some undecorated open space. The palette includes: red (persimmon), blue (bluish gray, bluish black or bluish green), yellow, black and aubergine (eggplant hue).

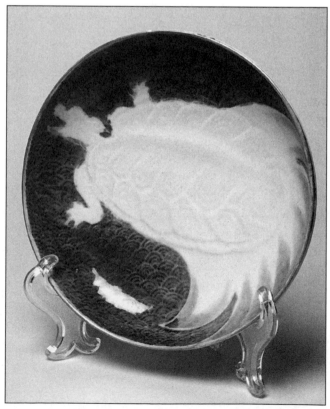

Arita Blue and White Porcelain Dish

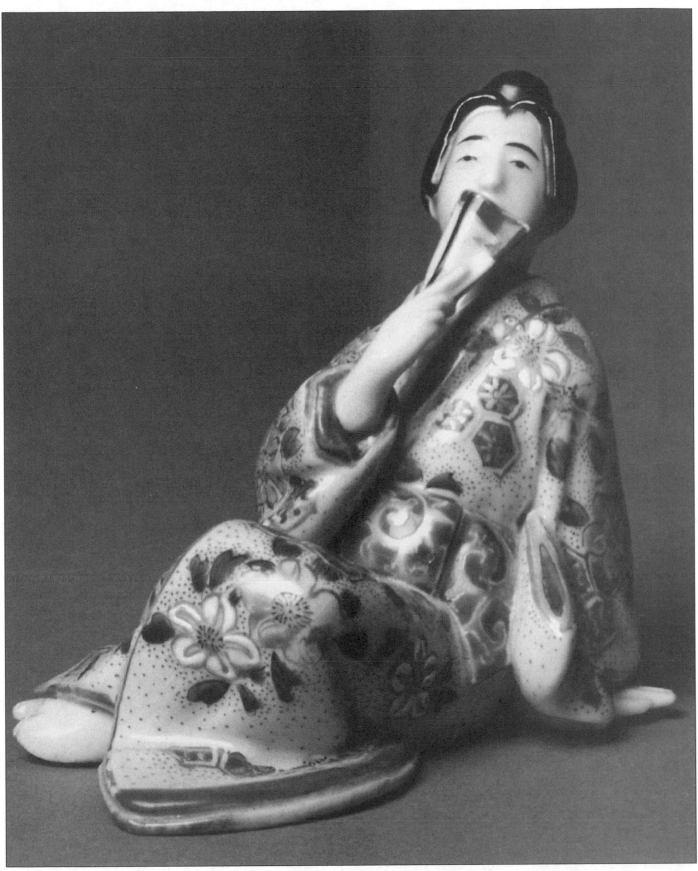

Imari Figure of Seated Bijin

Edges were sometimes decorated in chocolate brown or brownish red. Occasionally gilt was added to the designs. The collectible generations of the Kakiemon family go from I through XIV.

Nabeshima—Nabeshima wares were produced under the patronage of Lard Nabeshima of Saga Prefecture. Like other varieties of wares, they were not meant for domestic sale until the Meiji period. Nabeshima porcelain was produced with the same materials used at other Arita Factories, but it is much finer than other Arita ceramics. Nabeshima wares can have designs with underglaze-blue outlines, decorations being filled in with broad brush strokes. These wares are not as vibrant as their Arita counterparts. The palette includes: iron-red, underglaze-blue, yellow, green, celadon (seiji), and brown as well as blue and white.

Designs tend to be bold and simple and can cover the entire surface or as little as one-third.

Nabeshima wares are known for their high footrim which is decorated with an underglaze-blue diaper design. The most frequently used pattern is termed "comb" because it looks like the teeth on a comb. Back rims can have underglaze-blue designs similar to those found on other forms of Imari, but more finely executed.

Kutani wares—As early as the middle of the 17th century the Kutani kilns were set up at a remote mountain village in Kaga province called Kutani. This is where Ko Kutani (early Kutani) enameled porcelain was first produced. the Kutani kilns were founded under the patronage of the Maeda Family, Daimyo in Kaga province. The palette of Ko Kutani includes green, blue, aubergine, yellow and black. After some years. Kutani manufacture declined. it was at the beginning of the 19th century that the Kutani wares were revived. One of the many manufacturers was Yoshidaya. After the start of the Meiji period, Kutani wares of all varieties were produced for both domestic and foreign markets. In addition to traditional palettes, beautiful wares were made in reddish orange and gold. Styles conformed with orders form both the domestic and Western markets.

Kyoto wares—In the early 17th century Kyoto was the capital city of Japan. It was here that the wealthy merchant class had orders filled for ceramic articles including objects used in Cha no yu (tea ceremony), and other traditional vessels. Kyoto ceramics from the Edo through Taisho periods are highly collected in today's market. Kyoto pottery wares comes in a variety of pottery types including: cream colored, gray, buff, reddish brown, and can have incised and/or reticulated or painted designs.

Japanese Kyoto Ware Bowl and Cover

Nippon Era Ceramics—Porcelain and pottery wares made in Japan for Western export between 1891 and 1921 are called "Nippon." These wares are marked "Nippon" as the country of origin. Consumers should be careful with regard to reproduction marks which include the "M" in Wreath, pseudo-Maple Leaf and Rising Sun markings. The patterns "Antique Rose," "Wildflower" and "Green Mist" have been reproduced.

Occupied Japan—This backstamp, also used on stickers, was placed on all products exported from Japan to the United States from 1946 to 1952.

Satsuma—In today's market, Satsuma is synonymous with a pottery ware covered with a crackled glaze and decorated with polychrome and gilt.

Early versions of Satsuma wares, which included all the ceramic wares produced under the Daimyo of Satsuma (the head of the Shimazu family, in both Osumi and Satsuma provinces), consist of objects used in the tea ceremony (cha no yu), monochrome-glazed wares, shark's-skin-glazed pieces, tortoiseshell-glazed wares (Bekko), white-glazed pieces (Shiro), and Dragon Scale also termed "Serpent's Skin" or "Scorpion" glaze. From 1868 on Satsuma wares were exported in very large quantities. Western demand became even greater after Satsuma wares were produced in many other vicinities including Tokyo, Kyoto, Yokohama, etc., in addition to the productions of Kagoshima Prefecture.

Satsuma wares are judged on the quality of the pottery, its form and above all, the manner of technical skill in applying the decoration. Until the mid-19th century, for the most part, Satsuma wares were ornamented with elegant but simple decorations that were taken from nature as well as mythological and religious designs. Prior to the end of the Edo period (1850s), Satsuma wares were decorated with figures in the forms of processionals, warriors, bijin (beautiful ladies), karako (children), etc. (For markings found on Satsuma wares see marks section.)

Studio Ceramics—The Arts and Crafts Movement was born in 19th century England as a reaction against the mechanized cookie cutter assembly lines of the Industrial Revolution. It emphasized the human touch, the care and the craftsmanship and attention to detail that go into a decorative object. Arts and Crafts exemplified not just the product but the attitude that inspired it. Each piece was created with care. This movement was part of the Japanese art movement which included the Industrial Arts. The wares are listed according to the artist's name under Studio Ceramics. (The Japanese Folk Art Movement began in the 1920s and has become very popular since World War II. These wares are also listed by artist under Studio Ceramics.)

Satsuma Rooster Teapot and Cover

Sumida Gawa wares—The following is from an article which I wrote for *Antique Trader Weekly:*

"A great deal of confusion has resulted for the misinterpretation of Sumida Gawa wares. ...It is important to eliminate the misinformation surrounding these wares. This misinformation includes the following:

1. The wares were produced from 1840-1910 for the French and English markets.
2. They were made by Korean prisoners of war.
3. They were made on Poo Island (a nonexistent place) which was washed away by a typhoon.
4. They were made in Formosa.
5. They were produced by a colony of midgets.

"Unfortunately, many dealers and collectors have helped perpetuate the aforementioned myths.

"Sumida Gawa wares were produced in the Asakusa District of Tokyo by the Ryosai family. The earliest pieces date ca. 1898-1899. Following the earthquake of 1923 which struck Tokyo, the factory was moved to Yokohama. The name Sumida Gawa was retained. The characteristics of these wares include a porcelain body, thick walls, with interiors covered with glaze, generally green and exteriors decorated with applied decoration, generally figural, and in high-relief. The rims of objects have curtain glazes. Ground coloring can be red, black, green, orange, yellow, blue, purple, etc. These wares can have impressed markings or a cartouche with two or four characters." (See marks section.)

PRICE LISTINGS
for Japanese Ceramic Wares

Arita bottle, blue and white, late 17th or early 18th c., pear-form with a figure in a pavilion in a landscape, a border of stylized petals, reglued rim chip, lacquer restoration, 8" h. $3,500-4,500

Arita bottle/vase, blue and white, early 18th c., double-gourd with swirling panels of floral and geometric panels, Shonzui-style, 7¾" h. 3,000-5,000

Arita bowl, late 18th c., the design in red, green and blue, scalloped rim, 6" d. (ILLUS.) 300-375

Arita bowl and cover, ca. 1830, the decoration in red, blue, green, aubergine, yellow and gilt, reserves with flowers and foliage and flowers and birds (ILLUS.) 375-475

Arita charger, blue and white, late 17th or early 18th c., the center with fruiting branches of pomegranate below panels of emblems and flowers, 15½" d. 5,000-7,000

Arita dish, ca. 1800, center with phoenix and flowers, the rim with pine, plum and bamboo, Kakiemon-style, 8½" d. 1,500-2,500

Arita dish, blue and white, the kame (tortoise) in low-relief, high foot in Nabeshima-style, early 19th c., 6" d. (ILLUS. with Introduction) 1,000-1,500

Arita dish, late 19th c., blue and white flowers and foliage, 4" d. 35-75

Arita dishes, blue and white, early 19th c., each with landscape, the base with four-character Chenghua mark, 6" d., set of 5 500-700

Arita fish dish, blue, red and gilt, early 19th c., 10½" w. 800-1,200

Arita model of fish leaping waves, 19th c., red, blue and gilt, gilt rubbed, 6" h. ..800-1,200

Arita model of a cat, late 19th c., unglazed, 5" h. 500-700

Arita model of a monkey, late 19th c., unglazed, 5" h. 500-700

Arita model of a rabbit, 19th c., realistically modeled, 3" l. (ILLUS.) 900-1,500

Arita vases, late 18th or early 19th c., beaker-form, melon-ribbed, flowers and foliage in red, blue and gilt, 8" h., rubbed, chips on one rim, pr. 1,500-2,200

Banko box and cover, ca. 1850, circular form decorated with panels of repetitive designs in colors, the finial with floral design, base impressed "Banko," 5¾" d. 1,500-2,500

Arita Porcelain Rabbit

Japanese Arita Bowl and Cover

Banko bowl, early Meiji period, gray crackled glaze, decorated with insects, flowers and foliage, openwork rim, 8" d. **1,000-1,500**

Banko ewer, late 18th c., pear-shaped with scrolling handle and long spout, landscapes in shaped panels, the ground with roundels, the neck with palmettes, iron-red, blue, green and gilt, no stopper, stained, base impressed "Banko" **1,800-2,500**

Banko group, Three Wise Monkeys, ca. 1905, 4" h. **450-550**

Banko group, Three Wise Monkeys, ca. 1920s, 3½" h. **275-375**

Banko humidor and cover, ca. 1920, Seven Household Gods of Good Luck in relief, 6" h. **500-750**

Banko kogo, ca. 1910, the cover with Daruma, green, red and blue on gray pottery, 2¾" d. **375-500**

Banko kogo, ca. 1840-60, domed cover, circular body, overall grayish-cream glaze, impressed Banko mark on base, 2½" d. **350-550**

Japanese Arita Porcelain Bowl

Banko nodder, ca. 1900, Fukusukesan, gray with polychrome and gilt attire, 5" h. **550-775**

Banko nodder, ca. 1910, monkey reading a book, 4¾" h. **375-575**

Banko teapot, gray with enameled cranes and flowers, pivoting finial, ca. 1910 (ILLUS. with Introduction) **375-475**

Banko teapot, duck-form, ca. 1910, gray ware with polychrome and gilt details **150-175**

Banko teapot, house-form, ca. 1930, gray with brick red roof and polychrome details......................................**150-175**

Banko teapot, quail-form, ca 1900, gray ware with polychrome feathers, insect finial **450-575**

Banko teapot, ca. 1920, gray with Seven Household Gods of Good Luck in relief, decorated with primary colors, base with impressed Banko mark, 5½" h. **375-550**

Banko teapot, early 20th c., melon-ribbed, orange with green foliage, "Three Wise Monkeys" in low-relief **550-750**

Banko teapot, ca. 1900, gray ground with frogs, in various whimsical colors in relief, frog spout, loops form the handle (ILLUS.) **575-775**

Banko teapot, early 20th c., Vantine sticker on bottom, gray with sprigged-on prunus blossoms, and branches, cover glazed green, impressed Banko mark on base, 3" h. **275-350**

Banko teapot, gray with sprigged-on flowering branches in white, brown and yellow, lid and spout glazed brown, ca. 1910 (ILLUS.) **375-475**

Japanese Banko Teapot with Frogs

Japanese Banko Teapot with Branches

Banko teapot, early 20th c., tapestry-style, four-sided and elongated, gilt highlights **375-500**

Banko vase, gray, ca. 1875, bulbous with slender flared neck, decorated in colors and gilt with insects, impressed Banko mark on base, 6½" h. **700-900**

Bizen censer, late Edo period, modeled as birds, deep brown **2,000-3,000**

Bizen model of horse, late 19th c., deep steely gray, standing on all four legs, 4½" h. **550-750**

Bizen model of Hotei, ca. 1900, deep brown, his sack mottled, 7" w. **500-750**

Bizen model of a Shinto priest, Meiji period, late 19th c., seated with scroll in one hand, face meditative, dark brown overall 6¾" h. **500-750**

Bizen tokkuri (bottle for sake), 18th c., double-gourd form, dark ash glaze, 6¾" h. **1,200-1,800**

Fukagawa bowl, studio porcelain, ca. 1910, bamboo and karako in various poses, Mt. Fuji mark in underglaze-blue, 6" h., (Color Illus. pg. 37) **2,000-2,500**

Fukagawa dish, 19th c., Imari palette, fluted rim, panels of flowers, trees, the center with floral spray, Koransha mark on base in underglaze-blue, 9" d. **1,200-1,600**

Fukagawa dish, ca. 1980, pale blue ground with blue, white and yellow narcissus, Mt. Fuji mark, 6" d. **20-45**

Fukagawa vase, late 19th c., bulbous with elongated neck and wide mouth, blue foliage with red, light blue and yellow irises, Koransha mark on base, 10" h. **1,500-2,500**

Fukagawa vase, late 19th c., colors and gilt with courtesans, the shoulder, foot rim and neck with bands of lappets, the base with Koransha mark in red, 15" h. **2,500-3,500**

Fukagawa studio vase, ca 1880, red ground with chrysanthemums in shades of blue and white with gilt outlines below a double border of ruyi lappets, base with Koransha mark, 15" h. (ILLUS.) **3,000-4,000**

Fukagawa vase, 19th c., red and blue with gilt highlights, band of cranes above waves, the footrim and neck with bands of lappets and ruyi bands, 18" h. **3,500-5,500**

Fukagawa Porcelain Studio Vase

Fukagawa vase, ca. 1980, baluster-form with short waisted neck and flared rim, pink flowers on blue branches with blue foliage, Mt. Fuji mark, 11" h. **190-250**

Fukagawa vase, ca. 1980, broad shoulder and wide mouth with short waisted neck, designs of fruit in red and pale yellow with blue foliage and brown branches, Mt. Fuji mark, 8" h. **60-125**

Fukagawa vase, ca. 1910, bulbous with short neck, birds on branches, Mt. Fuji mark, 7½" h. **500-750**

Fukagawa vases, early 20th c., ovoid form with narrow waisted necks, the body of each with bands of dragons and phoenix, Mt. Fuji mark on bases, the gilt rubbed, 11" h., pair..............................**1,000-1,500**

Koransha tea set (often mistaken for 19th century Fukagawa): covered teapot and five covered teacups, ca. 1985, cylindrical in form with a design of bold flowers and foliage in blue, red and gilt, interiors of covers and bases of all pieces with blue orchid spray, the handle original to set, with plastic adornment, the set **125-175**

Hagi ware chawan (tea bowl), 18th or 19th c., rounded form covered with crackled white glaze, flat wide glazed foot, rim chips, 4¼" d. **1,200-1,500**

Hagi ware chawan (tea bowl), 19th c., summer bowl (wide), crackled mottled whitish-gray glaze, 4" d. **900-1,200**

Hagi ware sake cups, shell-form, Matsumoto family, 19th c., boxed, the set (ILLUS.)...**800-1,200**

Hagi Ware Sake Cups

Hirado bottle/vase, late 19th c., globular form with long neck, decorated with underglaze-blue frolicking shishi, 9½" h. **2,500-3,500**

Hirado bowl, early 19th c., blue and white, five karako (children) playing among butterflies, the blue rim with mokko shaped lappets below, 4" d. **1,500-2,000**

Hirado box and cover, 19th c., blue and white with seiji bands, decoration of morning glories and foliage, 5" d. **900-1,200**

Hirado bucket, 19th c., blue and white with designs of birds above foaming waves, 6" h. **900-1,200**

Hirado censer, 19th c., tripod base and globular body, the body and cover pierced with a honeycomb pattern, the three legs are figural shishi heads, blue clouds, minor chipping, 5½" h. **650-950**

Hirado censer, 19th c., globular, blue and white, cover with pierced honeycomb pattern, design of karako, minor chipping, 3½" h. **800-1,200**

Hirado dish, boat-shaped, 19th c., supported on three carved feet, the overall blue and white design features various mon, 7" w. (ILLUS.)....................................**700-900**

Hirado dish, 19th c., blue and white with Mt. Fuji in low-relief, 8" d. **1,000-1,500**

Hirado figure of dragon on rockwork, 19th c., overall white, the dragon with head erect and body coiled, minor chipping to spikes along dragon's back and tips of horns chipped, 6" w. **800-1,200**

Hirado figure of a horse, 19th c., very fine details, 7" w. (ILLUS.) **3,000-4,000**

Hirado figure of recumbent horse, 19th c., white glaze, 4" w. **1,800-2,500**

Hirado figure of a tiger, 19th c., white glaze, upturned tail with minor restoration, 7" l. **1,000-1,500**

Hirado vase, reticulated with beehive pattern, irises and foliage, signed "Hirado san Mikawa nai Imafusa sei," damages to openwork, 10¾" h. **1,800-2,400**

Hirado Ware Figure of a Horse

Hirado Ware Boat-Shaped Dish

Hirado vase, early 19th c., bulbous body with wide neck and wide trumpet form mouth, decorated with blue hydrangea, 15" h. **2,500-3,500**

Hirado vase, 19th c., globular body with tall neck, design of blue tiger and bamboo, 8¾" h. **2,500-3,500**

Hirado wine ewer, 19th c., bamboo-form, bamboo section finial and bamboo-form handle, decorated with underglaze-blue foliage, 5" h. (ILLUS.) **2,000-3,000**

Imari beaker vases, late 17th or early 18th c., blue, red and gilt with landscape panels reserved on a floral ground, one restored, 14" h., pair............................**3,000-5,000**

Imari bowl, late 19th c., rounded rom with steep sides, blue, colors and gilt, central panel of kirin encircled by radiating panels of geometric designs, 7" w. **375-550**

Imari bowl, Kenjo, late 19th c., fluted and floriform, the interior with kiku mon and medallions on a ground of brocade designs, the exterior similarly decorated, colors and gilt, minor rubbing, 8" d. **750-1,000**

Imari bowl, (Kenjo), late 18th c., the interior with center reserve featuring Kinko astride a carp, the bowl divided on interior and exterior with panels featuring peony blossoms, lotus and scroll, red, underglaze-blue, white and gilt, 10½" d. (ILLUS. next page)............................**2,000-3,000**

Japanese Hirado Ware Wine Ewer

Japanese Imari Bowl with Jewel Design Interior

Imari bowl, (Kenjo), 18th c., the interior with jewel design (necklace-form) below panels which match those on exterior, red, underglaze-blue, white and gilt, 12" d. (ILLUS. previous page) **3,000-4,000**

Imari bowl with cover, early 19th c., panels of birds and flowers on exterior of bowl, matching cover with center decoration of longevity symbol, gilt and colors, base with red and gilt leaf mark, 4" d. **375-500**

Imari charger, late 19th or early 20th c., three shaped panels of phoenix, flowers and landscapes on diaper ground, gilt rubbed, 18" d. **1,800-2,500**

Imari charger, early 18th c., blue, red and gilt with center scene of pavilions in a landscape, the everted rim with three medallions of phoenix and flowers, 18" d. **6,000-9,000**

Imari charger, early 18th c., petal-lobed form decorated in blue, iron-red and gilt with sprays of peonies bordered by floral patterns, the everted rim with a band of entwined pine, plum and bamboo, the reverse with scrolling flowers, 13" d. ..**1,800-2,250**

Imari charger, late 19th c., petal-form rim, chrysanthemums and foliage the reverse with blue lotus blossoms, 14" d. **800-1,200**

Imari dish, carp-form, late 19th c., decorated in blue, red, and gilt with gilt flowers and pomegranates, pseudo-Ming mark, 6" w. **700-900**

Japanese Imari Bowl with Interior Reserve of Kinko Astride a Carp

Imari dish, kenjo-style, late 19th c., kiku mon and medallions on ground of various brocade designs in colors and gilt, Fuku mark on base, 8" d. **800-1,200**

Imari dish, ca. 1850, red, blue and gilt decorations of medallions around central vase filled with flowers, 6" d. **200-285**

Imari dish, ca. 1830, red, blue and gilt with border reserves filled with flowers, the center medallion with phoenix above flowers, 6" d. **135-185**

Imari dish, 18th c., gosai, the back decorated with chrysanthemums and foliage in red, blue and gilt, 10" d. (ILLUS.) **2,500-3,500**

Imari figure of actor, late 17th or early 18th c., blue, red and gilt, he holds an open fan, old damages to foot and base, 12½" h. **1,500-2,500**

Imari figure of seated bijin, late 19th c., she holds a fan, attired in blue, red, yellow, green and aubergine, 4" h. (ILLUS. with Introduction) **475-675**

Imari figure of a woman, early 18th c., kimono and obi decorated with flowers and vines in red and gilt, her hands hidden in blue sleeves, 14" h. **3,500-5,500**

Imari figure group, 19th c., Shoki and his attendant who is cleaning his ear, 12" h., (Color Illus. pg. 39) **3,000-4,500**

Imari garniture set: baluster-form vase and cover with two beaker vases; late 19th c., bronze mountings, red, blue and gilt with floral decorations overall, tallest piece 11½", the set **3,500-5,500**

Imari shaving basin, late 17th or early 18th c., blue, red and gilt with flowers in vase in center, the everted rim with panels of flowerheads, 9" d. **2,000-3,000**

Imari vase, late 19th c., melon-ribbed, vertical designs of various flowers, foliage, birds, dragons and phoenix, 16" h. **2,000-3,000**

Imari vase, late 19th c., cobalt blue and colored designs, 8½" h. (ILLUS.) **225-300**

Imari vases and covers, late 19th c., hexagonal, domed cover with shishi finial, blue, red and gilt designs of shishi, peony blossoms and paulownia with foliage, 24" h., pair **3,000-5,000**

Imari Dish

Imari Vase

Kakiemon bowl, shallow, blue and white, ca. 1700, the well with design of rabbits leaping waves surrounded by foliate border with molded-in-relief diaper, interior filled with alternating panels of flowers surrounded by clouds which form petals below a band of underglaze-blue stylized dragons chasing the flaming pearl, the rim brown, base marked "Fuku" (ILLUS.) **12,000-18,000**

Kakiemon bowl, late 17th or early 18th c., blue and white with dragon roundel, the well with peony scroll, the rim brown, base marked "Fuku," 5¼" d. **1,000-1,500**

Kakiemon bowl, 18th c., blue and white with Three Friends design (pine, plum and bamboo), brown rim, Fuku mark on base, 6¾" d. **4,500-6,500**

Kakiemon bowl, late 19th c., pierced rim with coin decoration, decoration of flowerheads with gilt highlights, 4" d. **275-375**

Kakiemon bowl, late 19th c., decorated with pine, plum and bamboo, base marked "Fuku," 4½" d. **150-200**

Kakiemon cup, early 18th c., flared sided with yellow, green, blue and red decoration of flowers, 3" h. **750-1,200**

Kakiemon dish, late 17th or early 18th c., lobed form with barbed brown rim, blue and white decoration of fisherman, 4" d. **1,500-2,000**

Kakiemon dish, 18th c., colors and gilt, foliate rim, decoration of phoenix in flight with peony blossoms and scattered cherry blossoms, brown rim, two small rim chips, 6¼" d. **5,000-7,000**

Kakiemon dish, 18th c., fluted with scalloped rim, decoration of small bird and flowers, chipping in design, 6" d. **1,000-1,500**

Kakiemon dish, 18th c., foliate rim, phoenix and peony blossoms, brown rim, rubbed, 6" d. **2,000-3,000**

Kakiemon dish, late Edo period, the design of pomegranates and foliage in persimmon, underglaze-blue, green, yellow and aubergine, 7" d. (ILLUS.) ..**2,000-3,000**

Kakiemon dish, late 18th or early 19th c., blue and white with butterflies and flowers, brown rim, 8" d. **1,200-1,800**

Kakiemon dish, 18th c., the well with vase and flowers, the border with three rabbits, 8" d., (Color Illus. pg. 38) **2,000-3,000**

Kakiemon dishes, late 19th c., ribbed and scalloped, decoration of pomegranate and prunus, colors and gilt, 5" d., set of 5 ....**600-800**

Kakiemon ewer, late 19th c., hexagonal with porcelain bale handle, the panels decorated with flowers and foliage, finial on cover restored, 5½" h. **1,500-2,500**

Kakiemon saucer, early 18th c., blue and white, lobed form with brown edge, fishermen in a river landscape, the reverse with scrolling foliage, 4¼" d. **1,000-1,500**

Kakiemon Shallow Bowl with Rabbits

Kakiemon Dish with Pomegranates

Kakiemon saucer, 18th c., polychrome, molded petal-form with three peony sprays, 4½" d. **2,500-3,500**

Ko Kutani bottle, early 18th c., ovoid form decorated with phoenix and rockwork, flowers and bands of ruyi, cracked and rubbed, 8" h. **1,500-2,500**

Kutani bottle, late 19th c., hexagonal with panels depicting carp, birds and flowers,

figures the shoulder decorated with animals of the zodiac, 12" h. (Color Illus. pg. 38) **2,000-3,000**

Kutani bottle, late 19th c., double-gourd form, decorated in primary colors with zodiac animals in medallions, Fuku mark on base, 12½" h. **1,500-2,500**

Kutani censer, ca. 1900, tripod base, domed pierced cover, the body with design of a

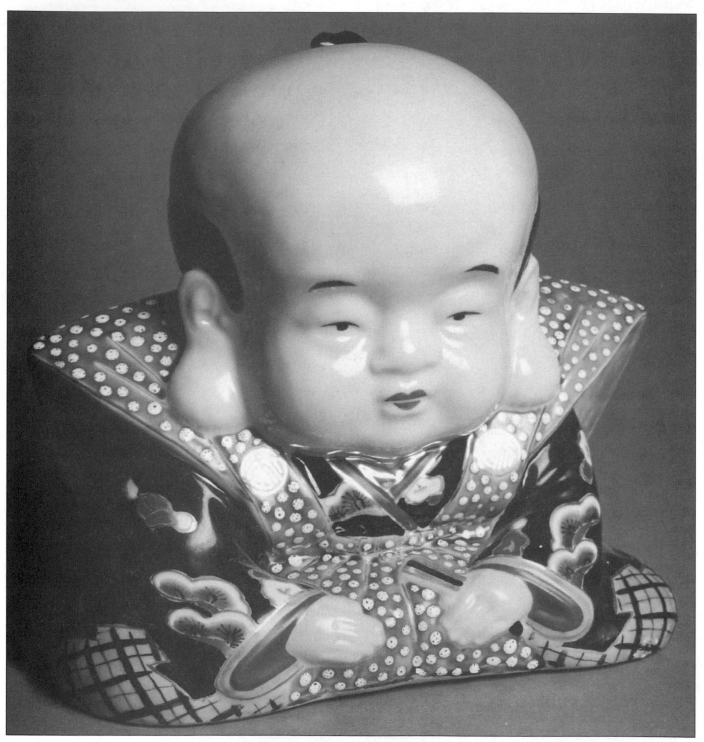

Kutani Figure of Fukusukesan

dragon and flaming pearl, in primary colors and gilt, base with Fuku mark, 4½" h. **350-550**

Kutani censer, ca. 1920, Shishi-form the head with open mouth, orange and gilt, the base marked "Kutani," 6" h. **275-500**

Kutani charger, late 19th c., red, green, blue and gilt with decoration of Daikoku, base marked "Kutani," 14" d. **1,200-1800**

Kutani charger, early 20th c., colors and gilt with decoration of the Seven Household Gods of Good Luck, 14" d. **1,000-1,500**

Kutani charger, ca. 1910, cranes in flight, primarily green and yellow, with gilt, 14" d. **1,000-1,500**

Kutani dish, ca. 1910, shaped panels with figures and flowers in reddish orange and gilt highlighs, base marked "Kutani," 7" d. **300-500**

Kutani (AO) dish, square, early 19th c., ca. 1830, with attested box, the design features two of the Seven Household Gods of Good Luck, Eibsu and Daikoku, 12" x 12" (Color Illus. pg. 41) **2,500-3,500**

Kutani dinner service for 6, ca. 1955, colors and gilt with scenic decoration of huts, trees and lakescape, 42 pcs., each piece with two-character Kutani mark, the set **375-575**

Kutani dish, late 19th c., Ko Kutani-style, landscape decoration, square with canted corners, the base with Fuku mark in a square, cracked, 6" w **350-650**

Kutani figure of Fukusukesan, ca. 1920s, colors and gilt, 6" h. (ILLUS.) **475-675**

Kutani figure of Hotei, ca. 1955, unglazed face, hands, body, his robes a pale celadon, base with two-character impressed mark, 6" h. **100-125**

Kutani figure of Hotei, ca. 1955, glazed face, hands and body, robe and sack in colors and gilt, 7½" h. **235-325**

Kutani figure of a woman, ca. 1920, her garments in orange and green with flowers in colors, impressed two-character mark on base, 8" h. **275-385**

Kutani figure of a woman, ca. 1905, one hand holding fan, the other hidden in her sleeve, colors and gilt, the base with two-character impressed mark, 9" h. **300-450**

Kutani figure of a woman, ca. 1900, her garments decorated with dragons amid clouds, one hand holding her garment the

other holding a fan, base marked "Kutani sei," 12½" h. **750-950**

Kutani tea set: six cups, six saucers, covered teapot, covered creamer, covered sugar, six cake plates; porcelain, ca. 1910, all decorated in orange, gilt and black with ladies among flowering cherry blossoms, each piece marked "Kutani" in gold in an orange rectangle, one cover chipped, the set **1,000-1,600**

Kutani tokkuri (sake bottle), early 19th c., double-gourd form, four-sided, panels of repetitive designs and calligraphy in reddish orange and gilt, base marked "Fuku," 8" h. **1,000-1,500**

Kutani vase, early 19th c., six spouts, scenic decoration in AO palette, 8" h. **1,500-2,500**

Kutani vase, late 19th c., six spouts, swirling decorations of rabbits, dragons, mandarin ducks, waves, flaming pearl, in orange and gilt, 9" h. **1,500-2,500**

Kutani vase, double-gourd form, Taisho period, reddish orange flowers, green foliage, gilt highlights, gilt rubbed, 8" h. ..**500-700**

Kutani vase, late 19th c., five spouts, overall scenic design, double-gourd form with the upper portion decorated with phoenix, 10" h., (Color Illus. pg. 41) ..**1,800-2,500**

Kutani vases, early Showa period, baluster-form, butterfly ears at shoulder, band of processional figures between bands of repetitive designs (diapers) predominately orange and gilt, bases marked "Kutani," 7" h., pair **700-950**

Kyoto ware bottle/vase, late 18th c., bulbous form, green, blue and gilt decoration of morning glories, gold lacquer repair to rim, 7" h. **4,500-5,500**

Kyoto ware bowl, 18th c., decorated with green, blue, white and yellow flowers and foliage, 6" d. **2,000-3,000**

Kyoto ware bowl and cover, 18th c., decorated in red, blue, aubergine, green and gilt, the rim set with metal, 6" d. (ILLUS. with Introduction) **1,200-1,800**

Kyoto ware box and cover, 18th c., the cover decorated in red, green, blue and gilt with circular decorations, 4" d. **1,500-2,000**

Kyoto ware censer, last half of the 18th c., cock and hen finial, supported on three legs, 4" h. (Color Illus. pg. 40).............**4,500-6,500**

Kyoto ware censer, late 19th c., beehive-shaped pierced cover, overall design of gourds, colors and gilt, Ninsei-style, 4" h. **1,000-1,500**

Kyoto ware chaire, 18th or 19th c., ivory cover, brown glaze, Ninsei-style **900-1,200**

Kyoto ware chaire, early 19th c., underglaze-brown decoration of dragon around shoulder **1,000-1,500**

Kyoto ware chaire, late 18th or early 19th c., blue, green and gilt "T" pattern overall, original cover, 3" h. **1,500-2,500**

Kyoto ware chawan, early 19th c., birds and camellia with foliage, signed "Kenya" (Color Illus. pg. 41) **1,500-2,000**

Kyoto ware chawan, black ground with white flowers and yellow centers with gilt highlights, 18th c., (ILLUS.) **1,500-2,200**

Kyoto ware chawan, late Meiji period, exterior decoration of maple tree, 4½" d. **900-1,200**

Kyoto ware chawan, late 19th c. polychrome and gilt flowers in two panels, 4"d. **800-1,200**

Kyoto Ware Chawan

Kyoto Ware Figure of Daikoku

Kyoto Ware Kogo

Kyoto ware chawan, early 20th c., signed "Kouun," maple leaves and stream in colors and silver (ILLUS.) **700-900**

Kyoto ware figure of Daikoku, late Edo period, colors and gilt, seated on rice bails, he leans upon his mallet, 8" h. (ILLUS.) **2,000-3,000**

Kyoto ware kogo (incense box), chrystanthem-form, late 18th or early 19th c., gilt highlights on the cover, interior in colors and gilt, standing up on aquatic forms including a starfish, 2½" w. (ILLUS.) **900-1,200**

Kyoto ware mizusashi (water jar), decorated with ginko leaves in red, green, yellow with gilt highlights, fan-form strap handle in black and gilt, signed, 6" h. (ILLUS.) **2,500-3,500**

Kyoto ware teapot and cover, early 19th c., pear-shaped with maple leaf design in colors and gilt, 5" h. **1,000-1,500**

Kyoto ware tokkuri (sake bottle), late 18th c., double-gourd form, with underglaze-blue and brown motif, 6½" h. (ILLUS.) **2,000-2,500**

Kyoto ware tokkuri (sake bottle), late 18th c., cylindrical with loops for handle, design of plum blossoms and foliage, 5½" h., (Color Illus. pg. 38)..................**2,500-3,000**

Kyoto Ware Mizusashi

Kyoto Ware Chawan with Maple Leaves

Double-gourd Kyoto Ware Tokkuri

Kyoto ware tokkuri (sake bottle), late 18th or early 19th c., hexagonal with gold, blue and green prunus blossoms and foliage, slightly rubbed, 7½" h. **3,000-4,500**

Kyoto ware tokkuri (sake bottle), early 19th c., the shoulder with kiku, the body with karakusa in green, blue and gilt with touches of red, 6" h. **4,500-6,500**

Kyoto ware tokkuri (sake bottle), late 18th c., elongated double-gourd form, gray with blue splashes, 8" h. **2,500-3,500**

Kyoto ware tokkuri (sake bottle), late 18th c., double-gourd form, green, blue and yellow flowers on branches, 7" h. **2,500-3,500**

Kyoto ware vase, late 19th c., baluster-form with flowers and birds in colors and gilt, 12" h. **300-500**

Nabeshima dish, late 19th c., underglaze-blue decoration of flowering branches, rim chips, 7" d. **500-750**

Nabeshima dish, early 18th c., blue and white, the inside with decoration of flower sprays, exterior rim with coin symbols, foot with comb-tooth pattern, 6" d. **15,000-20,000**

Nabeshima dish, late 18th c., blue and white chrysanthemums and foliage, exterior rim with floral sprays, comb-tooth pattern on footrim, 5¾" d. **1,500-2,500**

Nabeshima dish, early 19th c., blue and white trees and foliage, the exterior rim with large blossoms, footrim with comb-tooth pattern, 13" d. **6,000-7,000**

Nabeshima Dish with High Footrim

Nabeshima dish, 18th century, the pale blue ground with bold pattern of camellia and foliage, the high footrim with comb-tooth pattern, 7" d. (ILLUS. right)........**4,500-5,500**

Nabeshima dish, late 19th c., blue and white flowering tree, footrim with comb-tooth pattern, exterior rim with coin emblems, 8" d. **400-600**

Nabeshima dish, late 19th c., blue and white flower garden decoration, the exterior rim with floral decorations, footrim with comb-tooth pattern, 9" d. **800-1,200**

Nabeshima dish, late 19th c., blue and white mandarin ducks with aquatic foliage, exterior rim with coin and ribbon decoration, footrim decorated with comb-tooth pattern, rim chips shaved, 8" d. **900-1,200**

Nabeshima dish, blue and white design of bird on branch, the high footrim decorated with comb-tooth pattern, 18th c., 10" d. (scratches) (ILLUS.) **5,000-7,500**

Nabeshima-style dish, late 19th c., polychrome and gilt decoration of treasure ship, comb-tooth pattern on footrim in blue, 5" d. **300-500**

Nabeshima-style dish, late 19th c., polychrome and gilt decoration of flowers and cart, exterior rim with floral sprays in blue, the footrim decorated with comb-tooth pattern, 6" d. **500-700**

Oribe bowl, late 19th or early 20th c., shallow, landscape decoration, 6¾" d. **175-225**

Oribe bowl, late 19th c., unevenly potted, green and brown scenic design with bridge, 8" d. **300-400**

Oribe bowl, late 19th or early 20th c., landscape design in green and brown, exterior glaze in varied shades of green, 6" d. **200-250**

Oribe bowl, early 20th c., decorated with swallows, 8" d. **100-200**

Oribe censer, late 19th or early 20th c., shishi-form, head lifts off, cream with varied green glazes, 4" h. **250-375**

Oribe dish, late 19th or early 20th c., square with rounded corners, cream body covered with green, brown and pink glaze, 8" d. **200-400**

Oribe kogo (box and cover), Taisho period, peach-form with varied green glazes, 2" d. **75-150**

Nabeshima Dish with Camellia

Oribe mizusashi, late Meiji period, cream with green and brown flowers, 6½" h. **300-500**

Oribe vase, early 20th c., pear-form with irregular green glaze and mon patterns, impressed mark on base indicates Mino, 15" h. **400-650**

Oribe water dropper (suiteki), early Showa period, model of a dog, 3¼" l. **175-225**

Raku chawan (tea bowl), attributed to Raku Ryonyu (1756-1834), roughly thrown with red glaze and patches of green, rim repaired, 4½" d. **1,500-2,000**

Raku chawan, late 19th or early 20th c., black glazes extending over the wide foot, hairlines **1,000-1,500**

Raku chawan, 18th c., black glaze stopping short of the foot, 4½" d. **1,500-2,000**

Raku kogo, early 20th c., black glaze, in form of a nut, 2¼" d. **100-150**

Satsuma bottle/vase, late Edo period, early 19th c., bulbous form with elongated neck, decorated with chrysanthemums and bellflowers, a band of kame patterns just below the rim, 8½" h. **1,500-2,200**

Satsuma bowl, ca. 1912-1920, shallow, decorated with a scene of a party attended by ladies and attendants on the grounds of a temple in colors and gilt, the exterior in 1000 Flowers pattern, the base impressed "Kinkozan," 5¼" d. **3,500-5,500**

Satsuma bowl, ca. 1900, figures in shaped panels, the exterior decorated with butterflies, 9" d. **1,500-2,000**

Satsuma bowl, ca. 1910, decorated in color and gilt with dragon and Rakan on the interior, the exterior with Rakan and their attributes, base signed "Dai Nihon Satsuma Yaki Hodota sei," slightly rubbed, 12" d. **2,500-3,500**

Satsuma bowl, Meiji period, painted on inside with two women and a child surrounded by blossoming cherry trees, blue ground with gilt floral decorations, the exterior with blue ground and scattered flowers, impressed Kinkozan mark, 5⅜" d. **2,500-3,500**

Satsuma box and cover, early 20th c., rectangular, exterior of cover and base covered with small butterflies, 5" x 4" **500-750**

Satsuma box and cover, late Meiji period, the interior and exterior of the cover and interior of the box decorated with Rakan and their attributes in colors and gilt between diaper borders, base signed "Dai Nihon Satsuma yaki Hodota zo" (Satsuma ware made in Japan by Hodota), 7" d. (ILLUS.) **2,000-3,000**

Satsuma bucket, Meiji period, barrel-shaped, decorated with women and children, banded below with bats and flowers, above with birds, inside decorated with scattered butterflies, the crossbar on handle repaired, signed "Seikozan," 8¼" h. **2,500-3,500**

Satsuma charger, late 19th c., central scene of women carrying flower baskets, brick red and washed hues, gilt diaper border, 12½" d. **700-900**

Satsuma charger, late Meiji period, attendants gathered around Kannon in a landscape, colors and gilt, gilt diaper border, 14" d. **1,200-1,800**

Satsuma dish, ca. 1920s, the muted blue ground decorated with cranes on tree branch in colors and gilt, 7" d. (ILLUS.) **450-650**

Satsuma dish, ca. 1900, rectangular form decorated with figural procession and temple in colors and gilt, the base marked "Kinkozan," 7" w. **3,500-5,000**

Satsuma dish, late 19th c., colors and gilt with designs of various mon all outlined in gold, gilt rubbed, 7" d. **450-600**

Satsuma dish, ca. 1830, the decoration in red, blue, white and gilt with a basket in Moriage (low-relief) and vessels in black and gilt lacquer, tiny rim chip restored, signed, 7" d. (ILLUS.) **2,500-3,500**

Satsuma figures, ca. 1920s, colors and gilt, 1½" h., set of 5 dolls, (Color Illus. pg. 109) **1,750-2,125**

Satsuma jar and cover, ca. 1910, spherical form decorated with scattered reserves with images of the 36 Famous Poets (Sanjurokkasen), impressed "Kinkozan," 3" h. **3,000-4,000**

Satsuma Box and Cover

Satsuma kogo (incense box), ca. 1923-1927, impressed Kinkozan mark on base with original label, cobalt blue and gilt with interesting design on the interior of cha no yu (tea ceremony) utensils in colors and gilt, 3" d. (Color Illus. pg. 112) **2,000-3,000**

Satsuma koro (censer), early 19th c., each side decorated in colors and gilt with seasonal flowers, 4" h. (Color Illus. pg. 42) **4,500-6,500**

Satsuma koro (censer), ca. 1920, globular form on three elephant head feet, the domed cover with three openings, overall design of flowers and birds in gilt and muted colors. Buddhist lion finial, rubbed, repair to two legs, 36½" h. **2,500-3,500**

Satsuma mizusashi (water jar) with metal cover, early 19th c., ovoid form decorated in blue, red and gilt with medallions beneath a lappet border and above a key pattern at the foot, unsigned, 6½" h. **2,500-3,500**

Satsuma sake tokkuri, triple-gourd, 18th c., brown glaze with lacquer repair at rim, 8" h. (ILLUS.)......................................**3,500-5,500**

Satsuma Dish with Cranes

Satsuma Dish with Basket and Vessels

Triple-Gourd Satsuma Sake Tokkuri

Satsuma teapot and cover, early 19th c.,
spout in form of dog with long ears,
signed, 3" h., (Color Illus. pg. 109) **5,000-6,000**

Satsuma teapot and cover, ca. 1920,
cobalt blue with gilt flower sprays on
domed cover and globular body, two loop
handles, a medallion on each side filled
with flowers, gilt worn, signed "Kinkozan"
in gilt also worn, 3" w. **1,200-1,500**

Satsuma teapot and cover, early 19th c.,
in form of rooster, melon ribbed and
decorated with flowers in red, blue, white
and gilt (ILLUS. with Introduction), ...**4,000-6,000**

Satsuma tea set: covered teapot, covered
sugar and creamer; decorated blanks, ca.
1915, each decorated in shades of blue
and gold, gilt rubbed, the set
(ILLUS.) **1,000-1,500**

Satsuma vase, early 19th c., four-sided,
each side decorated with flowering plants
in blue, red and gilt with stiff leaf
decoration at the base and rim, "Issan"
with mon on base, 13⅜" h. **3,500-5,000**

Satsuma vase, late 19th c., design of irises
in color and gilt, Kinkozan mark, 5" h.
(ILLUS.) **2,000-2,800**

Satsuma vase, early 20th c., ca. 1910,
ovoid-form, the body decorated with
figures in a landscape during cherry
blossom season, signed "Ryozan" and
"Yasuda," 9" h. **2,500-3,500**

Satsuma vase, ca. 1915, two sides with
processionals and two sides with scenic
views, gilt and colors, 10" h.
(Color Illus. pg. 111) **5,000-7,000**

Satsuma vase, early 20th c., ca. 1915,
pearshaped with flared neck, decorated
overall with butterflies and karakusa on
blue ground, 10½" h. **800-1,200**

Kinkozan Satsuma Vase with Irises

Satsuma Decorated-Blanks Tea Set

Satsuma vase, early 20th, four-sided two with bijin and two with scenic views including a waterfall, colors and gilt, signed "Kameyama," 14" h. (Color Illus. pg. 108) **2,500-3,500**

Satsuma vase, early 20th c., colors and gilt with bijin and attendant, signed "Kameyama"(Color Illus. pg. 107) **2,000-3,000**

Seto chaire (tea caddy), late 18th or early 19th c., basket-form scored with vertical and horizontal lines, the shoulder with grayish white glaze dripping down to a yellowish-brown glaze, ivory cover, lacquer repairs to rim, 3" h. **800-1,200**

Seto chaire, 19th c., ovoid form covered with a mottled brown glaze, ivory cover, 3" h. **600-900**

Seto chaire, late Edo period, 19th c., blackish-brown glaze, repair in rim, 4½" h. **350-500**

Seto dish, 19th c., Horse's Eye pattern, brown glazed spiral patterns around a plain well, brown rim, 9" d. **300-500**

Seto dish, late 19th c., pale seiji (celadon) with tortoise decoration in colors, in slight relief, 5" d. **100-200**

Seto dish, late 19th c., dark green crackled glaze with enameled decoration of Gamma Sennin, 7" d. **250-350**

Seto figures, Meiji period, Owari, potters in colors and gilt trim, 8" h. (ILLUS.) **900-1,200**

Seto mizuasashi (water jar), 19th c., flattened waisted form with dark brown glaze with uneven white splashes, 6½" h. **1,000-1,500**

Seto model of two facing Shishi flanking Tama, 19th c., yellow and white glazes, 8" h. **700-900**

Seto vase, late 19th c., dark gray crackled glaze with enameled design of frogs in various poses, 8" h. **225-375**

Seto vase, late 19th c., dense greenish-gray crackled glaze with decoration of a Rakan in colors and gilt highlights, back with flowers, 10" h. **250-350**

Shigaraki storage jar, melon-ribbed, green stripes, 14" h. **900-1,500**

Shigaraki storage jar, 17th c., baluster-form, tapered to foot, rolled lip, four applied handles at the shoulder, green glaze overall, 18" h. **1,500-2,000**

Shigaraki storage jar, 17th c., ovoid body with short neck, textured surface, brown glaze, 20" h. **2,000-2,500**

Shigaraki storage jar, 19th c., ovoid form with brownish-gray glaze, 10" h. **300-500**

Shino chawan, early 20th c., underglaze decoration of a fan, 4½" d. **250-325**

(The markings used by various Japanese artists, factories and others, to denote manufacture are found in several forms. The most common are Zo, Sei, Tsukuru, and Kore. The first three mean the same thing - "manufactured," "produced," "made," and Kore means "this." These marks can be found written with a brush, stamped, or impressed.)

Studio dish, stoneware, ox design, made for the year of the ox, dated 1961, 8" d. (ILLUS.) **500-700**

Studio, Arakawa Toyozo, shino-style kogo, ca. 1970, square form with rounded edges, bluish-gray glaze, wood box, 2½" w. ..**2,000-3,000**

Studio, Eiraku, porcelain bowl, late 19th c., decorated in underglaze-blue with dragon in the well, the remainder with gold over reddish orange in repetitive designs, base marked "Dai Nihon Eiraku sei," 7" d. ..**1,500-2,500**

Studio, Eiraku, porcelain bowl, ca. 1900, Fahua-style, signed "Eiraku," 8" d. (Color Illus. pg. 111) **3,000-5,000**

Studio Stoneware Dish with Ox

Seto Meiji Period Porcelain Figures of Potters

Studio, Eiraku, porcelain sake bottle, ca. 1900, Fahua-style with silver (950) liner, base marked "Eiraku," 4½" h. (Color Illus pg. 114)............................**1,800-2,500**

Studio, Eiraku, sake cup and underplate, late 19th c., orange and gilt, interior of cup and plate with blue and white decoration, both pieces signed..............**1,000-1,500**

Studio, Eiraku, porcelain sake cup and underplate, the cup lined with silver (950), silver and gold foliage design on the orangish red ground, signed "Eiraku" and dated Meiji 40 (1907), with attested box (Color Illus, pg. 108) **3,500-4,500**

Studio, Hamada, flask, ca. 1950s, rectangular with tapered neck and everted rim, wax resist decoration of floral spray, wood box, 6⅞" h. **4,500-5,500**

Studio, Kanjiro, ca. 1950-60, wide necked vase decorated on either side with abstract designs in brown, blue and red on a mottled brown ground, with attested box which may belong to another vase, 8" h. **800-1,200**

Studio, Kanzan, porcelain bowl, 19th c., Meiji period, the design of ducks in shades of pinks and greens, gilt rim, base signed "Dai Nihon Kanzan" (Kanzan Denschichi), 7¾" d. **700-900**

Studio, Kawamoto, porcelain vase, late 19th c., blue and white decoration, signed "Masakichi (Kawamoto)," 8" h. (ILLUS,) **1,800-2,500**

Studio, Kawamoto Masakichi, vase, ca. 1885, celadon and white with overall circular (mon) decorations in relief, signed, 10" h. **1,800-2,500**

Studio, Kawamoto Masakichi, vase, ca. 1885, scene of snow upon trees, blue with red, white and gilt embellishment, signed, 8" h. **2,500-3,500**

Studio, Kawamoto Masakichi, vase, ca. 1885, blue and white diaper decoration around the shoulder and under the neck, base signed "Kawamoto" **2,500-3,500**

Studio, Kinkozan, pottery censer with open work metal lid, the shoulder with openwork chrysanthemum petals, a gray glaze with polychrome designs of diapers, the base marked "Kinkozan," 8" h., (Color Illus. pg. 116) **5,000-7,000**

Studio, Kinkozan, pottery kogo, ca. 1910, seiji (celery-like shade) with white slip decoration of a phoenix, signed "Kinkozan," 3" d. (ILLUS.) **1,500-2,500**

Studio, Kinkozan zo, pottery vase, ca. 1910, executed in muted shades of tan, brown, blue and cream tones with fan reserves featuring scenic designs, base signed "Kinkozan zo," 15" h. (ILLUS.) **5,000-7,000**

Studio, Kozan, pottery brush pot, early 20th c., unglazed with enameled design of flowerheads and flambé glaze at the rim and interior, impressed Kozan mark, 5" h. (ILLUS.) **2,000-3,000**

Kawanoto Studio Porcelain Vase

Kinkozan Studio Pottery Kogo

Kozan Studio Vase with Relief Coins

Kinkozan Zo Studio Pottery Vase

Kozan Studio Pottery Brush Pot

Studio, Kozan, dish, ca. 1915, circular form painted with green, purple and white wisteria, signed "Makuzu Kozan sei," 6½" d. **3,500-4,500**

Studio, Kozan, porcelain sake cup in the form of a tortoise, ca. 1909, the base marked "Kozan," with attested box (Color Illus. pg. 116) **3,000-4,000**

Studio, Kozan, porcelain vase, ca. 1900, petal-form rim, elongated neck, the blue ground covered with repetitive gilt diaper, the designs of coins in high-relief, Kozan, 6" h. (ILLUS.)..**3,500-4,500**

Studio, Kozan, porcelain vase, ca. 1910, the teal blue ground decorated with flying cranes, signed "Kozan," 7" h. (ILLUS.) **1,800-2,500**

Studio, Kozan, procelain vase, ca. 1905, blue and white with bamboo design, signed Kozan, 8" h. (ILLUS.) **3,000-4,000**

Studio, Kozan, vase, ca. 1910, pink ground decorated with herons, signed "Makuzu Kozan sei," 9" h. **2,500-3,500**

Studio, Kozan, porcelain vase, ca. 1900, with underglaze-blue flowering branches, signed "Makuzu Kozan sei," 12¼" h. ..**3,000-4,000**

Studio, Kozan, porcelain vase, ca. 1900, continuous scene of children at a party, 16" h., attributed to Kozan, (Color Illus. pg. 111) **4,000-6,000**

Kozan Porcelain Vase with Cranes

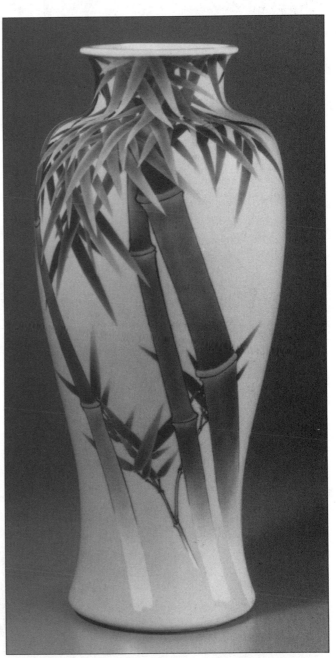

Kozan Bamboo Design Porcelain Vase

Matsumoto Studio Porcelain Vase

Meizan Studio Pottery Jar

Yabu Meizan Studio Pottery Cup and Saucer

Studio, Matsumoto, porcelain vase, ca. 1905, copper red simulating "peach bloom" glaze, signed "Matsumoto of Tokyo," 4" h. (ILLUS.) **750-950**

Studio, Meizan cup and saucer, ca. 1900, decorated with flowerheads and gilt vines, discoloration to cup **900-1,000**

Studio, Meizan, pottery cup and saucer, ca. 1905, design of wisteria and birds in polychrome and gilt, signed "Yabu Meizan," cup stained (ILLUS.) **700-900**

Studio, Meizan, pottery jar and cover, ca. 1920, maple leaf decoration in autumnal hues and gilt, signed "Yabu Meizan," 4" h. (ILLUS.) **1,200-1,500**

Studio, Meizan, vase, ca. 1915, ovoid-form with wisteria in colors and gilt covering shoulder, the body with several groups of karako (children) frolicking, base marked "Meizan," gilt rubbed, 4½" h. **3,000-5,000**

Studio, Meizan, vases, ca. 1900, each decorated in colors and gilt with 1000 Flowers pattern on neck and shoulder, the bulbous body covered with chrysanthemums, one vase marked "Meizan" in gilt, 2" h., pair **3,500-5,000**

Studio, Nishiura, porcelain vase, ca. 1910, green ground shaded to white, purple flowerheads and dark green foliage, signed "Nishiura," 3" h. **550-750**

Studio, Nishiura, porcelain vase, ca. 1910, with design of fruiting and flowering vines in muted shades of yellow and green on a white ground, signed "Nishiura, 3½" h. **1,000-1,600**

Studio, Nishiura Yedenji, porcelain vase, ca. 1910, muted shades of gray and white with design of Mt. Fuji, signed "Nishiura Yedenji," 4" h. (ILLUS.) **1,000-1,500**

Studio, Ryosai, jar and cover, supported in three long tapered legs, decorated with white flowers on muted shaded black to gray ground, silver cover with kiku, base signed in underglaze-blue, 6½" h.........**1,500-2,500**

Studio, Ryosai, porcelain jar and cover, ca. 1900, the jar supported on three long curved legs, the decoration of black and white chrysanthemums against a shaded gray body, pierced silver cover, signed "Ryosai," 7" h. (ILLUS.) **1,800-2,500**

Studio, Ryosai, vase mounted as a lamp, decorated with hydrangea in low-relief, base signed in underglaze-blue, 18" h. **3,500-4,500**

Nishiura Yedenji Studio Porcelain Vase

Ryosai Studio Porcelain Jar and Cover

Studio, Ryosai, vase, ovoid form with cylindrical flared neck, the ground shaded pink to white with lavender and blue morning glories and vines, base signed "Ryosai," 16" h. **4,000-6,000**

Studio, Ryosai, porcelain pieces, ca. 1910, both pieces signed "Ryosai": left - water coupe in copper red, with peach bloom blush in Chinese style, 3" d. (ILLUS.) **750-950**

Seifu Studio Porcelain Bowl

Right - vase with copper red glaze in Chinese style, 3½" h. (ILLUS.) **750-950**

Studio, Seifu, porcelain bowl, ca. 1910, underglaze-blue trees with brown rim, signed "Seifu," 8" d. (ILLUS.) **2,500-3,500**

Studio, Seifu, porcelain bowl, ca. 1900, Fahua-style with incised motifs, signed "Seifu," 8" d. (Color Illus. pg. 111) **3,500-5,500**

Studio, Seifu, porcelain vase, ca. 1900, yellow ground and green splashes, base marked "Seifu," 8" h. **2,500-3,500**

Studio, Seifu, pottery vase, ca. 1890s, muted gray ground decorated with cranes in polychrome, 18" h. **4,500-5,500**

Studio, Shoko Takabe, porcelain plate, polychrome decoration of mandarin ducks, signed "Shoko Takabe," dated in Japanese "May 10, 1891," 6½" d. (ILLUS.) **600-800**

Studio, Shozan, pottery bottle/vase, ca. 1910, shaded from ivory to orange, the scenic decoration includes Mt. Fuji, signed "Shozan (Okumura)," 5" h. (ILLUS.) **900-1,200**

Studio, Shozan, porcelain bowl, ca. 1890s, muted shades of yellow, gray and pink on exterior and continuing on interior, base signed "Shozan (Okumura)," 4" d. (ILLUS.) **1,000-1,500**

Ryosai Studio Water Coupe and Vase

Studio, Suwa Sozan, pottery, figure of No
dancer with mask, ca. 1900, decorated in
colors and gilt, the base bordered with
waves, the designs on the garment raised,
7" h. **9,000-12,000**

Shako Takabe Studio Porcelain Plate

Shozan Bottle/Vase with Mt. Fuji

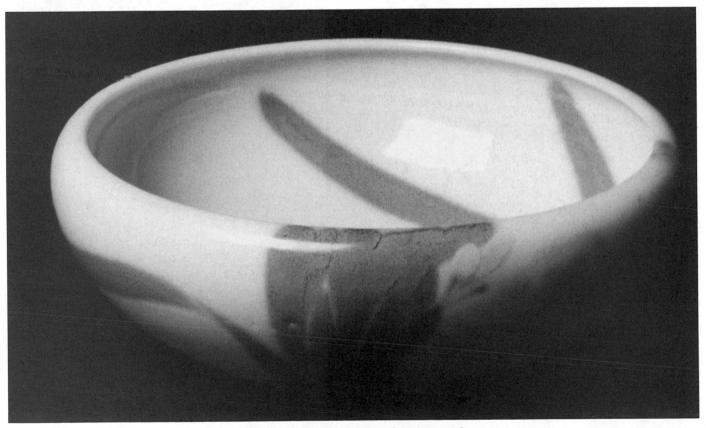
Shozan Studio Porcelain Bowl

Porcelain Sake Cup with Couple in a Boat

Taizan Studio Pottery Vase

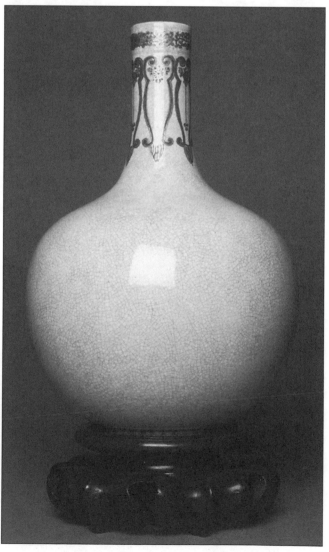

Tozan Studio Pottery Bottle/Vase

Studio, Taizan, pottery vase, ca. 1915, two panels in bright blue and two panels in yellowish gold with varied designs of birds and foliage (crane, heron, etc.), gilt diaper at neck and foot, signed "Taizan," 9" h. (ILLUS.) **500-700**

Studio, Tanzan, pottery vase, signed "Tanzan," with design in low-relief slip, 7" h. (Color Illus. pg. 113) **900-1,200**

Studio, Tanzan, pottery vase, ca. 1890, elongated pear-form, rolled neck, greenish blue ground decorated in various shades of brown, tan, ochre, ivory and black with geese and flowering branches, base signed "Tanzan," 8" h........................**1,000-1,500**

Studio, Tokyo, porcelain sake cup, 1881, the cup shows a scene on the Sumida Gawa (Sumida River) with a couple seated in a boat in high-relief, the boat decorated with gilt lacquer (ILLUS.) **1,000-1,500**

Studio, Tozan (Ito), pottery bottle/vase, ca. 1905, crackled glaze with red, blue and gilt design of jewels down the neck, base with impressed mark "Tozan (Ito)," 6" h. (ILLUS.)..............................**1,500-2,500**

Studio, Tozan (Ito), chawan, ca. 1915, bamboo, signed "Tozan (Ito)" (Color Illus. pg. 108) **1,500-2,500**

Studio, Tozan (Ito), porcelain sake cup, ca. 1900, black design around rim, base signed, 3½" d. **700-900**

Studio, Tozan (Ito), pottery sake pot, ca. 1900, pancake shape supported on three legs, overall design of flowers in gold, silver and three colors, signed "Tozan (Ito)" (ILLUS.) **3,000-4,000**

Studio, Tozan (Ito), pottery vase, ca. 1910, the unglazed body boldly decorated with large flowers in gunmetal, silver, gold, pink, aubergine and blue, Tozan (Ito), 10" h. (ILLUS.)....................................**1,500-2,500**

Studio, Tozan (Ito), pottery vase, ca. 1915, cylindrical with short neck, decoration on egrets in various poses, in color and gilt, the neck with a jeweled design, signed "Tozan" (Ito), 10½" h. **4,000-6,000**

Studio, Tozan (Himeji), porcelain mizusashi (water jar), seiji (celadon) of a bluish celery hue, design of incised rings, base marked "Tozan (Himeji)," ca. 1890s, 6" h. (ILLUS.)..**900-1,200**

Studio, Tozan (Himeji), porcelain vase, seiji (celadon) with a design of rings in low-relief, bluish celery hue, signed "Tozan (Himeji)," ca, 1890s, 12" h. (ILLUS.) ..**1,200-1,500**

Tozan Studio Pottery Vase

Tozan (Himeji) Studio Pottery Sake Pot

Tozan (Himeji) Studio Porcelain Vase

Tozan (Himeji) Studio Porcelain Mizusashi

Studio, Zoroku, chawan, pottery, impressed
mark "Zoroku," late Meiji period
(ILLUS.)..**900-1,200**

Studio, stoneware wine pot, late 1950s,
6" h. (ILLUS.)...**450-650**

Sumida Gawa ashtray, figure of a man
seated on rim, red ground rubbed..............**175-225**

Zoroku Studio Pottery Chawan

Studio Stoneware Wine Pot

Sumida Gawa basket, red ground with three karako on low-relief, handled with flambé glaze, 7" h. **275-375**

Sumida Gawa bowl, red ground with three children peering over rim, 5½" d. **350-450**

Sumida Gawa bowl, ca. 1920s, red ground with three karako (children) peering over rim, 6½" d. (ILLUS.) **250-350**

Sumida Gawa bowl, black ground with two monkeys peering over rim, 8" d. **700-900**

Sumida Gawa box with cover, orange ground, the cover glazed and mottled black, the cover surmounted with seated karako finial, 6" d. **750-950**

Sumida Gawa censer, red ground, with figure molded in low-relief on one side, 3" h. **375-500**

Sumida Gawa jar and cover, green ground, figures and birds in low-relief, cover with seated figure finial, 6" h. **1,000-1,500**

Sumida Gawa mug, red ground with elephant in relief **300-475**

Sumida Gawa pitcher, black ground with dragon in relief, 12" h. **900-1,200**

Sumida Gawa pitcher, red ground with dragon in relief, 12" h. **1,000-1,500**

Sumida Gawa teapot, Mt. Fuji-shaped, black ground, seated figure finial, handle missing, 6¾" h. **650-950**

Sumida Gawa teapot, pancake-form, red ground barely visible, mottled black and gray dragon relief, chipped, 7" w. **500-775**

Sumida Gawa vase, double-gourd pinched-form with irises and foliage on a red ground, 7" h. **500-750**

Sumida Gawa vase, black ground, decorated with applied children in high-relief, 7" h. **350-550**

Sumida Gawa vase, pinched-form, with elder and karako applied in high-relief, applied cartouche with two characters on reverse, ca. 1920, 8" h. (ILLUS.) **475-675**

Sumida Gawa vase, red ground, covered with crustaceans and aquatic plants, 10" h. **800-1,200**

Tamba chaire, late Edo period, temmoku glaze, ivory cover, 3" h. **1,000-1,500**

Sumida Gawa Bowl with Karako

Tamba chaire, late Edo period, temmoku glaze, wood cover, 3½" h. **800-1,200**

Takatori chaire, late Edo period, brown glaze, ivory cover, 3" h. **500-750**

Takatori chaire, 19th c., deep brown and chestnut brown glazes, with brocade pouch (20th c.), 5" h. **375-550**

Wakayama jar and cover, ca. 1915, brown glaze with silver overlay designs of flowers and scrolling foliage, signed, 5" h. **500-700**

Sumida Gawa Pinched-Form Vase

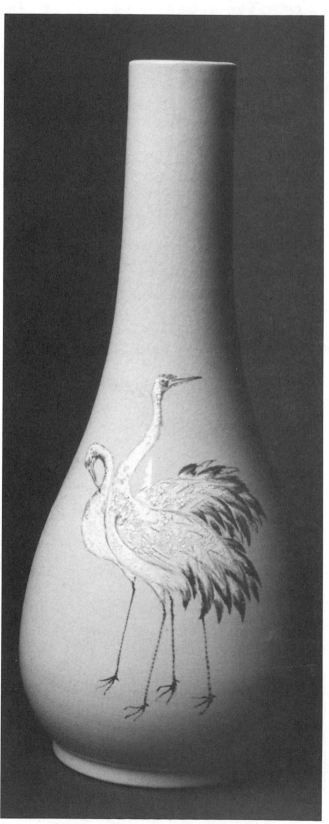

Wakayama Vase with Cranes

Wakayama jar and cover, ca. 1915, straw-colored glaze shaded to green, design of insects in blue and brown, signed, 8" h. **350-500**

Wakayama vase, straw ground with enameled cranes, pear-shaped with elongated neck, ca. 1905 (ILLUS.)..............**300-375**

Wakayama vases, ca. 1900, straw-colored glaze with tiger and cub in colors, Wakayama factory mark on base and decorated by Taizan, 12" h., pair **1,500-2,000**

PRICE LISTINGS
for Twentieth Century Japanese Export Ceramics Marked Nippon, Made In Japan, and Occupied Japan

Made In Japan bank, porcelain, model of a cat, the body with floral designs, 13" h. **$75-125**

Made In Japan bowl, set in silver basket frame, Kenzan-style, bold design and colors, ca. 1920s, 6" d. (ILLUS.) **100-175**

Made in Japan Kenzan-Style Bowl

Made In Japan cake plate, Geisha Girl pattern, apple green trim, fluted 6" d.............**20-30**

Made In Japan cake plate, ca. 1920s, "Geisha Girl," blue rim with gilt highlights, 6" d. (ILLUS.) **10-15**

Made In Japan cake plate, Phoenix Bird pattern, blue and white, 6" d. **10-15**

Made In Japan cigarette box, cover and tray, porcelain painted with red roses and gilt trim, the set **45-75**

Made In Japan cup and saucer, Geisha Girl pattern, cobalt blue border **10-18**

Geisha Girl Cake Plate

Made In Japan dinner set, blue and white, decorated with a landscape of Mt. Fuji and a lakescene:

Bread and Butter plate, 6" d. **10-20**

Breakfast plate, 8¼" d..............................**20-30**

Butter tub **60-85**

Creamer and sugar with cover, pair ..**100-135**

Cup and saucer, standard size..................**20-30**

Cup and saucer, demitasse **25-35**

Dinner plate, 9¾" d.................................**40-55**

Egg cup..**25-35**

Mayonnaise server and spoon, 6½" d...**50-75**

Oval platter, 10" l...................................**75-100**

Oval platter, 10½" l. **100-125**

Oval plater, 15" l. **175-225**

Salad bowl, 8" d. **50-85**

Soup bowl, 7¼" d....................................**45-75**

Teapot, cover, standard size **100-175**

Vegetable dish and cover, round, 10" d...**50-75**

Made In Japan figurine, porcelain, Hotei with his treasure sack, colors and gilt, 8" h. **275-385**

Made In Japan figurine, porcelain, woman, orange kimono with yellow and green flowers and foliage, holding fan in one hand, 8" h. **278-385**

Made In Japan figurine, porcelain, woman seated, her kimono decorated with small floral sprays in colors and gilt highlights, 5" h. **225-375**

Made In Japan figurines of a Dutch couple, porcelain, each with hanging baskets which are strung with cord, 4" h., pair..**35-75**

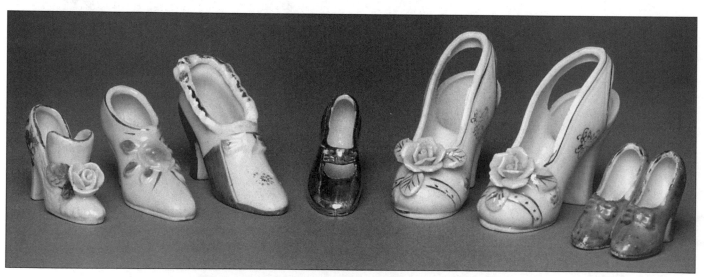

Made in Japan Porcelain Miniature Shoes

Made In Japan porcelain figures of Art Deco ladies, each marked "Made In Japan," 5" h., each (Color Illus. page 115) **250-400**

Made In Japan Dutch shoe, porcelain, 5" w. **25-50**

Made In Japan high heel shoe, porcelain, with red on front, bisque finish, 2" h.............**35-50**

Made In Japan high heel shoe, porcelain, decorated with gilt painted flowers, 2½" h. ..**25-45**

Made In Japan miniature porcelain shoes, ca. 1930s, all marked "Made In Japan," the average price range is $25-40 with the largest pair at (ILLUS.) **100-150**

Made In Japan high heel shoes, porcelain, blue with flower in relief, attached pair, 1½" h. **50-75**

Made In Japan high heel shoes, porcelain, white bisque with bows that turn, 2" h., pair...**45-75**

Made in Japan Satsuma-Style Monkey Group

Made In Japan lazy Susan sweet meat set, porcelain, with lacquer storage box, each section with designs of pink blossoms and gilt rims, 12" d., the set 150-200

Made In Japan Satsuma-style bowl, gilt landscape on black ground, border trimmed in gilt diaper, impressed "Made In Japan" on base, 7" d....................25-35

Made In Japan Satsuma-style figurines, Seven Household Gods of Good Luck, orange, blue, green, yellow and gilt attire, ca. 1925, each piece 2¾" h., the set 125-185

Made In Japan Satsume-style model of an elephant, brown with orange luster ears, saddle with colors and gilt, ca. 1930, 8" h. 125-200

Made In Japan Satsuma-style monkey group, ca. 1920-1935, colors and gilt on brown ground, 5" h., (ILLUS.) 300-500

Made In Japan Satsuma-style teapot and cover, elephant-form, brown with green, orange and gilt embellishment, ca. 1930 375-475

Made In Japan Satsuma-style tea set: covered teapot, covered sugar, open creamer, six cups and saucers; brown ground with Rakan surrounded with gilt haloes, ca. 1930 375-475

Made In Japan teapot and cover, Phoenix Bird pattern, blue and white, 5" h. 50-75

Made In Japan teapot and cover, Awaji ware, yellow crackled glaze, squat form, woven bail handle 175-225

Made In Japan teapot and cover, Awaji ware, turquoise blue crackled glaze, woven bail handle, ca. 1925 150-200

Made In Japan tea set: covered teapot, covered sugar, open creamer, six cups and saucers, six cake plates; blue and white Dutch scene, the set....................125-225

Made In Japan tea set: covered teapot, covered sugar, open creamer, six cups and saucers; orange and blue luster finish, with orange and yellow flowers, black trim, the set 175-250

Made In Japan tea set: covered teapot, covered sugar, open creamer, six cups and saucers; pearlized luster on interiors of cups, exteriors with floral designs on blue luster ground, the set....................185-250

Made In Japan tea set: covered teapot, open sugar, open creamer, six cake plates, six cups and saucers; hand-painted orange flowers with bright green foliage, interiors of cups with small floral spray near rim, all with gilt bands, the set 200-275

Made in Japan Pottery Vase

Awaji Ware Coffeepot

Made In Japan vase, porcelain, yellow with vertical black stripes, the yellow sections with bright red roses and green foliage, 11" h....................**100-150**

Made In Japan vase, porcelain, orange with black and white geometric diamond-shaped pattern around the neck and foot, 13" h. **150-220**

Made In Japan vase, porcelain, bold orange and yellow flowers on a chartreuse ground, 12" h. **200-300**

Made In Japan vase, pottery, ca. 1930, red glaze with rainbow hued flambé, 5½" h. (ILLUS.) **125-175**

Made In Japan coffeepot, Awaji ware, bamboo-form, bamboo-form finial, bamboo-form handle, lid and upper portion of pot green shaded to yellow, base marked with incised bird, ca. 1920s 7½" h. (ILLUS.) **350-500**

Made In Japan teapot and cover, Awaji ware, ca. 1920s, light blue muted ground with decoration of irises, woven bail handle (ILLUS.) **375-475**

Made In Japan vase, Awaji ware, bulbous with tall cylindrical neck, shaded turquoise to cream, ca. 1925, 8" h. **200-275**

Made In Japan vase, Awaji ware, baluster with short neck, shaded ivory to maroon, ca. 1930, 10½" h.................................**250-350**

Made In Japan vase, Awaji ware, bulbous body with elongated tapered neck, light to dark yellow, with dragon entwined around neck, ca. 1930, 14" h. **300-500**

Made In Japan vases, Awaji ware, modified pear-shape, yellow, ca. 1925, 7" h. (ILLUS.)...**350-450**

Nippon basket with handle, decorated with pansies in shades of pink and yellow, gilt rim, 8½" h. **125-175**

Awaji Ware Modified Pear-Shaped Vases

Awaji Ware Teapot with Irises

Nippon bowl, lakescape scene at sunset, "M" in Wreath mark, 5" d. **75-110**

Nippon bowl, open handles, autumnal hues with scene of lake and swans, 6½" d. **150-185**

Nippon bowl, Satsuma-style with brown ground and gilt halloed Rakans, 7" d. **175-225**

Nippon bowl, cobalt and gilt with red roses and foliage, 7½" d..................................**250-375**

Nippon bowl, scalloped with gilt rim, orchid design with gilt highlights, slightly rubbed, 10¾" d. **200-250**

Nippon candlesticks, two bands in Wedgwood-style, the stems with flowers and foliage, 5⅛" h...................................**550-750**

Nippon candlesticks, triangular form with Egyptian designs, 8" h., pair **300-375**

Nippon chocolate set: six cups and saucers, chocolate pot and cover; Egyptian decoration in panels, the set **1,000-1,500**

Nippon chocolate set: six cups and saucers, chocolate pot and cover; each piece with a band of flowers and foliage with gilt borders, slightly rubbed, the set **250-350**

Nippon cigarette box and cover, the sides with "swastika" symbols, the cover with a silhouette of cowboy with lariat riding his horse, 5¼" w..**275-375**

Nippon cracker jar and cover, melon-ribbed, footed, lappets at the rim and around edge of lid, scene of canoe and Native American, 7" h. **300-400**

Nippon dresser set: covered hair receiver, open hatpin holder, ring tree, pin tray and covered powder box; decorated with band of tiny flowers and gilt rims, tray 11" w., the set **350-450**

Nippon hatpin holder, four panels of yellow flowers and foliage between gilt bands, 4½" h..**75-150**

Nippon hatpin holder, upper and lower gilt band with small flowers, 4½" h. **65-100**

Nippon humidor and cover, decorated with Seven Household Gods of Good Luck, in colors and gilt trim, 7" h. **250-350**

Nippon humidor and cover, decorated with slip-trailed dragon against a muted gray ground, 7½" h., losses to dragon........**300-450**

Nippon lemonade set: pitcher with six handled cylindrical cups; underglaze-blue windmill scene, one handle cracked **100-150**

Nippon open handled dish, oval, gilt rims, yellow roses and buds on a muted brown ground, 9½" l. **175-250**

Nippon open handled dish, round, gilt rim, blue ground with lakeside scene at dusk, 9" d. **150-185**

Nippon nut set: 6" d. large bowl, 3" d. small bowls; decorated with irises and gilt scalloped rims, the set **150-200**

Nippon pitcher, cobalt blue and gilt with red roses, 8¼" h. **450-525**

Nippon tea set: teapot and cover, sugar and cover, open creamer, six cups and saucers and six cake plates; slip-trailed dragon on a muted gray ground, the set **800-1,500**

Nippon tea set: teapot and cover, sugar and cover, open creamer, six cups and six saucers; green shaded ground with silver overlay dragons chasing flaming pearl, the set **400-600**

Moriage-Decorated Nippon Vase

Nippon tea set: teapot and cover, sugar and cover, open creamer, six cups and six saucers; Kutani-style, the finial a double lotus blossom, design of ladies among cherry blossoms, the set..............**550-750**

Nippon vase, porcelain, marked "Nippon," green ground with celadon green Moriage designs in celery green, the body decorated with fuchsia flowers and green foliage, 8" h. (ILLUS.) **350-475**

Nippon vase, coralene-type, melon ribbed, the high shoulder with two looped handles, overall decoration of chrysanthemums and foliage, rim with gilt beading, ground shaded pink to yellow, 10" h. **600-700**

Nippon vase, coralene-type, cylindrical with scalloped rim and large loop handles, decoration of wisteria and foliage, 12" h. ..**375-550**

Nippon vase, Longwy-style, cylindrical, 8½" h. **300-400**

Nippon vase, Moriage birds on branches, two open handles, 11½" h. **400-500**

Nippon vase, Satsuma-style, a scene of Kannon and Rakan, color and gilt on brown ground, 8½" h. **300-450**

Nippon vase, shoulder with applied loop handles, short neck, lipped rim, sailboats in autumnal hues, 8" h..............**250-350**

Nippon vase, shoulder with applied squared handles extending about the short neck, heavy gilt trim above muted pink and yellow roses, 12½" h. **450-600**

Nippon vase, bulbous body supported on four circular legs, large loop handles, fluted rim, gilt trim, a scenic design with large pink roses from base to shoulder, 8" h. **300-400**

Noritake ashtray, blue luster finish, figural seated harlequin on rim, 5" w. **450-600**

Noritake ashtray, orange luster with yellow flowers and green leaves, 3¼" w. **75-100**

Noritake ashtray, orange luster finish with seated nude on the rim, 6½" d................**500-775**

Noritake bowl, open handles, windmill scene, orange and blue luster finish, 8" d. **150-185**

Noritake bowl, the center with facing parrots surrounded by garland of small flowers, the border with orange luster trimmed in black with black openwork handles, 7½" d. **200-325**

Noritake bowl, the plain center surrounded by an orange luster band filled with large brightly painted flowers, trimmed with black band and black loop handles, 7" d................**125-175**

Noritake box and cover, figural bird finial, pale blue luster finish, 4" d.............**250-350**

Noritake cake plate, open handles, cobalt blue and gilt border, the center with lake scene in muted shades of yellow, gray, brown, 10" d..............................**225-325**

Noritake candlesticks, autumnal lakeside scene, 7" h. **225-350**

Noritake demitasse set: covered pot, covered sugar, open creamer, six cups and saucers; orange luster ground with blue luster band, decorated with large poppies, the set **350-475**

Noritake luncheon set: six plates, square with rounded corners, and six cups; blue luster border, decorated with large reddish orange flowers and green trailing foliage, the set **300-400**

Noritake model of a squirrel, 3" h. (ILLUS.) **700-900**

Noritake Model of a Squirrel

Noritake Model of a Spaniel

Noritake model of a spaniel, 4" h. (ILLUS.)...**800-1,200**

Noritake tea set: teapot and cover, sugar and cover, open creamer, six cups and saucers and six cake plates; lavender luster border, pale orange luster ground with two facing perched parrots in green and yellow, the set **450-650**

Noritake tray, porcelain, ca. 1925, sunset scene with cobalt blue and gilt open handles, 10" d. (ILLUS.) **275-375**

Noritake vase, ca. 1925, orange luster ground with Art Deco girl wearing purple dress and green hat, black tripod curved feet, 7" h. (Color Illus. pg. 114).................**575-775**

Noritake vase, splayed orange luster foot, blue luster elongated body with fluted rim, decoration of brightly colored birds in flight, 7½" h. **175-225**

Noritake Scenic Tray

Noritake vase, baluster-form with loop handles at the shoulder, short neck and flared rim, two square panels filled with sailing ships at sunset, gilt trim, 12" h. **500-700**

Noritake vase, elongated form with dark orange luster finish, light orange luster band at neck, decorated with a standing female harlequin, 8" h. **400-550**

Noritake vase, jack-in-the-pulpit-style, interior a shaded yellow, exterior with a sunset scene in autumnal hues, pale orange foot, 8" h..........................**400-500**

Noritake vase, fluted rim, gold luster finish, decorated with peacock feathers, 8½" h. ..**375-500**

Noritake vase, fan-shaped orange shaded luster with green and white geometric band at the top, floral bouquet in bright primary colors, 6" h. **450-600**

Occupied Japan ashtray, round, decorated with red roses, 3½" d. **10-15**

Occupied Japan box and cover, flowers and foliage in colors and gilt trim, 6" d. **50-85**

Occupied Japan cigarette lighters, ceramic, figural Toby jug-form, 2½" h., each (ILLUS.) **50-75**

Occupied Japan figure of a ballerina, ruffled lace skirt with applied flowers, 4" h. **50-75**

Occupied Japan figure of a clown standing on his hands, 4" h. **60-85**

Occupied Japan figures of a Colonial man and woman, pair, 5" h......................**75-100**

Occupied Japan figures in the style of Hummel figurines, marked "Occupied Japan," 5" h., (ILLUS.) each **50-75**

Occupied Japan planter, porcelain, supported on four curved legs, cherubs scattered around the front, gilt trim, 7" w. ..**75-125**

Occupied Japan tea set: covered teapot, sugar and creamer; in the forms of chickens, teapot 5" h., the set **100-125**

Occupied Japan tea set: covered teapot, covered sugar, creamer, six cups and saucers; Kutani, scenic design with huts and lake in black and gold, the set **100-125**

Occupied Japan vase, bisque with applied pink roses and leaves in low-relief, 6" h. **20-35**

Occupied Japan vase, porcelain, painted design on front of Japanese lady, 8" h. **50-70**

Occupied Japan Toby Jug-Form Cigarette Lighters

Occupied Japan Hummel-Style Figurines

KOREAN CERAMICS

The following varieties of Korean ceramics are of interest to both dealers and collectors:

Blue: Also termed lapis lazuli. This glaze is an azure blue made of oxidized cobalt. Korean potters may have tried to produce this glaze after seeing a similar hue used during the Qing (Ch'ing) Dynasty. Korean potters simply coated white porcelain heavily with natural cobalt. The finished pieces sometimes are closer to white porcelain.

Blue and White wares: This is white porcelain with underglaze designs executed in blue. The blue was rare and expensive, having to be imported from China. Blue and white porcelain was used by the aristocracy. During the Reign of King Sejo (1455-1468), a native supply of cobalt is said to have become available, though small in quantity. Korean blue and white porcelain was fired at lower temperatures than its Chinese counterpart.

Celadon wares: The color of celadons, whose clay and glaze contains small amounts of iron, shows a greenish blue when baked with a reduced fire. When the fire is oxidized the color has a yellowish tone. Koryo celadons show a deep greenish color.

Celadon wares, inlaid: Before the paste of the body of an object dried, the design was incised, filled with black and/or white slip, and then glazed and fired.

Copper Red (underglaze): This glaze, made of copper oxide, turned red in a reduction firing, and green in an oxidizing firing. Korean copper red can be found used in combination with inlaid Koryo celadons as well as blue and white Yi Dynasty wares, and wares produced in the 20th century.

Iron Black (underglaze iron): This kind of ware was made of clay that contained a high percentage of oxidized and was fired in an oxidizing kiln. There were two underglaze methods of decorating, both dating from the early Yi Dynasty: underglaze painting in iron black, and underglaze painting applied over previously engraved decorations. The underglaze iron ware is related to the Japanese E-hakeme (brushed slip over which a pictorial design is executed) and the Japanese E-gorai (Koryo wares with painted designs).

Iron Black wares: Tenmoku (Japanese-Temmoku, Ame, Saki, Soba, Namako) glazes. In these kinds of wares, an iron glaze is applied to the entire surface of an unfired object. Depending upon the shade of glaze these wares are termed either Tenmoku (Temmoku = "almost black" or Ame = amber; Soba = green; Kaki = persimmon; Namako = gray). These various colors resulted from differences in the amount of iron contained in the clay and the temperatures used for firing. Tenmoku glaze was derived from the black tea bowls made during the Song Dynasty at the Chien yao kilns in the province of Fukien.

Punch'ong (White slipped celadon):

1. Kamhwa Punch'ong (Inlaid)—Same technique as Koryo inlay but with bolder designs.

2. Inhwa Punch'ong (Stamped)—An inlay technique which used the whole space, having dots or floral patterns impressed overall with stamps. The incised patterns were filled with white slip.

3. Sgraffito Punch'ong—Instead of inlaying, the whole space of an object was covered with white slip and then scraped off, in part, leaving designs.

4. Kakhwa Punch'ong (Incised)—Similar to sgraffito but after the slip was applied the background was not cut off.

5. Cholwa Punch'ong (Underglaze iron designs)—This form was covered with slip and fired, a design was drawn and the piece was refired.

White wares: Probably the most representative of Yi Dynasty ceramics, the white can vary in hue and include: grayish white, milk white, egg white, etc. Most of the blue and white wares were produced in the later Yo Dynasty and 20th century.

PRICE LISTINGS
for Korean Ceramics

Korean bottle, 18th-19th c., blue and white, pear-form with design of auspicious characters, the neck and mouth restored, 6¼ " h. **$12,000-18,000**

Korean bottle, 14th c., Tenmoku glaze, 5" h. **900-1,200**

Korean bottle/vase, 19th c., with quick brush stroke design in underglaze-blue, 8" h. (ILLUS.)..**400-600**

Korean cosmetic box and cover, 12th c., inlaid celadon, slightly domed cover with inlaid decoration of central chrysanthemum encircled by a dotted band, the sides with key fret border, 2" d. **1,200-1,500**

Korean dish, 19th c., blue and white with roundrel of landscape, four bats, key fret border, high footring, 7½" d. **3,500-6,000**

Korean Bottle/Vase

Korean dish, 15th c., Punch'ong, stamped and inlaid overall in white slip, the center with calligraphy, overall thick glaze, 6" d. **3,500-5,500**

Korean dish, 15th c., Punch'ong, stamped and incised overall in white slip with twist rope pattern, the center with calligraphy, crack in center, 5½" d.................................**700-900**

Korean jar, 18th-19th c., underglaze-blue and white, 5½" h. (Color Illus. pg. 112) **7,000-9,000**

Korean jar, ca, 1910 or later, the swift brush design in green, 6" h. (ILLUS.) **300-500**

Korean jar, 19th c., white glaze, globular and rounded with tall neck, minor hairlines, 10½" h. **1,500-2,000**

Korean Green-Decorated Jar

Korean oil bottle, 13th c., celadon, sloping shoulders decorated with inlaid band of four cranes and clouds below a flared mouth, silver lacquer repair on rim, 2½" h. **3,500-5,500**

Korean stem bowl, Silla Dynasty, gray pottery, spreading conical foot divided by rectangular apertures, supporting a bowl with two bands of lines, restored, 9" h. **400-500**

Korean stem dish, 18th c., white glaze, flat dish with raised straight rim, the foot splayed, 6" d. **10,000-15,000**

Korean vase, Silla Dynasty, gray, ovoid form with tall neck set on high foot pierced with squares, 11" h. **500-700**

Korean water dropper, porcelain, post-World War II, model of a duck, reproduction of early Korean celadon (ILLUS.) **250-350**

Korean water dropper, post-World War II, lion dog glazed in blue, 2¼" w. **300-400**

Korean water dropper, ca, 1910, lion dog glazed in blue and white, 2⅞" w. **1,000-1,500**

Korean water dropper, 19th c., model of a carp, underglaze-blue and white (Color Illus. left, pg. 115) **2,500-3,500**

Korean water dropper, 19th c., model of a pomegranate, copper red glaze (Color Illus. right, pg. 115) **3,500-5,500**

Post-World War II Korean Water Dropper

Illustrated right:
Japanese Satsuma vase, early 20th c., colors and gilt with bijin and attendant, signed "Kameyama"

$2,000-3,000

Illustrated left:
Japanese Satsuma, base of kogo shows impressed Kinkozan mark and the label which was affixed, ca.1923-1927. The labels can be found in blue, brown, green, etc. If the label were not intact, it is likely that this kogo would be attributed to an earlier dating by many dealers and collectors. Later dating does not diminish values.

Illustrated top left:
Japanese studio porcelain sake cup and underplate, the cup lined with silver (950), silver and gold foliage design on the orangish red ground, signed "Eiraku" and dated Meiji 40 (1907), with attested box.

$3,500-4,500

Illustrated bottom left:
Japanese Satsuma vase, early 20th, four- sided, two with bijin and two with scenic views including a waterfall, colors and gilt, signed "Kameyama," 14" h.

$2,500-3,500

Illustrated top right:
Japanese Satsuma figures, ca. 1920s, colors and gilt, 1½" h., set of 5 dolls.

$1,750-2,125

Illustrated bottom right:
Japanese Satsuma early 19th c. teapot, spout in form of dog with long ears, signed, 3" h.

$5,000-6,000

Illustrated below:
Japanese chawan, ca. 1915, bamboo, signed Tozan (Ito).

$1,500-2,500

Illustrated left:
    Japanese studio porcelain vase, ca. 1900, continuous scene of children at a party, 16" h., attributed to Kozan

$4,000-6,000

—————————●—————————

Illustrated top right:
    Japanese bowl, studio porcelain, ca. 1900, Fahua-style, signed "Eiraku," 8" d.

$3,000-5,000

—————————●—————————

Illustrated bottom right:
    Japanese Satsuma vase, ca. 1915, two sides with processionals and two sides with scenic views, gilt and colors, 10" h.

$5,000-7,000

—————————●—————————

Illustrated below:
    Japanese bowl, studio porcelain, ca. 1900, Fahua-style with incised motifs, signed Seifu, 8" d.

$3,500-5,500

Illustrated left:
Korean jar, 18th - 19th c., underglaze-blue and white, 5½" h.

$7,000-9,000

Illustrated right:
Japanese studio pottery vase, signed "Tanzan," with design in low-relief slip, 7" h.

$900-1,200

Illustrated below:
Japanese Satsuma kogo (incense box), ca. 1923-1927, impressed Kinkozan mark on base with original label, cobalt blue and gilt with interesting design on the interior of cha no yu (tea ceremony) utensils in colors and gilt, 3" d.

$2,000-3,000

Illustrated left:
Japanese Noritake vase, ca. 1925, 7" h.

$575-775

———————————●———————————

Illustrated top right:
Japanese porcelain figures of Art Deco ladies, each marked "Made In Japan," 5" h., each

$250-400

———————————●———————————

Illustrated bottom right:
Korean water droppers, 19th c., carp, underglaze-blue and white $2,500-3,500; pomegranate, copper red glaze

$3,500-5,500

———————————●———————————

Illustrated below:
Japanese studio porcelain sake bottle, ca. 1900, Fahua-style with silver (950) liner, base marked "Eiraku," 4½" h.

$1,800-2,500

Illustrated left:
Japanese studio porcelain sake cup in the form of a tortoise, ca. 1909, the base marked "Kozan," with attested box

$3,000-4,000

Illustrated below:
Japanese studio pottery, censer with openwork metal lid, the shoulder with openwork chrysanthemum petals, a gray glaze with polychrome designs of diapers, the base marked "Kinkozan," 8" h.

$5,000-7,000

The term "cloisonné" comes from the French term *cloison* meaning "cell". Standard cloisonné has a metal body covered with designs made of wire cells which were filled with enamels.

STANDARD CLOISONNÉ PRODUCTION TECHNIQUES

1. A sheet of metal is bent and hammered into the desired shape.

2. An artist paints the design onto the metal.

3. The wires are bent into shapes and placed on their edges to form partitions (cells) or cloisons.

4. A layer of enamel (powdered glass) is sifted over the wires and gently fired to secure it in place.

5. The cells are packed with enamel in powdered form. The colors of the fused enamel depend upon the mixture of natural minerals with the crushed glass.

6. The cells are packed again and refired until they are filled to the top of the wires.

7. The piece is polished with stones of various coarseness and then with charcoal and, finally, powdered horn mixed with oil until the proper finish is obtained.

Illustrated left:
Chinese cloisonné vase, 18th c., decorated with large lotus blossoms and scrolling foliage between ruyi head borders, exterior and interior of the flared neck with matching motifs, a splayed gilt foot, the underside countersunk, one of a pair, restored, 3½" h.

$1,500-2,500

———————●———————

Illustrated right:
Chinese cloisonné vase, Ming Dynasty, meiping shape, 16th or 17th c., overall design of lotus and scrolls between a border of upright leaves around the base and lappets on the shoulder, short neck with floral scroll, 12 1/2" h.

$8,000-12,000

———————●———————

Illustrated below:
Japanese cloisonné vases, silver wire design of facing phoenix, ca. 1930, 6" h., pair

$3,500-5,000

Illustrated right:
   Japanese cloisonné vase, early 20th c., silver and gold wires, base with Ando mark, 12" h.
$4,500-6,500

Illustrated below:
   Japanese cloisonné vase, early Showa period, bulbous body with elongated neck, the wireless motif of camellias in muted shades of bluish green on a deeper bluish green ground.
$2,000-3,000

Illustrated top right:
   Japanese cloisonné box and cover, hammered copper with Moriage motif of peony blossom and foliage, Ando mark on base, 4" w.
$2,500-3,500

Illustrated bottom near right:
   Japanese cloisonné vase, akasuke, late 19th c., modified pear-shape decorated overall with flowers, silver wires, silver mounts, Ando Jubei, 6" h.
$3,000-4,000

Illustrated bottom far right:
   Japanese cloisonné vase, ca. 1910, hammered copper with Moriage designs of grapes and leaves, the base with Ando mark, 16" h.
$4,500-6,500

Illustrated left:
Japanese cloisonné vase, early 20th c., midnight blue ground decorated with birds and flowers, silver wires, silver mounts, signed "Ando," 8" h.

$1,800-2,500

Illustrated left:
Japanese tortoiseshell sake cup, late 19th c., the interior with gold lacquer design of carp.
$1,000-1,500

●

Illustrated below:
Chinese black lacquer armchairs, Shanxi Province, 18th c., each with scrolled crestrail with a bowed, paneled splat, and panel seat, pr.
$3,500-4,500

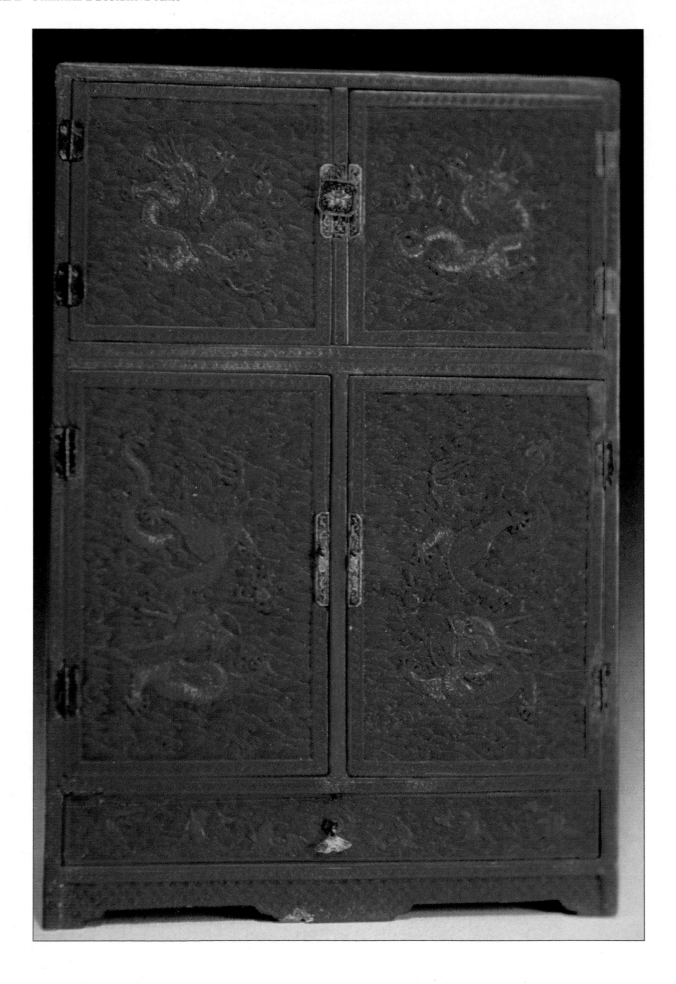

Illustrated left:
Chinese carved cinnabar lacquer cabinet, 19th c., two main doors carved with large dragons chasing the flaming pearl, smaller doors above with similar motif, shallow drawer at the bottom, key fret borders, replacement mounts, restored chips and cracks, 25½" h.

$5,000-7,000

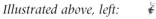

Illustrated above, left:
Chinese mah jongg set, wood case with brass hardware, bat-form longevity symbol painted green on sliding door, the interior fitted with drawers containing ivory and bamboo tiles and ivory counting pieces, complete, ca. 1920s

$250-350

Illustrated above, right:
Korean red lacquer cosmetic case, Yi Dynasty, the hinged cover, black lacquer interior, fitted drawers, iron mounts, tortoiseshell-form lock, four bracket feet, restored, 11" x 9" x 13"

$3,500-5,500

Illustrated right:
Japanese doll, ca. 1920s, face hands and instrument of ivory with silk attire, tortoiseshell hair ornaments, 4½" h.

$1,000-1,500

Illustrated above, right:
　　Left: Vase, yellow Peking glass, 18th c., compressed globular body, long cylindrical neck, 12 vertical flutes from the foot to rim, wide footrim, circular base, yellow, base polished, 6⅞" h.

$5,000-7,000

　　Right: Vase, blue Peking glass, 18th c., tapered ovoid body, cylindrical neck, transparent blue, base polished, 8" h.

$2,500-3,500

———————●———————

Illustrated above, left:
　　Chinese ivory card case, mid-19th c., peony blossoms and openwork

$500-700

———————●———————

Illustrated left:
　　Japanese ivory carving of a young boy, Taisho or early Showa period, signed, 4" h.

$2,500-3,500

Illustated above, left:

Jewelry, Satsuma pendant, ca. 1910, dragon and flames, in gilt and colors, set in new silver mount designed by Mike Kaye

$900-1,200

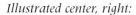

Illustrated above, right

Japanese lacquer footed bowl and cover, late Edo period, the nashiji ground covered with mon in gold and silver lacquer, 7" h.

$2,000-3,000

Illustrated center, right:

Japanese lacquer koro (censer) tray, late Edo period, 18th c., nashiji ground decorated with mon in gold and silver hiramaki-e and togidashi, supported on three legs, 8" dia.

$4,000-6,000

Illustrated right:

Chinese Mandarin necklace, 108 beads with stations, 19th c., amber glass beads as well as glass beads simulating lapis lazuli, jadeite, and Imperial yellow glass

$1,200-1,800

Illustrated right:
> Japanese lacquer bowl and lid, one of a set of ten, in original box, early Showa period, the set
>
> $3,500-4,500

Illustrated right, center:
> Japanese lacquer kogo (incense box), early Edo period, the red lacquer rubbed to reveal the black underlying lacquer, the cover decorated in gold with dragon, the base with floral mon, 2" d.
>
> $7,500-9,500

Illustrated below, right:
> Japanese lacquer and ivory carving of Bijin reading, Taisho or early Showa period, seated before her table which is ornamented with ivory flower vase, ivory books with legible calligraphy and ivory poem box with polychrome designs of flowers, Bijin, 4" h.
>
> $1,500-2,200

Illustrated below:
> Japanese lacquer tray, maple leaves on black ground, 7" x 7", Showa period
>
> $400-650

Illustrated top:
Japanese Komai table screen, ca. 1915, a continuous scene in three shades of gold and silver, below and gold design of maple leaves, 6" h.

$2,500-3,500

Illustrated above:
Japanese iron tetsubin (kettle), signed, signature in bronze lid "Kinryudo zo," signature on kettle "Okuni zo," the body with elaborate overall relief work of a warrior slaying a tiger, handle with gilt inlay

$1,800-2,500

Illustrated above:
Japanese Komai box, dated 1923, the design features women beside a stream, in silver and gold, 5" w.

$4,000-5,000

Illustrated left:
Japanese enameled silver box and cover, ca. 1900, with designs of flowers and foliage raised at various levels of relief, supported on four bracket feet, 3" x 4"

$2,000-2,500

Illustrated center, left:
Japanese enameled card case, ca. 1900, the design of flowers, foliage and insects raised at various levels of relief, 3" l.

$2,000-2,500

Illustrated below, left:
Japanese match safe: Right—Match safe, mixed metals in the form of Oni, late Meiji period

$500-700

Left—Silver match safe, late Meiji period, design of dragons in relief

$375-475

Illustrated below:
Japanese silver kogo, ca. 1920s, rectangular box with incised flowers, 2" x 1", marked gin and signed

$375-575

Japanese silver kogo, teardrop-form, 2½" l.

$375-575

Illustrated left:

Korean iron brazier, 19th c., hexagonal, inlaid with silver, each side decorated with a key fret-bordered roundel with each enclosing a turtle and a crane beneath the moon, an oversized conch shell, fruit on a branch, a pomegranate, a floral branch, or a pair of deer, the neck supporting a flat everted hexagonal rim with a floral design and diaper ground, the base with six bracket feet, 7½" h.

$3,500-6,500

———————————————●———————————————

Illustrated below:

Japanese bronze and mixed metal tea set on lacquer stand, early Showa period, black lacquer with silver and gold mon, the utensils of silver and bronze with silver liners and incised motifs filled with gold, signed

$3,500-4,500

Illustrated above:
    Korean painting, 19th c., mandarin ducks and
    lotus, color on paper, frame size 25 x 12"

$900-1,200

Illustrated left:
    Chinese painting, Qi Baishi (1864-1957), Bird
    and Flower, hanging scroll; ink and color on
    paper, signed and sealed, approximate size 54"
    x 18"

$12,000-18,000

Ilustrated above:
   Chinese painting on silk, vegetables and fruit, signed "Sun Xiaguang," 9½" x 12", early 20th c.

$300-500

Illustrated above:
Chinese painting on silk, scenic view with sailboats and setting sun, signed "Chen Gungchao," Guangxu period, 10" x 12½"

$300-500

———————————●———————————

Illustrated left:
Japanese painting, water color of Beauty walking in the snow, ca. 1910, 14" x 18"

$400-600

Illustrated left:
Japanese painting of boats with tall sails, ca. 1905, 12" x 18".

$500-700

———————————●———————————

Illustrated above:
Chinese paintings, Zhang Daqian (1899-1983), flowers, ink and color on board, framed, framed sizes approximately 10½" x 9¼", each signed and sealed, pair.

$5,000-7,000

Illustrated above:
    Chinese painting on silk, ca. 1900, figures on a
verandah, one adjusts her hair by gazing at a
bronze mirror, 10½" x 14".

                        $175-225

Chapter 4
CLOISONNÉ

●

The term "cloisonné" comes from the French term *cloison* meaning "cell". Standard cloisonné has a metal body covered with designs made of wire cells which were filled with enamels.

STANDARD CLOISONNÉ PRODUCTION TECHNIQUES

1. A sheet of metal is bent and hammered into the desired shape.

2. An artist paints the design onto the metal.

3. The wires are bent into shapes and placed on their edges to form partitions (cells) or cloisons.

4. A layer of enamel (powdered glass) is sifted over the wires and gently fired to secure it in place.

5. The cells are packed with enamel in powdered form. The colors of the fused enamel depend upon the mixture of natural minerals with the crushed glass.

6. The cells are packed again and refired until they are filled to the top of the wires.

7. The piece is polished with stones of various coarseness and then with charcoal and, finally, powdered horn mixed with oil until the proper finish is obtained.

1	2	3	4	5
Plaster form is made and wire mesh is wrapped around form.	Form is removed.	Enamels are added and fired.	Repeated process.	Finished piece.

A Method for Producing Plique-A-Jour

CHINESE CLOISONNÉ

Chinese cloisonné is termed *Ching tai lan* after the period in the Ming Dynasty in which is was developed. Characteristics include:

1. Pieces can have a gold, bronze, copper or brass body.

2. There can be pitting in the surface.

3. Ground coloring includes rust, black, oxblood, white, turquoise, green, etc.

4. Designs, in addition to the prime motif, can include background designs of diapers (repetitive patterns).

5. Objects include: animals, figures, water pipes, snuff bottles, as well as ornamental, occasional and functional wares.

6. Chinese cloisonné can be marked with reign marks (period markings).

JAPANESE CLOISONNÉ

Characteristics of Japanese Cloisonné include:

1. The body of an object can be silver, brass, ceramic (pottery or porcelain), bronze, copper, papier-mache or lacquer.

2. Japanese cloisonné can have factory marks, artist's signatures or seals.

3. Enamels can be opaque, transparent or translucent.

4. Designs are naturalistic and do not have to cover the entire piece.

5. Objects include: netsuke, belt buckles, tsuba, pins, inro, as well as ornamental and functional wares.

Japanese cloisonné, also termed *Shippo Yaki*, includes the following techniques:
Yusen (with wires), **Musen** (wireless), **Yu Musen** (wire and wireless); **Shotai** (plique-a-jour—bodiless cloisonné with transparent enamels); **Moriage** (cameo-a motif in relief); **Totai** (ceramic bodied); **Ginbari** (silver foil wrapped around a metal body having translucent or transparent enamel); **Akasuke** (pigeon blood) red .

The term "goldstone" applies to the enamel which glitters like gold. The enamels had iron pyrite and/or copper filings added to it. "Fishscale" simply refers to a repetitive decoration that resembles the scales of a fish.

RELATED TERMS:

Counter enameling is found on both Japanese and Chinese cloisonné. Usually used inside and/or on bases to counteract the expansion and contraction of the enamel and metal. It strengthens the body.

Repoussé is relief formed by pressing or hammering a decoration from the back.

Basse Taille has a translucent enamel over metal. The metal has designs of various heights in relief. It was produced by the Chinese and was usually machine-made.

Champleve is a technique where the metal body is engraved, etched, stamped or chiseled to form sunken designs and enamels are then used to fill the depressions, leaving the divisions in relief. It uses no wires.

PRICE LISTING
for *Chinese Cloisonné:*

Canton enamel on bowl with matching cover and underplate, 19th c., dragons and flames on a blue ground, the interior of the bowl and cover and underside of underplate are pale green, 4" d., the set...**$600-800**

Canton enamel on copper dish, 18th c., the interior with a scenic design of figures in a garden, Famille Rose palette, the underside with flowers and fruit, chipping and scratches, 6" d. **500-700**

Canton enamel on copper dish, Qianlong, Famille Rose palette, the center with European subject of a gentleman standing beside a seated lady in a landscape within

Canton Enamel Sweetmeat Box

a border filled with small repetitive diapers and reserves filled with scenic vignettes, 10" d. **3,500-4,500**

Canton enamel on copper sweetmeat box and cover, Famille Rose palette, yellow and blue designs of flowers, early 18th c., 10" d. (ILLUS.)...........................**900-1,200**

Champleve figure of a seated Buddha, late 18th or early 19th c., seated in dhyanasana on double lotus throne, both hands in dhyanamudra, champleve-decorated robe, downcast face, elongated ears, hair in a usnisa, 7" h. **1,200-1,800**

Cloisonné basin, late Ming Dynasty, shallow, decorated with red and yellow lotus blossoms and scrolls on a turquoise ground, 9" d. **3,000-5,000**

Cloisonné candlestick, 20th c. in 18th c. style, a white enameled goose standing on a dish, the rim with dragon scrolls, the underside with petal forms and lappets, 8" h. **800-1,200**

Cloisonné and gilt-metal clock, 19th c., rectangular, set between a domed top and tiered base, the cloisonné with panels of flowers on a bright blue ground with key fret diaper, 19" h...........................**2,500-4,500**

Cloisonné jar and cover, ca. 1935, dark green ground with flowerheads in colors marked "CHINA," 6¼" h., ...**100-150**

Cloisonné jar and cover, ca. 1935, decorated overall with chrysanthemums and leaves on diapered ground of T-pattern, domed cover, 6" h........................**150-200**

Cloisonné plaque, 19th c., circular with a design of birds perched in blossoming prunus branches, framed, frame size 28" x 28" **4,500-6,500**

Cloisonné plaque, 19th c., rectangular, scenic design with pagoda and boat, framed, frame size 14" x 10" **700-900**

Cloisonné quails, 18th c., each standing with heads turned sideways, yellow enamel with gilt wires, black markings, the backs form detachable covers, the feet and beaks gilded, 5" h., pair **2500-3,500**

Cloisonné smoking set, ca. 1930, ashtray, match box holder, cylindrical cigarette jar; diaper on a black ground, the set **150-200**

Cloisonné vase, 18th c., decorated with large lotus blossoms and scrolling foliage between ruyi head borders, exterior and interior of the flared neck with matching

motifs, a splayed gilt foot, the underside countersunk, one of a pair, restored, 3½" h. (Color Illus. pg. 118) **1,500-2,500**

Cloisonné vase, Ming Dynasty, meiping-form, lotus and scrolls in red, green, white and yellow on a turquoise ground, dents, enamel missing, 11" h. **2000-3000**

Cloisonné vase, Ming Dynasty, meiping shape, 16th or 17th c., overall design of lotus and scrolls between a border of upright leaves around the base and lappets on the shoulder, short neck with floral scroll, 12½" h. (Color Illus. pg. 119) ..**8,000-12,000**

Cloisonné vase, 19th c., Gu-form, green lappets, white lotus on a blue ground, the foot with lotus and scroll, 12" h.................**700-900**

Cloisonné vase, Qianlong mark and of the period, the body decorated with wide bands of alternating phoenix, archaistic designs, turquoise ground and primary hues, the handles of taotie form, the tall waisted neck with further bands, 2' 1" h. **25,000-45,000**

PRICE LISTING
for Japanese Cloisonné

Champleve vase, ca. 1930, decoration of blossoms and foliage in band around the center, base marked "Japan," 10" h. **75-125**

Champleve vase, ca. 1925, three bands of flowers and scrolls in red, blue and green, mounted as a lamp, 14" h. **100-175**

Cloisonné bowl, 20th c., plique-a-jour technique, translucent enamels within

Japanese Cloisonné Box

Japanese Cloisonné Vase

silver wires with flowers, chrome rim and foot, unsigned, 4" d. **800-1,200**

Cloisonné box and cover, ca. 1920, the cover with Moriage design of deer on hammered copper, the base marked "Ando," 6" w. (ILLUS.) **2,500-3,500**

Cloisonné box and cover, hammered copper with Moriage motif of peony blossom and foliage, Ando mark on base, 4" w. (Color Illus. page 121) **2,500-3,500**

Cloisonné box with cover and undertray, early 20th c., hammered copper with Moriage motifs of pomegranates and foliage, impressed Ando mark, tray 6" w., the set **2,500-3,800**

Cloisonné censer, ca. 1910, tripod-form, black ground, extended handles, alternating shields of phoenix and dragon, floral borders above and below, on three straight legs, 4¾" h. **800-1,200**

Cloisonné censer and cover, ca. 1900, sperhical form with midnight blue ground, decorated overall with cranes in flight, the cover with lappet border, bud-form finial, 6" h. **400-650**

Cloisonné charger, ca. 1900, bird and flowers on a turquoise ground, 12" d. **200-300**

Cloisonné charger, ca. 1910, three birds in flight above flowering branches, black ground, 12½" d. **250-375**

Cloisonné jar, in the-style of Namikawa Yasuyuki, early 20th c., copper and silver wires, two cream-colored panels filled with insects and foliated branches, the shoulder and sides with floral bands, cover missing, 6" h. **1,500-2,500**

Cloisonné vase, early 20th c., gin bari, with wire and wireless designs of hydrangea against a deep blue ground, the underlying silver foil embossed with flowers, silver wires, silver mounts, 4" h. (ILLUS. left) **1,500-2,000**

Cloisonné vase, akasuke, red enamel with underlying silver foil, flowers and foliage, the footrim with Ando mark, 6" h. This piece is contemporary and current secondary market values are not very high. (ILLUS. below) **150-200**

Cloisonné vase, beaker-form ,early 20th c., pink ground with silver wires, design of bamboo and foliage in green, 5" h. (ILLUS. next page) **900-1,200**

Cloisonné vase, Meiji period, ovoid form tapering toward the base, pale muted shaded blue ground decorated with sparrow and paper whites with long leaves, wire and wireless, the rim and base silver, minor star crack, signed "Namikawa Sosuke," 10½" h. **15,000-25,000**

Modern Japanese Cloisonné Vase

Cloisonné vase, ca. 1910, hammered
   copper with Moriage designs of grapes and
   leaves , the base with Ando mark, 16"h.
   (Color Illus. pg. 121) ....**4,500-6,500+**

Cloisonné vase, yu musen, early 20th c.,
   pink ground, the base surrounded with
   white heron, damaged, 5" h......................**400-600**

Cloisonné vase, late Meiji period, ginbari,
   silver mounts, short neck, ovoid body
   decorated with gold fish, base signed
   "Kawaguchi," cracks and oxidation
   to silver, 6" h................................**300-450**

Cloisonné vase, akasuke, late 19th c.,
   modified pear-shape decorated overall
   with flowers, silver wires, silver mounts,
   Ando Jubei, 6" h. (Color Illus.
   pg. 121) **3,000-4,000**

Cloisonné vase, early 20th c., midnight
   blue ground decorated with birds and
   flowers, silver wires, silver mounts, signed
   "Ando," 8" h. (Color Illus. pg. 122)......**1,800-2,500**

Cloisonné vase, early 20th c., ovoid form
   with flared rim, the body with colored
   enamels on a pale blue ground, birds
   flying above a lakescape, silver rims,
   signed "Ota," 10¾" h. **3,000-5,000**

Cloisonné vase, early 20th c., ovoid form
   with waisted neck and everted rim,
   opaque and translucent enamels with
   archaicistically-shaped panels filled with
   birds above lappets, signed
   "Ando," 6¾" h. **1,800-2,500**

Cloisonné vase, early Showa period,
   bulbous body with elongated neck, the
   wireless motif of camellias in muted
   shades of bluish green on a deeper bluish
   green ground (Color Illus. pg. 120)......**2,000-3,000**

Cloisonné vase, post -World War II,
   akasuke (red) on silver foil stippled with
   a design of a bird and branch, silver
   wires with designs of white roses and
   green foliage, the rim marked "Ando,"
   8" h. **300-500**

Cloisonné vase, style of Ando, early
   20th c., shouldered ovoid form, green
   ground decorated with three carp,
   wire and wireless, silver mounts,
   8¾" h. **1,000-1,500**

Cloisonné vase, ca. 1900, ovoid form with
   blossoming flowers and birds on branches,
   silver wires, black ground,
   unsigned, 8" h......................**1,500-2,200**

Cloisonné vase, post-World War II, beaker-
   form, red, white and pink orchids, the
   interior red,the foot rim marked "Ando" ..**500-750**

Cloisonné vase, as above, green with white
   narcissus, the interior green, some damage
   (dings), Ando mark on foot rim **250-500**

Cloisonné vase, early 20th c., ovoid-form,
   copper wires, the ground alternating from
   oxblood to pale brown in vertical bands
   filled with insects, 4¾" h. **600-900**

Cloisonné vase, early 20th c., silver and
   gold wires, decorated with large pink roses
   on a white ground, base with Ando mark,
   12" h. (Color Illus. pg. 120)..................**4,500-6,500**

Cloisonné vases, silver wire design of facing
   phoenix, ca. 1930, 6" h., pair
   (Color Illus. pg. 119) **3,500-5,000**

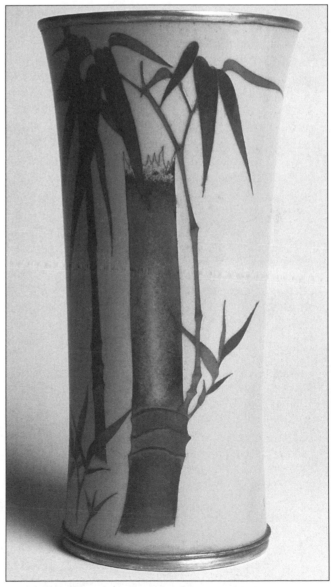

Japanese Cloisonné Beaker-form Vase

Chapter 5
EPHEMERA AND BOOKS

●

Ashton, Leigh & Gray, Basil. *Chinese Art,* Boston: Hale, Cushman & Fling **$15-25**

Backhouse, E. & Bland, J.O.P. *Annals and Memoirs of the Court of Peking,* London 1914 ....**100-150**

Ball, J. Dyer, *Things Chinese.* Hong Kong, Kelly & Walsh, 1903 ....**40-65**

Blacker, J.F. *The ABC Of Japanese Art.* Boston: Cornhill Pub. Co. **35-50**

Brockhous, Albert. *Netsuke.* New York: Duffield & Co., 1924 ....**100-150**

Cox, Warren, *Chinese Ivory Sculpture.* New York: Crown Publishers, 1946 ....**75-125**

Davids, T.W. Rhys. *Buddhism.* London, 1877 ....**50-85**

Edkins, Rev. Joseph. *Chinese Buddhism.* Boston: Houghton, 1880 ....**35-55**

Etherton, Colonel P.T. *Manchuria.* London: Jarrokis, 1932 ....**20-30**

Fought, Harold & Alice. *Unfathomed Japan.* New York: Macmillan Co., 1928 ....**50-75**

Franks, Augustus W. *Japanese Pottery Being A Native Report.* Piccadilly: Chapman & Hall, 1880 ....**150-200**

Gichner, Lawrence E. *Erotic Aspects of Japanese Culture.* USA, 1953 ....**400-600**

Giles, Herbert Allen. *China And The Chinese.* New York: Columbia U. Press, 1902 ....**40-65**

Hartshorne, Anna C. *Japan And Her People.* Philadelphia: John C. Winston Co., 1902 (2 vols.) **150-200**

Jarvis, James Jackson. *A Glimpse At The Art Of Japan.* Philadelphia: Albert Saifer, 1970 ....**20-25**

Joya, Mock. *Quaint Customs And Manners Of Japan.* Tokyo: New Servicek, 1955 (4 vols.) ..**50-75**

Laufer, Berthold. *Ivory In China.* Chicago: Field Museum of Natural History, 1925 ....**1,500-2,000**

Leibowitz, Aldophe. *Japanese Prints And Their Creators.* Shoreline Press, 1935 ....**35-55**

Loti, Pierre. *Madame Chrysantheme.* Paris: 1889 ....**300-400**

Masuda, Tomoya. *Living Architecture: Japanese.* New York: Frosset & Dunlap, 1970 ....**30-40**

McKune, Evelyn. *The Arts Of Korea.* Rutland: Charles E. Tuttle, 1962...............................**50-75**

Michner, James A. *The Floating World.* New York: Random House, 1954 ....**50-75**

Miln, Louise Jordan. *Quaint Korea.* New York: Charles Schribner's Sons, 1896 ....**50-75**

Nakamura Tanio. *Contemporary Japanese Style Painting.* New York: Tudor, 1969 ....**75-100**

Narazaki, Muneshige. *The Japanese Print.* Tokyo & Palo Alto: Kodansha International, 1978 ....**125-150**

Okuma, Count. *Fifty Years Of New Japan.* New York: 1909 ....**65-95**

Priest, Alan. *Costumes From The Forbidden City.* New York: Metropolitan Museum of Art, 1945 ....**15-25**

Ralph, Julian. *Alone In China.* London: Hutchinson, 1958 ....**15-25**

Rockhill, William Woodville. *The Land Of The Lamas,* New York: Century Co., 1891 ..**175-225**

Scidmore, Eliza Ruhamah. *China: The Long Lived Empire.* New York: The Century Co., 1900 ....**30-50**

Siren, Osvald. *Chinese Paintings In American Collections.* Paris and Brussels: Les Editions G. Van Oest, 1928 ....**250-300**

Statler, Oliver. *Shimoda Story.* New York: Random House, 1969 ....**25-35**

Sze Mai-Mai. *The Tao Of Painting, A Study Of The Ritual Disposition Of Chinese Paintings.* New York: Bollingen/Pantheon, 1956 ......**100-150**

Takaki, Masayoshi. *The History Of Japan Paper Currency.* John Hopkins Press, 1903 ......**20-35**

Tatsui, Matsunosuke. *Gardens Of Japan.* Tokyo: The Zauho Press, 1935 ....**250-300**

Valla, Alene. *The Secret Diary Of Lady Takayama.* Kyoto, 1960 ....**65-85**

Werner, E.T.C. *Myths & Legends Of China.* New York: Brentano's (1920s) **50-75**

Williston, Teresa Peirce. *Japanese Fairy Tales.* Rand McNally & Co., 1904 ....**50-75**

Chapter 6
EROTICA

Chinese album, 19th c., ten silk leaves painted with various scenes of lovers in erotic pursuits, each painting mounted on board, 13" l. **$2,500-3,500**

Chinese album, early 20th c., 35 paintings on silk executed in ink and color on silk and mounted on boards, foxing, stains, 11" l. **500-700**

Chinese fan, ca. 1890s, one side painted with vegetables, the other when partially open reveals an erotic scene, bamboo guards and ribs.....................................**1,500-2,000**

Chinese ivory carving of nude seated on garden stool, holding fan, polychrome, 20th c., 7" h. **600-800**

Chinese porcelain group, couple engaged in love making, base marked "CHINA," 3" w. **800-1,200**

Chinese porcelain cups, Tongzhi period, the set of nine with Famille Rose decoration, the largest 4" h., the smallest 1", each with scenic exteriors and interiors with figures engaged in amorous poses, men with women and women with women **5,000-7,000**

Chinese reverse-painting on glass, 20th c., nine rectangular panels of glass, each with couple in amorous activities in an interior setting, some with attendants, all mounted within a wood frame, the reverse with plain mirror, 18" x 14" **2,500-3,500**

Chinese snuff bottle, porcelain, each side with a couple engaged in amorous pose, ca. 1900 ....**700-950**

Japanese cup and saucer, early 20th c., colors and gilt with couple in amorous pose watched by attendant, interior of cups filled with floral decorations, 3½" h. **600-800**

Japanese netsuke of a nude, post-World War II, ivory, ...**100-175**

Japanese netsuke, Okame fondling Tengu's nose, early 20th c., ivory **300-500**

Japanese netsuke, Okame with a large suggestive mushroom, ivory, late 19th or early 20th c. **600-800**

Japanese netuske, Okame being intimate with Tengu, ivory, early 20th **350-550**

Japanese netsuke, 20th c., pillow-form, ivory, man looking through pillow, the interior view of a woman bathing.............**200-300**

Japanese painting on silk, ca. 1920s, a couple in amorous encounter, with voyeurs, 8" x 8" **500-750**

Japanese scroll, late 19th-early 20th c., ink and colors on silk depicting various couples in amorous pursuits, foxing and stains, 70" l. **600-900**

Japanese woodblock print, couple in amorous pose, with voyeurs, from "Molds for Loving Couples," attributed to Hokusai, very good impression, color, creased, trimmed, oban yoko-e, early 19th c. **1,500-2,500**

Japanese woodblock print, a couple in amorous encounter in a boat, "Sumidagawa yosuru geisha" (Geisha approaching the Sumida River), from a series attributed to Keisai Eisen, ca. 1824, good impression, color, centerfold, soiled, wormage, trimmed **1,200-1,800**

Japanese woodblock print, a couple engaged in erotic pursuit from the book (Ehon) "Komachi biki," attributed to Utamaro, ca. 1802, good impression, color, slight fading, restored at bottom and left.............................**1,000-1,500**

Chapter 7

EXOTIC MATERIALS

CHINESE

Rhinoceros horn libation cup, 17th or 18th c., carved in high-relief with eight chilong around the sides, four shaped cartouches filled with repetitive patterns (diapers), with a band of petal-form lappets below a band of key fret at the rim, pedestal foot, handle in form of a dragon, color overall shaded from deep honey to blackish brown at the foot, restored, 4½" h. **$8,000-12,000**

Rhinoceros horn libation cup, 17th or 18th c., carved in the form of a blossom, one side with two wufu (bats), buds and blossom at the base, mostly honey color, minor chips overall, 6¾" h. **4,500-6,500**

Rhinoceros horn libation cup, 18th c., elaborate cloud patterns with seven dragons chasing flaming pearls, one dragon forming the handle, shaded light honey to deep brown at the foot, 6" h. **6,000-9,000**

Rhinoceros horn libation vessel, 18th c., carved and pierced designs, the horn a dark brown hue, cracks and losses, 16" h. (ILLUS.).....................................**4,500-6,500**

Tortoiseshell box and cover, 19th c., circular, the top and bottom carved with figures in landscapes, 2½" d. **900-1,200**

Tortoiseshell box and cover, early 19th c., circular with carved village sccne on cover, 4¾" d. **650-950**

Tortoiseshell hair comb, 19th c., six long teeth, pierced and carved with an oval panel of figures in a boat, 4" w.................**600-900**

Tortoiseshell hair comb, 19th c., six short teeth, pierced with panel of blossoming branches, 3" w. ....**300-500.**

JAPANESE

Tortoiseshell Cigarette case, openwork decoration, ca. 1930s, 4" w. (ILLUS.) **$250-350**

Chinese Rhinoceros Horn

Tortoiseshell comb and hairpin, ca. 1916-1926, gold lacquer decorated with cranes and pine, comb 3½" l. **700-900**

Tortoiseshell comb and hairpin, ca. 1902-1910, roiro ground with shibayama inlay forming flowers, signed "Matsuyama," 4" l. **1,000-1,500**

Tortoiseshell dish, late 19th c., interior decorated with gold lacquer flowers and foliage, minor wear, scratches, 6" d.........**800-1,200**

Tortoiseshell hair ornaments, ca. 1910, with gilt lacquer and shibayama flowers (ILLUS.)...................................**800-1,200**

Tortoiseshell sake cup, late 19th c., interior decorated with gold lacquer aquatic designs, 3¾" w. **1,200-1,500**

Tortoiseshell sake cup, late 19th c., the interior with gold lacquer design of carp (Color Illus. pg. 123) **1,000-1,500**

Japanese Tortoiseshell Cigarette Case

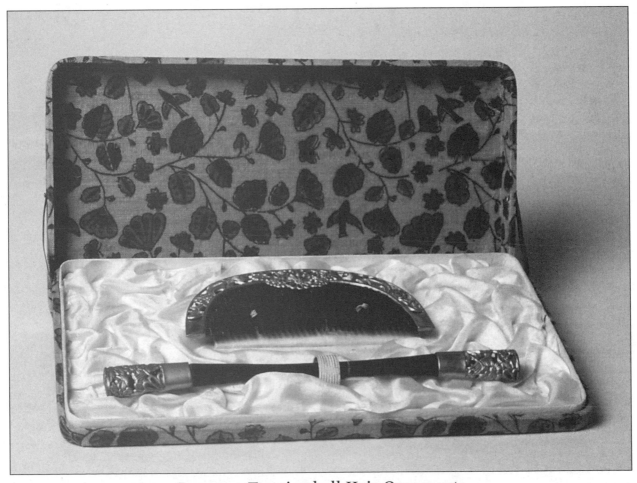

Japanese Tortoiseshell Hair Ornaments

Chapter 8
FANS

———————————————●———————————————

In the West, the use of the fan was confined to women. In the Orient fans were used by both genders.

Chinese Fans: As there is fashion in all things, fashion decreed that women use one sort of fan, men another. The difference lies principally in the number of ribs in the fans. A man's fan could have nine, sixteen, twenty or twenty-four ribs. A woman's fan would not have less than thirty ribs.

The three basic types of fans are the folding fan, the ceremonial fan and the *pien-mien*. The Chinese word for fan is 'shan.' There are three basic types of folding fan. One is made of feathers, another of paper supported by individual sticks and the third is a brisé or folding fan made from rigid segments joined at the base by a rivet and at the top by a thread or ribbon.

China Trade fans are popular in today's market. Typical of these are those which were decorated with silk embroidery in long and short stitches; fans decorated with painted gouache landscapes and figures (figures having ivory faces); and water-color on silk.

Fan cases were made from a variety of materials, the most common in the 19th and early 20th centuries being pasteboard boxes covered with fabric having geometric designs or lacquered boxes with gold designs and fitted silk interiors.

Japanese Fans: There are three basic types of Japanese folding fan, the feather, the folding paper and the brisé. The *Uchiwa* is a flat non-folding fan. *Ogi* is a folding fan which has two forms: the *Hi-ogi*, or slatted form, came first and consisted of thin wooden slats generally made of hinoki (cypress), riveted at the base and threaded at the upper end; the *Sensu*, the other form, made of paper or silk, pasted on flat or round ribs of bamboo, ivory or wood, with a rivet that holds the ribs together at the base, while the upper end unfolded in accordion fashion. Those with small ribs having spaces between when opened are termed *suehiro*. Those with flat ribs are termed *kawahori*.

Gyoji no uchiwa is the fan used for making signals by the referee of a Sum (wrestling)match. *Kome ogi* is a lady's hinoki fan. It should have 39 slats ornamented with designs.

PRICE LISTINGS
for Fans

Chinese fan, 19th c., silk, painted on one side with landscapes, the other with houses and figures, the faces of the figures picked out in painted ivory, the ribs and guards ivory, fitted box, some restoration, 22" w. when open **$500-700**

Chinese fan, 19th c., Canton school, 23 slats carved with figures in gardens, slight damage **700-900**

Chinese fan, silver-gilt and enamel, filigree floral design, ca. 1850, minor repair to one rib **1,000-1,500**

Chinese fan, early 19th c., circular form with ivory stick, painted on silk in colors with design of a lady and attendants in a garden, silk worn, 10" l. **300-500**

Chinese fan, folding-type, Qian Hui'an (1833-1911), scene of a fisherman in a boat, ink and colors on paper, inscribed and signed by the artist, one seal, reverse with calligraphy and two seals, 9" h. **700-900**

Chinese fan, Wang Jielin (20th c.), prunus decoration, signed and sealed, 9" h. **400-600**

Japanese fan, late 19th c., ivory, the guards with lacquer designs of birds and maple leaves, the ribs with lacquer decorations of cranes and bamboo on both sides, 9" h. **2,000-3,000**

Japanese fan, late 19th c., ivory with shibayama decoration, both sides of fan with hiramakie lilies, trees and birds, the insects of carnelian, coral, and mother-of-pearl, 9" h. **2,000-3,000**

Japanese fan, ivory with shibayama inlay, late 19th c., the fan a woodblock print of bijin, the other side showing karako, rabbit ojime with coral eyes, 10" h. **1,800-2,500**

Chapter 9
FURNITURE

●

IDENTIFICATION OF WOOD

CHINESE

In addition to bamboo and fruit woods the following woods and decorative treatments have been used in the production of Chinese furniture:

Hong mu *(hung mu)*—red wood

Hua li—pear tree flower wood

Huang hua li—yellow pear tree flower wood

Huangyang—boxwood

Ji chi mu *(chi ch'ih mu)*—chicken wing wood

Jumu—elm from S. China

Li—pear tree

Luodianqian—mother-of-pearl inlay

Muqian—wood inlay

Nanbai—southern cypress

Nan mu—southern wood (Lauraceae family)

Chinese Zitan Table

Ti hong *(t'i hung)*—carved red lacquer (carved cinnabar, *cinnabar* being a name for "red")

Wumu—ebony

Yingmu—burl wood

Yinxing—Ginkgo wood

Zitan *(tzu-t'an)*—purple sandalwood

Zuomu—a type of oak

JAPANESE

The Japanese used many varieties of wood for the making of furniture. In addition to bamboo and various fruit woods the following were popular:

Hinoki—cypress

Keyaki—zelkova (elm)

Kiri—paulownia

Kuri—chestnut

Kuwa—mulberry

Matsu—pine

KOREAN

Woods commonly used by Korean carpenters are zelkova (elm), pine, pear, gingko, persimmon, mountain ash, paulownia, walnut, oak and bamboo. There are over 30 kinds of woods known to have been used in the making of furniture.

PRICE LISTINGS
for Oriental Furniture

Chinese bamboo cabinet, 19th c., two rectangular shelves above two doors enclosing a shelf, all in an angular open work pattern, 17" x 40", 74" h., ...**$3,500-5,500**

Chinese bamboo table, 19th c., with black lacquer top above angular openwork, 20" x 40", 33" h. **1,200-1,800**

Chinese black lacquer armchairs, Shanxi Province, 18th c., each with scrolled crestrail with a bowed, paneled splat, and panel seat, pr. (Color Illus. pg. 123) **3,500-4,500**

Chinese cabinet, 18th c., black lacquer, the upper section with two paneled doors, the lower section with two larger doors opening to reveal a shelf and two drawers, painted with figures in extensive garden scenes with elaborate borders filled with shaped panels, old restorations disintegrating, 95" x 45" x 24" **4,000-5,000**

Chinese carved cinnabar lacquer cabinet, 19th c., two main doors carved with large dragons chasing the flaming pearl, smaller doors above with similar motif, shallow drawer at the bottom, key fret borders, replacement mounts, restored chips and cracks, 25½" h., (Color Illus. pg. 124) ..**5,000-7,000**

Chinese chair, 17th c., Huanghulai, 'U'-shaped crestrail with outscrolled handgrips and bowed rectangular splat carved with cloud medallion, caned seat, scrolling apron, 16" x 21", 39" h. **5,500-7,500**

Chinese chairs, 18th c., black lacquer armchairs, each with scrolled crestrail with a bowed, paneled splat, and panel seat, pair....................................**3,000-4,000**

Chinese hardwood sideboard, 19th c., inlaid with marble, the rectangular marble panel with cloud-like markings shaded

Chinese Side Table

Chinese Medicine Chests

white to reddish brown to pink, supported on a high pierced apron and with a carved back panel, damages, 60" x 45" x 30" **3,000-4,500**

Chinese Hung Huali cabinet, silver inlay and jade handle, two drawers, cupboard and open shelf, first half 19th c., 20" x 15" **2,000-3,000**

Chinese Hung Mu scholar's bench, back with four carved panels, birds and flowering plants, the apron with carved fruit in low-relief, early 20th c., 75" l. **1,000-1,500**

Chinese Huang Huali low tables, early 20th c., the tallest 6" h., set of 4 ....**400-650**

Chinese elmwood coffer, 18th c., rectangular top with everted ends above a frieze of three drawers and two doors, each side with a long carved spandrel, 34" x 68½" x 17"................................**3,500-4,500**

Chinese medicine chest, late 19th c., original mounts and labeling, restored, 52" x 70" x 20½" (ILLUS. right) **1,200-1,500**

Chinese medicine chest, mid-19th c., 45 drawers, original labeling and mounts, restored, 35" x 50" x 19" (ILLUS. left) **1,000-1,500**

Chinese side table, 18th c., Huanghuali, rectangular with double cushion molded edge, arched wrap around stretcher, oval pierced brackets, legs of circular section, underside with three transverse braces, 19" x 48", 34" h. (ILLUS.) **15,000-20,000**

Chinese stools, 19th c., soft cane seat, legs of circular section, 16½" w. x 19" h., pair..**1,000-1,500**

Chinese table, 19th c., walnut, rectangular form, rounded sides with carved stylized dragons, front carved with clouds and two drawers, 14 x 48", 14½" h. **1,200-1,800**

Chinese table, 19th c., lacquered with carved dragons above foaming waves, the borders with lotus blossoms and foliage, repeated on the shaped apron, cabriole legs, the patterns in colors and gilt on a black ground, old restoration, 15½" x 40" x 20" **2,500-3,500**

Chinese Zitan table, 18th c., soft cane seat, columnar section legs, arched high stretchers, vertical braces, 18½" h. (ILLUS. with introduction) **5,500-8,500**

Japanese armchair, carved overall, the arms with dragon terminals, the back with flowers and foliage, cabriole legs, carved apron with foliage, early 20th c. **500-700**

Japanese birdcage, spherical with canes made in two separable halves strengthened with wood hoops and a hinged door, upon a stand of roiro, red and gold lacquer, cracking and old restoration, late 19th-early 20th c., 29" h. **500-850**

Japanese desk, inlaid lacquer, bow-fronted with large hinged door at its center and shelves at either side, as well as one hinged compartment, cabriole legs, deep bombé apron, roiro ground and designs of birds, foliage and flowers in gold and colored togidashi, the door with shibayama inlay, losses, cracking, 55" x 44" x 22" **1,500-2,500**

Japanese hibachi, elmwood, two drawers, early 20th c., 37" x 24" **300-500**

Korean Chests

Japanese kimono rack, cedar wood, 65" x 65", 20th c...................**200-400**

Japanese Sendai tansu, six drawers, iron mounts, carved with passion flowers, early Meiji period, 35" h. **2,000-3,000**

Japanese table, ca. 1925, ebonized and carved with dragons and clouds in relief, approximately 30" x 32" **400-600**

Japanese tansu, captain's chest, iron hardware, hinged door concealing six drawers, 18th c., 14" x 17" x 12½", fair condition...................**900-1,200**

Japanese tansu, kiri wood with copper mounts, three drawers over four drawers, 20th c., 34" w., 38" h., good condition **600-800**

Japanese tansu, rectangular form, three rows of double drawers above two single drawers, iron fittings, worn, late Meiji period, 28½" w., 30" h. **600-800**

Korean chest-on-chest, rectangular form, four drawers, doors opening below, the lower section with doors, brass fittings, raised on sled, early 20th c., 34" w., 55" h. **400-600**

Korean chest-on-chest, burl inlay, two door cupboards with white metal mounts, sled base, 20th c., 34" w., 54" h...................**400-600**

Korean low chest, rectangular form, three drawers, central doors flanked by two side doors with single drawers below, brass hardware, 20th c., 40" w., 18" h. **300-500**

Korean red lacquer cosmetic case, Yi Dynasty, the hinged cover, black lacquer interior, fitted drawers, iron mounts, tortoiseshell-form lock, four bracket feet, restored, 11" x 9" x 13" (Color Illus. pg.125) **3,500-5,500**

Korean coin chest with iron mounts, resting on brace feet, 18" x 32¼" x 12½" (ILLUS. right) **800-1,200**

Korean wood storage chest, 19th c., with fall front opening, iron hardware, brace feet, 27" x 40½" x 20" (ILLUS. left) **1,000-1,500**

Korean low table, rectangular with pierced apron, rounded legs with mid-section stretchers and two base stretchers, 19th c., 19" w., 10" h....................**8,000-12,000**

Korean low table, twelve sided top with cabriole legs, two base stretchers, early 20th c., 18" d., 10½" h. **300-400**

Chapter 10
GAMES AND DOLLS

●

Chinese doll furniture, ca. 1900, two carved soapstone armchairs with mother-of-pearl inlay, 3" h., pr. **$250-500**

Japanese doll, ca. 1920s, seated lady with musical instrument, face, hands and instrument of ivory with silk attire, tortoiseshell hair ornaments, 4½" h. (Color Illus. pg. 125) **1,000-1,500**

Japanese doll, boxed, ca. 1920-1930s, with various wigs, fair condition **50-125**

Japanese doll, Hakata, "Wisteria Lady," label on base, 11" h. **125-185**

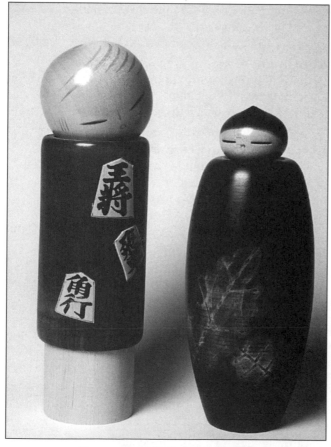

Japanese Kokeshi Dolls

Japanese doll, Hakata, elder with washbasin, 7" h. **125-175**

Japanese doll, lacquer, ca. 1930, wearing silk attire and holding a drum, silk somewhat worn, 14" h. **100-175**

Japanese dolls, ca. 1900, two girls playing, original clothes, 6" h. pair **100-200**

Japanese dolls, Kokeshi, ca. 1950s , 8" h. & 12" h., both artist-signed, each (ILLUS.) **200-300**

Japanese dolls, ca. 1915, depicting a prince and princess, original silk clothing, oyster shell faces, 6½" h., pair **150-250**

Japanese dolls, ca. 1920s, depicting Emperor and Empress in traditional silk costumes, oyster shell faces, good condition, pair **300-500**

Japanese kobe toy, late Meiji period, wood, depiction of a man with lantern, inlaid with ivory, minor crack to base, 3½" h. **375-550**

Mah Jongg set, Chinese, ca. 1920s, in wood box, complete with ivory and bamboo tiles, five drawers, green painted bat on front sliding door, two brass handles at top, the set **250-450**

Mah Jongg set, Chinese, wood case with brass hardware, bat-form longevity symbol painted green on sliding door, the interior fitted with drawers containing ivory and bamboo tiles and ivory counting pieces, complete, ca. 1930s (Color Illus. pg. 125) ..**250-350**

Mah Jongg set, ca. 1950, box covered with black leather, matching trim on handle, five wood racks, ivory tiles, the set **400-500**

Mah Jongg set, ca. 1960, alligator-covered box, plastic racks, ivory tiles dyed mint green, the set **350-500**

Chapter 11
GLASS

———————————●———————————

Glass was recorded in Wen Wei as having been introduced via the silk route to China during the reign of Emperor T'ai Wei (424-452 A.D.). At the same time, in south China, during the reign of Wan Ti (424-452 A.D.), it is said that travelers brought presents to the Court that included glass and the knowledge of how to convert stones into glass. They demonstrated to the Court how crystal could be made from common quartz, potash and sand. That was the beginning of glass production in China.

For the most part, European glass contains soda for lowering the melting point. Soda is a dissolving agent for sand (silica). Chinese glass contains potash as well as lime, which stabilizes and hardens and makes the glass easier to work. The proportions are about the same. Lead gives the glass its brilliance. Borax gives it its hardness. The main ingredients of glass are silica (sand) and an alkali. Added are minerals such as iron, lead alumina, magnesium, etc., to give clarity and hardness to the end product. Mineral oxides can be added to the liquid glass to produce specific colors e.g.: iron or copper for greens and reds, cobalt for blue, magnesium for purple, black and lavender.

Chinese glass can be opaque, clear or transparent. Also used was an overlay technique, with a minimum of two colors. Chinese glass can be made to resemble other materials such as hardstones. For further glass information see *Snuff Bottles*.

REVERSE-PAINTINGS ON GLASS

Among the most decorative of all the China Trade objets d'art were the reverse-paintings on glass and the paintings on mirrors (which are also termed "back paintings"). Reverse-paintings on glass were produced, for the most part, in Canton and Macao. In addition to Chinese subjects, European scenes, still lifes (birds and flowers), portraits, erotica, mythological and political subjects were fashionable.

The mirror paintings were more difficult to produce. The mirrors were manufactured at Vauxhall (England) and shipped to China for decorating and framing. Much of the framing was done in the Western-style, copying American, English and French frames.

PRICE LISTINGS
for Chinese Glass

Glass bowl, blue, rounded sides rising to an everted rim, 20th c., 5" d. **$100-200**

Glass jars, 19th c. with Qianlong markings, each with oval panels of birds on flowering plum branches, both fitted with wood covers, lemon yellow, 9½" h., pair. **1,000-1,500**

Glass Mandarin necklace, beads of yellow, amber and green, 19th c., 30" l., missing stations **600-900**

Glass vase, yellow Peking glass, 18th c., compressed globular body, long cylindrical neck, 12 vertical flutes from the foot to rim, wide footrim, circular base, yellow, base polished, 6⅞" h. (Color Illus. pg. 126) **5,000-7,000**

Glass vase, 18th c., milk glass with deep blue overlay designs of blossoming branches rising from rockwork, 7¾" h. **2,000-3,000**

Glass vase, blue Peking glass, 18th c., tapered ovoid body, cylindrical neck, transparent blue, base polished, 8" h. (Color Illus. pg. 126) **2,500-3,500**

Glass vases, 19th c., yellow Peking glass carved in low-relief with patterns of archaistic dragons with lappets above and below, a lemony hue, 8½" h., pair **6,000-8,000**

Reverse-Painting on Glass—Woman with Blue Dress

Glass vases, 18th c., snowflake glass with ruby red overlay cut to form phoenix and flowering branches on the tall neck, the shoulder with lappets, flared foot, 10" h., pair. **10,000-15,000**

Mirror painting (back painting), late 18th c., figures in a boat, Chinese school, framed, frame size 12" x 20" **3,500-5,000**

Reverse-painting on glass, late 18th c., Famille Rose palette, a seated lady holding a closed fan, in black lacquer frame with gilt details (frame late 19th c.), frame size 11" x 15" **2,500-3,500**

Reverse-painting on glass, late 18th c., Famille Rose palette, various flowers, including peony blossoms and chrysanthemums with foliage in a vase, framed, framed size 8" x 10", frame damaged..**1,800-2,500**

Reverse-painting on glass, ca. 1920, woman with blue dress, hardwood frame, frame refinished, framed size 11" x 14" (ILLUS.) **200-400**

Reverse-painting on glass, Famille Rose palette, man and woman drinking wine, ca. 1900, approximately 18" x 15" **400-600**

Chapter 12

HARDSTONES

———————————●———————————

Hardstones are judged on a scale of 1 to 10, a scale devised by Frederich Mohs (1773-1839), a German mineralogist. He selected ten stones, the softest was talc and the hardest was a diamond. Any mineral on the list can be scratched by the one with the next highest number. Any unlisted mineral that is as hard as any mineral appearing on the list will rate at the same hardness number. The minerals he selected were:

1. Talc 2. Gypsum 3. Calcite 4. Flourspar 5. Apatite 6. Feldspar 7. Quartz 8. Topaz 9. Corundum 10. Diamond.

Agate—In the quartz family (cryptocrystalline) it is translucent and microfibrous. It generally shows straight or curved color bands. Shades of gray and brown are common. Agate may have inclusions which appear to be branch-like or patch-like.

Amber—Not a hardstone, but petrified tree sap, it was used by the Chinese. Amber, imported from Burma, can be red, red to yellow, red to orange, reddish brown and black. Testing: A negative charge of electricity will develop when amber is rubbed (a piece of wool is suitable). After rubbing the amber you should be able to pick up a small piece of paper just as a magnet picks up metal objects. Amber will retain heat and after it is rubbed it should feel warm and give off a faint woodsy aroma. If the smell is more like turpentine or pine pitch then the material is possibly new resin or re-constituted amber flakes.

Amethyst—This hardstone ranges from light to deep violet (purple).

Aquamarine—A transparent stone that varies in color range from light bluish green to blue.

Aventurine—A form of quartz (crystalline) with mica or hematite inclusions that sparkle. The best specimens of aventurine have such minute specks that one needs to use a magnifier to see them. The colors range from light to dark green and a reddish brown. It is also known as "Indian jade."

Bloodstone—This stone is usually opaque dark green with dark red spots.

Bowenite—A compact form of serpentine that is uniform in color. The cream color and green variety resemble jade (nephrite). On the Mohs scale is has a hardness of 6.

Carnelian—A translucent stone. The color range is reddish brown to red.

Chalcedony—A microfibrous stone in the quartz family. It is translucent and a neutral hardstone without patterns. This term is also used when referring to microfibrous stones in the quartz family.

Chrysopase—This hardstone is often mistaken for jadeite. It is uniform apple green in color with a high luster. Chrysopase is translucent.

Coral—Opaque and white, cream-colored, pink to red, coral is calcium carbonate deposited by marine animals.

Hematite—A shiny blackish gray opaque stone. Most often used in jewelry. Synthetic hematite is part powdered steel and part iron sulfides.

Jadeite—Siliate of sodium and aluminum. The hues are vivid and include: snow white, emerald green, lavender, blue, apple green, and mixtures of the aforementioned. Jadeite became popular in China during the 18th century. Jadeite is harder than nephrite but both are termed "Jade." To test for jade: select a smooth area in an inconspicuous place on an object, such as under a foot. Press the steel blade of a pocket knife firmly against the stone and draw the blade a quarter of an inch. If there is a white mark it means the knife has scratched the stone. This indicates the stone is not jade. If the mark is black or steely gray looking it means the stone has scratched the steel. This indicates the stone is jade. Many contemporary jade objects are not completely polished by the lapidary. A wax polish is often used to give a piece a finished look. If wax polish remains on the area tested you will not get an accurate result.

Jasper—Generally light to dark shades of red, green, gray and brown. It is opaque and sometimes patterned.

Lapis Lazuli—An opaque blue stone ranging from light to dark blue.

Malachite—An opaque deep green stone with striations (bands). A soft stone, 3 or 4 on the Mohs scale, it is a favorite of the Chinese and revered for its color.

Marble—Chosen for its markings and used much like jadeite. Some pieces look as though they were painted by brush with a landscape design.

Quartz—Rock Crystal (colorless) quartz is transparent. Rose Quartz (pale pink) can be translucent or transparent. Smoky Quartz is pale brown to dark brown.

Nephrite—It too can be tested with the steel blade of a pocket knife. Nephrite is duller that jadeite. Colors include grayish black, spinach green, brown, pale celadon and white as well as mixtures of the aforementioned.

Rhodonite—It can be pink or red with gray mottling. It is usually opaque.

Serpentine—It is structurally similar to nephrite. Colors include white, light celadon, brown, blackish green. Use the pocket knife test on any stone which resembles jade.

Soapstone—This stone is actually Talc. The Chinese produced finely carved soapstone objects.

Sodalite—Similar to lapis lazuli but more purple.

Thulite—Pink with dark green inclusions.

(Also see Snuff Bottles)

PRICE LISTINGS
For Hardstone Objects

Agate group of grapes, ca. 1900, the stone with varied shades of brown, 4" l. **$1,000-1,500**

Agate figure of Buddhist lion, 20th c., carved in two sections, removable head, 8" h. **1,000-1,500**

Agate vase and cover, ca. 1900, flattened baluster-form with dragon handles, each side carved with phoenix and flowers, the stone gray in hue, 5" h. **900-1,200**

Amber carving of water buffalo, 20th c., a boy seated on its back, 4½" w...**500-700**

Amber carving of a sage, 20th c, shown reclining against pierced rockwork, 3" l. **300-400**

Chinese Carnelian Carving

Jadeite carving of a Rabbit

Amethyst water coupe, late 19th or early 20th c., gourd-form with leaves and fruit, 6" l., damages...**250-350**

Archaic Nephrite tablet, Neolithic, rectangular form, circular hole at one end, one corner with semicircular cut, brown, deteriorated **500-700**

Carnelian carving, 18th c., Chinese, man in boat, the stone shaded white to reddish orange, 2" h, (ILLUS.) **1,000-1,500**

Carnelian figure of a Meijin, shown holding a flower, 9" h...............................**150-250**

Jadeite figure of Buddha, white, seated, hands in dhyanamudra, holding a bowl, fitted wood base carved with lotus petals, Qing Dynasty, figure 5" h. **10,000-15,000**

Jadeite figure of Meiren, white, standing holding a whisp, long flowing robes, 6" h., 20th c. **700-1,000**

Chinese Nephrite Carving

Jadeite model of a rabbit, Chinese, white
stone uniform in color, early
20th c., 3" w. (ILLUS.) 500-750

**Lapis Lazuli carving of a recumbent
water buffalo,** the stone with gilt
inclusions, 4½" l. 350-550

Lapis Lazuli vase, 19th c., formed as a
section of bamboo, one side with
flowering branch, deep blue,
4" h. 800-1,200

Malachite vase and cover, 20th c.,
flattened ovoid form, carved and pierced
in relief with flowering branches
extending onto the cover, 6" h.............1,000-1,500

Marble panel, ca. 1900, mounted into a
table screen, 12" x 12"..............................600-900

Moss Agate brushwasher, 19th c.,
carved as a lotus leaf with curled
sides, 3" w. 300-500

Nephrite abacus, 92 spinach green beads
on brass wires, 13" x 6"........................1,000-1,500

Nephrite carving, 18th c., Chinese, boy on
water buffalo, the stone varying in hue
from light to dark gray, 2" h.
(ILLUS.)..900-1,200

Nephrite Pi, greenish brown with central
circular form carved with chilong and
animal masks, 10" 400-700

Nephrite staff handle, grayish
green, animal head finial,
20th c., 4½" 200-300

Rock crystal staff handle, 19th c., Chinese
Moghul-style, lion head above a floral
design, 4½" h. 500-750

Rock Crystal seal, late 19th c., carved with
a landscape, 2¾" h. 175-250

Rock Crystal ball, flawed, 8" d. 1,000-1,500

Rose Quartz vase, ca. 1900, carved with
lion dog handles, peony blossoms
and phoenix, mounted as a lamp,
8¾" h. 300-500

Serpentine cup and saucer, late 19th or
early 20th c., flared form, the stone dark
gray with darker speckles 100-150

**Soapstone figure of Meijin holding a
flower,** ca. 1920s, mounted as a lamp,
7" h. 250-350

Soapstone group, early 20th c., Shou Lao
and a crane, 6" h. 150-225

Soapstone recumbent ox, 18th or 19th c.,
its legs tucked underneath, mottled
brown, 3¾" w. 400-600

Soapstone seal, 20th c., circular form with
lion dog finial, base cut with "Longevity"
character, 2" h....................................75-100

Soapstone seal, 19th c., the top
surmounted with a dragon, base carved
with two characters, 2½" h. 200-400

Soapstone seals, 20th c., Chinese, left: the
seal surmounted by woman holding a fan,
5"h.; right: seal surmounted by a dragon,
3¾" h.; bottom of each uncarved,
(ILLUS.) each 100-175

Chinese Soapstone Seals

Chapter 13
IVORY AND
RELATED MATERIALS

Boar's tusk—The upper canine of the wild boar. It is very white. The carvings from these are of a triangular section which is usually less than 6" in length. The grain looks triangular.

Bone—Shin bone and the tibia were most often used for carvings. They were obtained from almost any available animal source. Bone is hollow and the center is filled with spongy material. A bone carving will usually show a pattern of dots resembling beard stubble.

Elephant ivory—It shows a criss-cross pattern unique to elephant ivory. Also visible is a pattern of lines which can be longitudinal. Elephant ivory has a density of 1.70 to .95 times that of water which often serves to distinguish it from plastic or other light materials.

Hippo teeth (canines and incisors)—This is the hardest of all the ivory-like materials. The grain consists of wavy lines and they all flow in one direction.

Narwhal tusk—This tusk comes from the elongated left tusk of a species of whale which is now an endangered species. The center of the tusk is hollow and the transverse and longitudinal sections resemble the pattern of a tree trunk.

Stag antler—The antler of reindeer, elk, deer or related animals. Antler will have a spongy center but the outer areas are denser than bone. The color can vary from yellow to brown with irregular openings.

Vegetable ivory—This comes from the nut of a South American palm and has a grain that is circular and dull. It is softer than bone and was used for okimono and netsuke as well as for buttons.

Japenese Ivory Group

Walrus tusk—These are the upper canines and have a mottled or marbled effect.

Whale teeth—Whale teeth will show a striated pattern or striated grain pattern which is very faint.

Today you must be aware of composition ivory copies which are basically plastic substances. Objects made from composition may be termed "Ivorine." Ivory shavings can be mixed with polymer to form a product which resembles ivory. Ivorine and other plastic imitations can be pierced with a red hot sewing needle.

(See Inro, Netsuke, Ojime, Snuff Bottles)

Japanese Ivory Father and Child

PRICE LISTINGS
for Chinese Ivory Objects

Basket and cover, 19th c., eight-lobed tapering circular section with inverted rim, carved and pierced on each lobe with figures in landscapes, surmounted by knob finial, the sides set with a bail handle, damages to pierced work, 11" to top of handle **$800-1,200**

Box and cover, early 19th c., carved overall with figures, boats, trees, minor damages, 10½" w. **2,000-3,000**

Card case, early 19th c., low-relief aquatic design on one side, the other side with a landscape, damages **350-550**

Card case, early 19th c., rectangular with carved panels of figures in villages bordered by dragons, 4" l. **1,000-1,500**

Card case, mid-19th c., peony blossoms and openwork (Color Illus. pg. 126) **500-700**

Figure of a reclining female nude, 20th c., loose bracelet, 12" l. **500-700**

Figure of a reclining female nude, 20th c., woman reading book while resting on leaf, 6" l. **400-600**

Figures of Guardians, early 20th c., one holding a sword, the other a lute, 11" h., pair. **700-900**

Figures of Meijin, 20th c., one holding a basket, the other a candle, 10" h., pair **600-900**

Figure group, 18th c., two Lohans (Po Chien and Lohan Lo mi), each holding an attribute, 9" h., some cracks **1,800-2,500**

Vase and cover, Qianlong mark but late 19th c., oval baluster shape, carved in relief with continuous scene around the body, numerous elegant figures strolling in walled garden with numerous pavilions, the shoulder with ruyi lappets, the neck with figural panels, loose ring lion mask handles, waisted foot, the cover with further figures and pavilion, losses, 19½" h. (ILLUS.) **2,500-4,500**

PRICE LISTINGS
for Japanese Ivory Objects

(Japanese ivory carvings are termed Okimono)

Ivory Okimono of bijin, signed "Shingyoku," she is dressed in formal attire, her hair dressed with cherry

blossoms, she holds a parasol,
10½" h. **3,500-4,500**

Ivory Okimono of karako, the young boys
hold a puppy, ca. 1900-1920, minor
cracks, 6" h. **2,500-3,500**

Ivory Okimono of a dragon, signed
"Masatatsu (seiryu)," a large scaly dragon
with eyes inlaid with mother-of-pearl,
chips to spine and whiskers, Meiji
period, 9" l. **5,000-7,000**

**Ivory Okimono of a farmer and young
child,** signed "Koho," the man wearing a
kasa (straw hat)and holding a basket of
fruit, the boy holding a small hand drum,
realistically modeled, 9" h. **2,500-3,500**

Ivory Okimono of a farmer and child,
signed "Hosui," the farmer standing
and smiling, he holds the child in
his arms, Meiji period, 13" h.,
minor cracks **2,000-3,000**

Ivory Okimono of a female musician,
signed "Soshin," standing and wearing
formal attire, holding small hand drum
which is strapped to her waist, one hand
holds a stick, the other a fan, Meiji
period, 14" h. **2,000-3,000**

Ivory Okimono of a quail, its beak open
revealing a pointed tongue, inlaid horn
eyes, two talons missing, late 19th or early
20th c., 4⅞" h. **2,000-3,000**

Ivory Okimono of a rat, finely detailed,
inlaid eyes, late 19th c., 3½" h. **1,500-2,500**

Ivory Okimono of rats, tumbling over
each other as they grapple for grapes and
gourds, inlaid horn eyes, ca. 1900,
minor cracks, 4½" d. **2,000-3,000**

Ivory Okimono of a young boy, Taisho or
early Showa period, signed,
4" h. (Color Illus. pg. 126)....................**2,500-3,500**

Ivory Okimono group, Meiji period,
19th c., father and child, the child pulling
a toy topped by a figural fish, the father
holding a cat, 7" h. (ILLUS.) **2,500-3,500**

Ivory Okimono group, Meiji period, ca.
1905, each figure with attribute,
6" w. (ILLUS.) **3,000-4,500**

Staghorn Okimono of a lotus pod,
naturalistically carved with movable
seeds, late 19th c., 4" d..........................**500-700**

Chinese Ivory Vase and Cover

Chapter 14
JEWELRY

———————————●———————————

PRICE LISTINGS
for Oriental Jewelry

Chinese amber necklace, 51 graduated ovoid beads, each honey colored.............**$600-800**

Chinese amber and hardstone court necklace, 19th c., 108 amber beads intersected by three jadeite foudou, a gourd-shaped fodouda supporting a large jadeite pendant, the silk cord intersected with three small strands of coral beads with a jadeite finial attached **5,000-7,500**

(These necklaces were traditionally worn by nobles and persons of rank at the Qing Dynasty court. The court necklace evolved from the Buddhist rosary. It is always composed of 108 beads of the same material, it was divided in the front, each group of 27 beads by a larger bead of a different material, the foudou, and also supported three chinien strands, each of ten small beads and terminating in finials of contrasting drops, two on one side and one of the other side of the foudouda, suspending an extension.)

Chinese archer's ring, Qing Dynasty, yellowish green stone suffused with emerald green, approximately 30.5 mm in diameter, 5.2 mm in thickness **10,000-15,000**

Chinese jadeite bangle bracelet, ca. 1920, mottled apple green, cracked, interior measurement 60 mm............................**4,500-6,500**

Chinese jadeite belthook, 18th-19th c., white, spade-form, carved in relief with a pair of chilong, the hook formed by the head of a dragon, the stone an even pale greenish white, 4" l...............................**1,000-1,500**

Chinese jadeite cuff links, Hong Kong, ca. 1960, mounted in 14kt yellow gold, apple green discs with shou character in center, approximately 15.5 mm, pair. **500-750**

Chinese jadeite ring, post-World War II, set with oval-shaped cabochon of mottled apple green, approximately

14.7 mm x 10.8 mm x 5.9 mm, 14kt gold mount **1,000-1,500**

Chinese jadeite pendant, white, rectangular with dragon and cloud decoration on both sides, 36.1 mm x 29.3 mm...**1,000-1,500**

Chinese Mandarin necklace, 108 beads with stations, 19th c., amber glass beads as well as glass beads simulating lapis lazuli, jadeite, and Imperial yellow glass (Color Illus. pg. 127) **1,200-1,800**

Chinese pendant, pink tourmaline, late Qing Dynasty, translucent and intense in color, carved with a deer and two bats, approximately 40 mm x 30 mm **5,000-7,500**

Chinese pendant, pink tourmaline, Hong Kong, post-1950, carved on the front with a fish and on the underside with a lotus, 14kt gold bail **500-700**

Japanese belt, Satsuma in medallions set in silver with silver links, designs of flowers in colors and gilt, ca. 1910, 24" w. **475-775**

Japanese cuff links, round, each set with Satsuma with a design of a bamboo tree in green and gilt, ca. 1925, pair. **200-300**

Japanese komai bar pin, scenic design in silver and gold, ca. 1905 ....**350-650**

Japanese komai bracelet, set with seven rectangular medallions, plain silver links, each medallion with a floral design in gold and silver, ca. 1930 ....**700-900**

Japanese cloisonné pendant, gin bari, ca. 1915, bird, flower and bud, set in new silver mount designed by Mike Kaye (ILLUS.) **950-1,250**

Japanese komai pendant, scenic motif in gold and silver, ca. 1915, set in new silver mount designed by Mike Kaye (ILLUS.) **1,000-1,500**

Japanese satsuma pendant, ca. 1910, dragon and flames, in gilt and colors, set in new silver mount designed by Mike Kaye (Color Illus. pg. 127) **900-1,200**

Japanese komai pin, round with a design of ladies and a flower cart, marked "S. Komai," ca. 1910 ....**550-750**

Japanese pin, cloisonné ginbari with lilies and foliage, ca. 1920, 3" d. **200-275**

Japanese silver belt buckle, oval, decorated with plum blossoms, ca. 1920....**175-225**

Japanese wrist watch, ca. 1915, Swiss movement, silver case, marked "Arthur Bond Yokohama" (ILLUS.) **500-700**

Indian silver bracelet, hinged-form, three rows of pierced rosettes and two large clusters of plain silver beads attached to the terminals **450-600**

Nepalese silver belt buckle, with turquoise stones, filigree scrolls, 6" d. **375-450**

Nepalese silver-gilt, turquoise and coral pendant necklace, star-form with deity in low-relief in center **50-100**

Tibetan silver belt buckle, 19th c., chased with blossoms, center inlaid with malachite, 3" l...**100-150**

Japanese Komai Pendant

Japanese Cloisonné Pendant

Japanese Wrist Watch

Chapter 15
LACQUER WARES

●

PRICE LISTINGS
for Chinese Lacquer Wares

Black lacquer gaming box and cover, 19th c., export-type, rectangular form decorated in gold lacquer on the black ground with a lake scene, the interior with seven fitted covered compartments and two stacks of trays, all supported on eight feet in the form of animal claws, 15" l. **$1,000-1,500**

Black lacquer gaming box and cover, 19th c., export-type, the cover with a design of buildings and figures, the interior with six shaped and covered compartments, twelve trays and a set of mother-of-pearl gaming counters, 14½" l. **1,500-2,000**

Black lacquer box with hinged cover, 19th c., export-type, gold lacquer designs of figures in pavilions, 10¼" w. **750-950**

Black lacquer sewing box, 19th c., export-type, rectangular, four dragon feet, hinged cover, gilt lacquer decorations of figural processions, the front with one drawer, the interior with compartments containing ivory sewing implements, 9" x 15" x 14" **1,500-2,500**

Carved cinnabar bowl, 18th c., carved on the exterior with dragons and flaming pearl, the foot with a band of key fret pattern, interior of bowl in black lacquer, 6½" d. **2,500-3,500**

Carved cinnabar box and cover, late Ming Dynasty, circular with designs of leaves and branches and diapers, interior plain black lacquer, losses, 3" d. **4,000-6,000**

Carved cinnabar box and cover, ca. 1920, patterns of figures in relief, interior and base of black lacquer, cracks to base, 5" d. **150-250**

Carved Cinnabar Stacked Box

Carved cinnabar stacked box, mid-18th c., the lid carved with a pavilion and figures, the exterior of each compartment carved with seasonal flowers and foliage designs, interior of each section, base and interior of lid in black lacquer, losses, 6" h. (ILLUS.)..**900-1,200**

Carved cinnabar lacquer dish, late 18th c., flower and sprigs with fretwork, the sides with lotus and scrolls, minor restoration to rim................................**3,000-4,000**

Carved cinnabar lacquer picnic box, circular, each section with figures in a landscape, late 19th c., minor wear and chipping, 8" h. **300-500**

Carved cinnabar lacquer vases, late 19th or early 20th c., carved with peony blossoms, foliage and birds, 15" h. some chipping, pair....................................**700-900**

Japanese Black Lacquer Box

Carved cinnabar lacquer wig stand,
octagonal with overall designs of lotus and
scrolls, key fret on borders, late 19th c.,
losses **800-1,200**

Lac burgaute box and cover, 19th c.,
circular, inlaid with gilt and silver foil
around a mother-of-pearl flower, 3" d. ..**900-1,200**

PRICE LISTINGS
for Japanese Lacquer Wares

Black lacquer box, ca. 1930s, the design in
low-relief, features pagoda and Mt. Fuji,
metal mounts, 5" w. (ILLUS.) **$375-475**

Black lacquer box, ca. 1930, gilt design of
mon, 7" l. (ILLUS.) **150-225**

Black lacquer natsume (tea caddy), ca.
1930, snowflake pattern overall in gold
hiramakie, 2½" h. **200-300**

**Black lacquer poem slip box
(tanzakubako),** 19th c., slender form,
the base and cover domed, on four
small bracket feet, the ground decorated
with gold and silver takamakie
chrysanthemums and inlaid mother-of-
pearl, nashiji interior damaged,
15¾" x 3¼" **700-900**

Black lacquer suzuribako (writing box),
late Edo period, rectangular form with
canted corners, decorated with a rooster
and hen among grass, gold and colored
takamakie with kirigane details, the
interior nashiji, 9" x 7¾" **2,500-3,500**

Black lacquer tray, red maple leaves on
black ground, 7" x 7", Showa period
(Color Illus. on pg. 128) **400-650**

Black lacquer tray, late 19th c., rectangular
shape with indented rounded corners,
four bracket feet, the design of figures in a
boat executed in iro-e tagadashi, nashiji
and okibriame, the underside in mijingai-
nuri (shell dust), silver rim, 14¼" x
10½" **2,000-3,000**

Gold lacquer footed bowl and cover, late
Edo period, the nashiji ground covered
with mon in gold and silver lacquer,
7" h.(Color Illus. pg. 127) **2,000-3,000**

Gold lacquer kobako, late 19th c., rounded
rectangular form with indented corners,
fitted with an interior tray resting just
beneath the cover, nashiji ground inside
and out, the exterior with a scenic design,
the tray with silver edge, all gold
takamakie, with kirigane details, crack in
one side, rubbed, 4½" x 9⅞" x 7½" **3,000-4,000**

Gold lacquer kobako, late 19th c.,
rectangular form, canted corners, colored
takamakie, interior nashiji, the cover inset
with ivory monkey and monkey trainer,
6" x 5", cover worn, rim chips **900-1,200**

Gold lacquer kogo, early 20th c., square
shape with canted corners, surface design
of pine tree and stream on a kinji ground,
interior nashiji, 1½" x 1½" x 1½" **550-750**

Gold lacquer kogo, ca. 1925, round metal
base and cover, the cover with low-relief
peony on kinji ground, the interior
cream colored, 3" d....................................**350-750**

Gold lacquer koro (censer) tray, late Edo
period, 18th c., nashiji ground decorated
with mon in gold and silver hiramaki-e

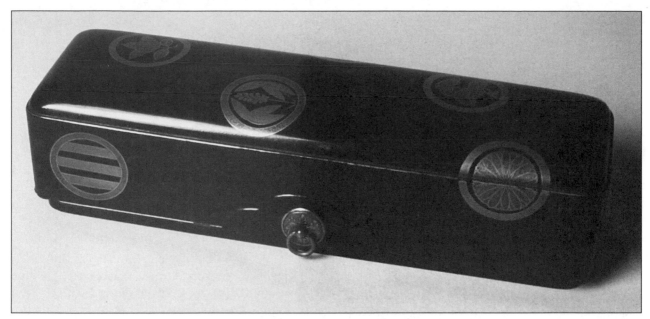

Black Lacquer Box with Design of Mon

Red Lacquer Sake Cup

and togidashi, supported on three legs, 8" dia. (Color Illus. pg. 127) **4,000-6,000**

Gold lacquer natsume (tea caddy), late Edo period, circular with flat cover, the decoration of gold hiramaki-e chrysanthemum cover extending onto side, interior black lacquer, slightly rubbed, 2" h. **700-900**

Lacquer and ivory carving of Bijin reading, Taisho or early Showa period, seated before her table which is ornamented with ivory flower vase, ivory books with legible calligraphy and ivory poem box with polychrome designs of flowers, Bijin 4" h. (Color Illus. pg. 128) **1,500-2,200**

Red lacquer bowl and lid, one of a set of ten, in original box, early Showa period, the set (Color Illus. pg. 128) **3,500-4,500**

Red lacquer kogo (incense box), early Edo period, the red lacquer rubbed to reveal the black underlying lacquer, the cover decorated in gold with dragon, the base with floral mon, 2" d. (Color Illus. pg. 128) **7,500-9,500**

Red lacquer sake cup, Meiji period, red lacquer with silver Kiku mon in low-relief (ILLUS.) **1,000-1,500**

PRICE LISTINGS
for Korean Lacquer Wares

Tray, 19th c., octagonal, black lacquer inlaid with mother-of-pearl flowers and leaves in each border panel, the center with an inlaid mother-of-pearl bamboo design, losses to mother-of-pearl, cracks and chipping, 15½" d.............................**10,000-15,000**

Tray, 19th c., flat with central design of a peony blossom made of oxhorn and surrounded by small mother-of-pearl blossoms, the rim enhanced with silver wire, losses to inlay, cracks, chips, nicks, 10" d. **15,000-20,000**

Vase, ca. 1955, red ground on brass with small inlaid mother-of-pearl flower, 6" h. **25-75**

Vase, ca. 1955, pear-shaped, black ground, small inlaid mother-of-pearl flower on front and back, 3½" h...................................**25-50**

Chapter 16
METALWARES

BRONZE CASTING
The Lost Wax Method

For this process a clay core, roughly following the shape of the object being produced, was dried and then coated thickly with bees' wax. The wax was also modeled to the desired form. A thin clay of creamy consistency was applied to the wax until a thick coat was obtained. This composite core had pins pushed through to support the inner core. The whole was then inverted in an iron box or flask. It was filled with loam which was packed solid and had a cutting runner and breathers so that the metal would run up and ensure a sufficient amount of molten metal to cover any shrinkage. The molten metal filled the spaces between the core and the clay which had been filled by the wax. A few holes were left in the clay mold so that the melted wax could be drained out and the molten metal poured in. Prior to the metal being poured the whole mold was subjected to great heat so as to melt the wax and all the moisture. When the bronze was hardened, the mold was broken off. Sometimes a mold was composed of several pieces which could be separated to remove the cast bronze. This type of mold was reusable.

CHINESE METALWARES

BRONZE

Of special interest in today's market are Chinese bronzes of the Ming and Qing Dynasties. During the Ming Dynasty new processes for variegating the surface of the metal were developed. Vessels were based on ceramic shapes. Handles in the form of fish, rope, elephant, phoenix, etc., were developed. The bronze surface finishes included chestnut brown, yellow gold, and crab apple. Some of these had gilt trim. Objects included both functional and ornamental wares.

SILVER

Silver has always been abundant in China. Kiangsi, Szechwan, Fukien, etc. are places where silver has been mined. Chinese silver, alloyed with tin and lead, was produced in desired shapes and generally finished with hammering. Handles and the ringfoot were generally soldered on.

China Trade Silver (Chinese Export) is very popular in today's market. The earliest Chinese maker of export silver was Pao Yun (ca. 1810-1840). He was joined by many other makers who worked during the 19th and early 20th century. The following will list maker's marks found on China Trade Silver. It is important to remember that the maker's used English initials with or without Chinese marks: CS (Cum Shing); CUT (Cutshing); H (Hoaching); KHC (Khecheong); SS (Sun Shing); CW (Cum Wo); TS (Tien Shing); WH (Wang Hing); LC (Lee Ching); HC (Hung Chong); LK/KH (Luen Hing); LW (Luen Wo). Many of the silversmiths also produced objects in gold, ivory, wood, tortoiseshell, mother-of-pearl, bamboo, and other materials.

PRICE LISTINGS
for Chinese Metalwares

Chinese bronze belt hook, Eastern Zhou period, inlaid with gold and turquoise, rounded on one side, the other side tapering toward the dragon's head hook, malachite encrustation overall, losses, repaired, 7¼" l. **$2,500-3,500**

Chinese bronze censer, late Ming Dynasty, cylindrical form with three tab feet, wide band of gilt flowers and foliage between bands of gilt diapers, signed "Hu Wenming of Yunjian," rubbed, 5" d. **3,500-5,500**

Chinese bronze censer, late Ming Dynasty, bombé-form, inlaid with silver blossoms and vines, the base with six-character "Xuande" mark, 5" d. **4,500-5,500**

Chinese bronze gu, Ming-style, 19th c., cast with taotie masks on a ground sectioned by flanges, 11¾" h. **500-800**

Chinese bronze tripod censer, the body splashed with gilt, supported on three animal-form legs, the sides with pierced rectangular handles, Ming Dynasty Xuande, 5" d. **8,000-12,000**

Chinese bronze mirror, Tang Dynasty, cast with animal-form knop with decoration of grapevines and beaded borders, silver patina on bronze with green encrustation, 4" d. **1,500-2,000**

Chinese bronze tripod vessel (ding), archaic, late Shang Dynasty, bulbous body raised on three tapering columnar feet, cast on the upper body with band of taotie masks, two bail handles, the patina a mottled greenish color with encrustation on both interior and exterior, 12" h. **10,000-15,000**

Chinese bronze lion dog (fu lion) **scroll weight,** Ming Dynasty, four paws outstretched, shaggy mane, bushy tail, two cubs on its back, 2½" l...................**1,500-2,500**

Chinese bronze storage vessel (hu), Western Han Dynasty, broad pear-form, cylindrical foot, short waisted neck, four plain raised bands encircling the body, loose ring handles at the top of the shoulder, malachite encrustation, repaired, 18" h. **7,500-10,500**

Chinese bronze vase, 18th c., gilt-splashed, ovoid with loose rings at the shoulder, 6½" h. **2,000-3,000**

Chinese silver bowls, mid- to late-19th c., hallmarked "CW," 4" d., pair (ILLUS.) **600-800**

Chinese silver filigree card case, with relief motif of dragon chasing flaming pearl, late 19th c. (ILLUS.) **900-1,200**

Chinese silver and gilt stem cup, Song Dynasty, exterior slightly lobed, incised with birds and peony, 4" d. **1,500-2,500**

Chinese silver vase, ovoid body with tall slender neck, engraved with lotus and scrolls, 20th c., 16" h. **1,200-1,600**

Chinese silver-inlaid bronze vase, 18th c., baluster-form, the shoulder with a band of flowerheads in low-relief, the details picked out in silver, 12" h...................**2,500-3,500**

Chinese Silver Filigree Card Case

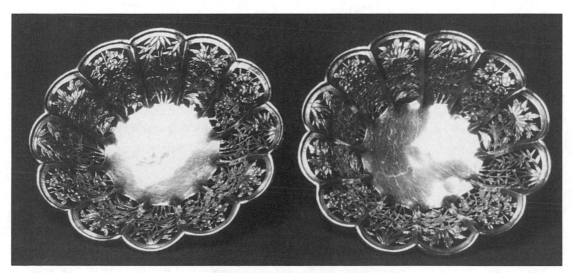

Chinese Silver Bowls

JAPANESE METALWARES

In addition to standard bronze the Japanese used a variety of mixed alloys to produce ornamental and functional objects.

Copper: Used chiefly in alloys like bronze, shakudo, and shibuichi. Copper has also been used for inlay.

Gold: The use of gold was restricted in Japan. However, it was popular to use gold in the gilding of other alloys.

Gold Plating: Gold foil was burnished to the metal base. The metal base was covered with mercury, then the gold was cleaned and heated. Finally, the gold was applied over the mercury. Another term for gold foil is "gold leaf." In the heating process the mercury would evaporate and the amalgam formed would leave a gold surface adhered to the metal base.

Komai (also called "Damascene"): In today's market, damascene wares produced by S. Komai, O. Komai and the Amita Co. are highly collectible. The following describes the production process: On a ground of steel, double hatch lines were cut with a chisel. The outline of the design was drawn on paper and transferred onto the ground by tracing. The design was copied through paper onto the metal ground with a small needle point. Combinations of gold, silver and/or copper were pounded into the ground with dots created by the needle point. After each application a coat of lacquer was applied to the object and then the object was baked. This was repeated many times, until the design was even with the surface or in slight relief. To finish the process the object was rubbed and polished to form a bright finish to the portions which were inlaid.

Shakudo: An alloy invented by the Japanese which consists of copper with 3-6% gold. Treated by pickling and polishing it has a glossy patina of bluish black or deep brown. It forms a perfect ground for inlaid designs of gold, silver, shibuichi, and/or copper. It can be cast, hammered or drawn into wire.

Shibuichi: An alloy made of one part silver to three of copper. When used in sword furniture the proportions vary (the silver can be 50%). Like shakudo, it is suitable for receiving inlaid designs of other alloys. It varies in hue from gray to misty silver.

Silver: The Japanese have used silver in conjunction with cloisonné and enameling as well as inlaying. Silver objects can also be embellished with other metals.

KOREAN METALWARES

Bronze casting on the Korean peninsula dates back to the first millennium B.C. From ca. 300 B.C. to the Christian era bronze objects increased in quantity and quality all over Korea. As Buddhism flourished in Korea so did the development of metal crafts for Buddhist objects. In addition to ritual objects, the aristocracy required elegant utensils for daily use at court and at home. Ornamental objects such as hair pins, buckles, etc., were produced. Korean metalwares include bronze wares and iron wares inlaid with silver. Bronze wares contain copper, tin and traces of silver. Gold and silver were used for jewelry and ornaments worn in the hair and on clothing.

PRICE LISTINGS
for Japanese Metalwares

Bronze bell, mid-19th c., elongated form cast with suspension loop, the body with panels of bosses, 17" h...........................**$750-1,250**

Bronze figure of Hotei, ca. 1910, seated, he rests his arm on his treasure sack, the brown patina enhanced with shakudo and gilt, 7" h. **1,200-1,800**

Bronze figure of warrior, signed "Miyao," ca. 1900, his garments with copper and gilt trim, on wood stand, 9" h. **3,500-5,000**

Bronze model of an elephant, late Meiji period, ivory tusks, patinated ears, 26" w., 11" h. (ILLUS.) **2,500-3,500**

Bronze model of a phoenix, ca. 1910, the feathers embellished with silver, gilt and copper, 14" l. **1,000-1,500**

Bronze model of sea demon, signed "Miyao," late Meiji period, copper patination with gilt details on a lacquered wood stand, minor losses, 13" h...........**5,500-7,500**

Bronze Model of an Elephant

Bronze Vases with Facing Dragons

Meiji Bronze Vase with Dragons

Bronze mirror, 17th c., circular form, decorated with birds and plum blooms, stylized minogame at the center, 4¾" d. **550-750**

Bronze vase, ca. 1910, ovoid form, cast with five carp in low-relief, the fish with inlay of shakudo and gilt, 12" h. **1,000-1,500**

Bronze vase, ca. 1920, ovoid form worked in wickerwork (plaited) design with various patterns and bands, dented, base replaced, 9" h. **400-600**

Bronze vase, Meiji period, 19th c., decorated with dragons in very high-relief, 21" h. (ILLUS.)......................................**3,000-5,000**

Bronze vases, 19th c., signed "Moryuken Sori," inlaid with gilt iroe takazogan and silver nunome with birds above peony blossoms and foliage, 9" h., pair **2,000-3,000**

Bronze vases, late 19th c., with birds on flowering branches in low-relief, 10" h., pair, ...**1,000-1,500**

Bronze vases, late 19th c., facing dragons in relief, 10" h., pr. (ILLUS.) **1,500-1,800**

Bronze and mixed metal tea set on lacquer stand, early Showa period, black lacquer with silver and gold mon, the utensils of silver and bronze with silver liners and incised motifs filled with gold, signed (Color Illus. pg. 131) **3,500-4,500**

Enameled card case, ca. 1900, the design of flowers, foliage and insects raised at various levels of relief, 3" l. (Color Illus. pg. 130) **2,000-2,500**

Enameled silver box and cover, ca. 1900, with designs of flowers and foliage raised at various levels of relief, supported on four bracket feet, 3" x 4" (Color Illus. pg. 130) **2,000-2,500**

Iron cabinet, late 19th or early 20th c., Komai-style, in the form of a shrine, hinged doors open to reveal three drawers, the designs worked overall in gold and silver inlay, 4¼" w., 6" h. **2,500-3,500**

Iron box and cover, ca. 1900, rectangular, rounded corners, the cover and sides with various flowers in low-relief and finished in silver and gilt, 5" sq. **1,200-1,500**

Iron box and cover, ca. 1920, Komai-style, square with hinged cover, the cover decorated with gilt dragons, the base with Mt. Fuji mark in gilt, 4" x 3" x 3¼" **1,000-1,500**

Iron tetsubin (kettle), signed and ascribed to the 11th generation of Suzuki Hihachi Iesada (died 1847) (ILLUS.)..................**1,500-2,500**

Iron tetsubin (kettle), signed, signature in bronze lid "Kinryudo zo," signature on kettle "Okuni zo," the body with elaborate overall relief work of a warrior slaying a tiger, handle with gilt inlay (Color Illus. pg. 129) **1,800-2,500**

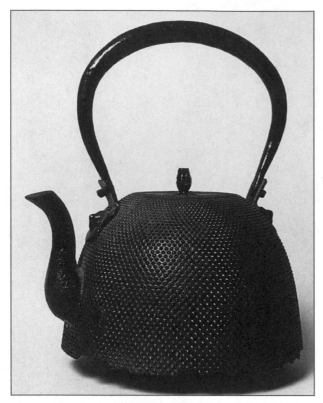

Iron Tetsubin

Komai Shoe Buckles

Komai-style Box

Komai belt buckle, ca. 1910, oval scenic views of Japan, signed, 2¼" oval **1,000-1,500**

Komai box and cover, early 20th c., round with detailed landscape, the borders with repetitive patterns, gilt and silver, signed on the base, 3¾" d. **3,500-5,500**

Komai box and cover, late Meiji period, oval with shaped panels filled with landscapes, yellow, pink and greenish gold with silver and copper highlights, 4" d. **3,500-5,500**

Komai box and cover, dated 1923, the design features women beside a stream, in silver and gold, 5" w. (Color Illus. pg 129)............................**4,000-5,000**

Komai cigarette case, ca. 1915, scenic designs..**1,000-1,500**

Komai shoe buckles, gilt, original box, label with Komai trademark, buckles marked with trademark in Japanese, ca. 1920, pair (ILLUS.)................................**375-575**

Komai table screen, ca. 1915, a continuous scene in three shades of gold and silver, above panels of maple leaves, 6" h. (Color Illus. pg. 129)...................**2,500-3,500**

Komai-style box supported on four legs, ca. 1950s, pattern includes feathery tailed tortoise, 3" w. (ILLUS.) **300-500**

Mixed metal vase with relief design of a warrior, ca. 1920, 6" h. (left) **$500-750;** Mixed metal dish, late Meiji period, painter with brushes painting flowers, all in low-relief (right) (ILLUS.) **800-1,200**

Shakudo and Shibuichi censer and cover, signed "Kuroda," ca. 1910, square form supported on four bracket feet, four panels containing flowering branches, domed cover pierced with flowerhead, 5" h. **5,000-7,500**

Silver box, ca. 1910, octagonal, the cover set with a shakudo panel decorated with magnolia and branches all in silver, gold and copper, 3" d. **1,000-1,500**

Silver box and cover, early 20th c., square form with blossoms and foliage in various heights of relief, enameled in primary colors, some losses **1,000-1,500**

Silver kogo, ca. 1920s , rectangular box with incised flowers, 2 " x 1", marked gin and signed (right) **$375-575;** Silver kogo, teardrop-form, 2½" l. (left) (Color Illus. pg. 130) **375-575**

Silver match safe, late Meiji period, design of dragons in relief (left) **$375-475;** Match safe, mixed metals in the form of Oni, late Meiji period (right) (Color Illus. pg. 130) ..**500-700**

Silver model of a hen, early 20th c., realistically detailed, 6" h........................**900-1,200**

Silver napkin rings, dated 1925, incised flowers with gilt embellishments, original box, the set (ILLUS.) **550-775**

Silver sake pot, Showa period, signed and dated 1933, 2½" h.(ILLUS.)..................**1,000-1,500**

Silver vases, early 20th c., ovoid with short neck and slightly flared rim, the overall design of flowers and foliage highlighted in gilt, 6¼" h., pair................................**3,500-5,500**

PRICE LISTINGS
for Korean Metalwares

Bronze Buddha, 16th c., seated dhyansana with hands in dhhyana mudra, draped in loose robes, face tilted down, long earlobes, hair arranged in rows of tight curls, smooth usnisa, interior hollow, 10¾" h. **$9,000-15,000**

Bronze Buddha, Unified Silla period, hands in vara and abhialya mudra, seated on lotus base, gilt very rubbed, 3" h. **1,000-1,500**

Bronze Buddha, 19th c., seated hands held in abhayamudra, loosely draped robes, some old restoration, 4½" h. **3,500-6,500**

Copper and silver damascened iron censer and cover, 19th c., square-form, rounded sides, decorated with roundels of cranes, tortoise and assorted trees and foliage, the cover with openwork trigrams, 11" h. **4,500-7,500**

Iron brazier, 19th c., hexagonal, inlaid with silver, each side decorated with a key fret-bordered roundel with each enclosing a turtle and a crane beneath the moon, an oversized conch shell, fruit on a branch, a pomegranate, a floral branch, or a pair of deer, the neck supporting a flat everted hexagonal rim with a floral design and diaper ground, the base with six bracket feet, 7½" h. (Color Illus. pg. 131) **3,500-6,500**

Mixed Metal Dish and Vase

Silver Napkin Rings

Silver Sake Pot

Chapter 17
PAINTINGS

●

Chinese album, 12 paintings, 19th c., painted in colors with scenes of figural processions, 7½" x 12", some damage.................................**$1,500-2,000**

Chinese painting, Mao Qiling (1623-1716), "Viewing the Bamboo," ink on paper, signed and sealed, 11"x 47".................**3,500-5,500**

Chinese painting, Chen Gungchao, scenic view with sailboats and setting sun, on silk, signed "Chen Gungchao," Guangxu period, 10" x 12½" (Color Illus. pg. 135) ..**300-500**

Chinese painting, Chen Shuren (1883-1948), "Bird Perched On Branch," ink and color on paper, signed and one seal of artist, 37" x 12" **5,000-7,000**

Chinese painting, Chinese school, late 18th or 19th c., "Figures in a Boat," oil on canvas, original black lacquer frame, framed size 11" x 19", restoration to painting and frame **4,000-5,000**

Chinese painting, Chinese school, mid-19th c., "View of the Canton Waterfront," oil on canvas, original black lacquer frame, frame size 10" x 8" **3,000-5,000**

Chinese painting, Chinese school, ca. 1870, "A View Of Victoria, Hong Kong," oil on canvas, original frame, painting and frame restored, frame size 15" x 20½"...**8,000-12,000**

Chinese painting, ca. 1900, figures on a verandah, one adjusts her hair by gazing at a bronze mirror, on silk, 10½" x 14" (Color Illus. pg. 138) **175-225**

Chinese painting, Qi Baishi (1864-1957), "Bird and Flower," hanging scroll; ink and color on paper, signed and sealed, approximate size 54" x 18" (Color Illus. pg. 132).............................**12,000-18,000.**

Chinese painting, Qi Baishi (1864-1957), "Grasshopper With Gourds," ink and color

on paper, signed and with one seal, 39" x 13½"...**5,000-7,000**

Chinese painting, "Snow in the Song Chien Mountain," ca.1890, Shu Yuan, scroll, ink on paper, sealed, water damage, 27" l. **175-225**

Chinese painting, 18th c., Song Xu, hanging scroll, Xi Wangmu, ink and color on silk, two seals of the artist, two collector's seals, 74" x 36" **4,500-6,500**

Chinese painting, Sun Xiaguang, vegetables and fruit, on silk, signed "Sun Xiaguang," 9½" x 12", early 20th c. (Color Illus. pg. 133) **300-500**

Chinese painting, an Immortal with a tiger, color on silk, 19th c., unsigned, restoration to silk, 65" l. **300-500**

Chinese paintings, Tingqua School, 19th c., each a river scene with boats and houses, 6¾" x 9¾", pair **1,000-1,500**

Chinese paintings, Zhang Daqian (1899-1983), flowers, ink and color on board, framed, framed sizes approximately 10½" x 9¼", each signed and sealed, pair (Color Illus. pg. 137) **5,000-7,000**

Japanese painting, "A Courtly Tale," late 18th or early 19th c., ink and color on silk, 55" x 26" **1,800-2,500**

Japanese painting, water-color of beauty walking in the snow, ca. 1910, 14" x 18" (Color Illus. pg. 134) **400-600**

Japanese painting, boats with tall sails, ca. 1905, 12" x 18" (Color Illus. pg. 136) **500-700**

Japanese painting, "Kannon," early Edo period, ink and color on silk, some deterioration, 15" x 31½" **2,500-3,500**

Japanese painting, "Processional," 18th or 19th c., portion of handscroll mounted on brocade, ink and color on paper, 12"x 50" **900-1,500**

Japanese painting, Hokusai-style, "Tea Whisk Vendor," ink and color on paper, 10" x 15" **500-750**

Japanese painting, Kano Tanyu School, "Landscape with a Temple," ink on paper, 37" x 16" **1,500-2,000**

Japanese painting, Kogyo, "Spirit of Courtesan with Skull," ink on paper, signed "Kogyo," 50¼" x 11½" **1,000-1,500**

Japanese painting, "Mt. Horai," signed and sealed "Haneda Mitsuo," ink and color on silk, 19" x 19" **800-1,200**

Japanese painting, "Persimmon with Bird on Branch," Nakatani Taisen, signed and sealed, mineral pigment on paper, framed, frame size 12"x 15" **1,200-1,800**

Japanese painting, "Birds on Branches with Oranges," Taguchi Noboru (b. 1951), signed and sealed, ink and mineral pigment on paper, framed, frame size 12" x 16" **1,200-1,800**

Japanese painting, Tsuji Seika (1870-1931), "Eggplant on Branches," signed and sealed, ink and color on paper, framed, frame size 18" x 19" **800-1,200**

Japanese painting, Tsuji Seika (1870-1931), "Eggplants and Insects," ink and color on paper, signed and sealed, framed, frame size 14" x 16" **800-1,200**

Japanese painting, Utagawa School, 19th c., woman seated on a bench, ink, color and gofun on paper, 31" x 18", framed, glazed **600-800**

Japanese painting, Utamaro School, 19th c., woman riding on an elephant, Kakemono, ink, color and gofun on paper, 43" x 10" **800-1,200**

Japanese water-color on paper, 20th c., tropical fish, framed and glazed, 18" x 22" **250-450**

Japanese water-color on paper, early 20th c., a street scene with rickshaw, signed "Y. Matsumoto," framed and glazed, 12" x 17½" **200-375**

Japanese water-color, landscape with houses and mountains, signed "Y. Kanashiro," dated "1948," framed, framed size 14" x 18" **500-700**

Korean Minwha (folk art) painting, "Three Buddhist Priests," 19th c., colors on cloth, framed, framed size 23" x 19"..............................**850-1,200**

Korean Minwha(folk art) painting fragment, Buddhist disciples, 19th c., colors on cloth, framed, frame size 27" x 20" **1,000-1,500**

Korean hanging scroll, 19th c., long-tailed rooster in color on silk, stained, 44½" x 12 7/8" **1,000-1,500**

Korean hanging scroll, 19th c., flowering prunus branches, color on silk, foxing, 42" x 13½" **500-700**

Korean hanging scroll, 19th c., "Bird and Clouds," ink and color on paper, mounted on silk brocade, trimmed, 31" x 18" **1,000-1,500**

Korean hanging scroll, 19th c., "Dragon In Clouds," ink on silk, 45½" x 20½" **2,500-4,500**

Korean painting, "Mountain Spirit," 19th or early 20th c., ink and color on silk, framed, framed size 34" x 28" **1,200-1,800**

Korean painting, 19th c., Tok Song and Attendants, ink and color on silk, framed, frame size 50" x 40" (ILLUS.) **4,500-6,500**

Korean painting, 19th c., mandarin ducks and lotus, color on paper, frame size 25" x 12" (Color Illus. pg. 132) **900-1,200**

Korean portrait, 19th c., ink and colors on paper, a depiction of a military official, toned, faded, framed, frame size 16" x 14" **3,000-5,000**

Tok Song and Attendants

Chapter 18
SAGEMONO
(Inro, Netsuke, Ojime and Related Objects)

Netsuke is a toggle used to prevent a cord attached to an object from slipping through the *obi* (sash). Japanese objects were suspended in this manner because garments had no pockets. The *ojime* is the slide which controls how tight or loose the string is. The *inro* is the principal object that was suspended in this manner. The whole assemblage of suspended objects is termed *Sagemono* or "wear thing." Inro were developed into compartmented cases. They were used for carrying medicine, ointments, etc. Additional objects which were suspended include: *tonkotsu* (tobacco container); *tabako ire* (pouch); *kinchaku* (money pouch); *yatate* (case containing brush and ink). Netsuke are usually 1"-2" in length (there are, of course, exceptions which can be as long as 5"). There are many forms of netsuke including: ryusa (mirror cover); manju (bun form); seal form; masks, sashi (rod shaped); hyotan (made of dried gourds); trick or toy (netsuke having moving parts); katabori (studies of animals or figures); ichiraku (woven or plaited) and *Kagamibuta* (round hollowed form with opening covered by a disk).

Inro, netsuke, ojime, etc., were made of varied materials including ivory, wood, lacquer, metal, pottery and porcelain.

PRICE LISTINGS
for Inro

Lacquer, two-case, shibuichi, shakudo, gold and silver, carved coral ojime, ivory netsuke with silver inlay, miniature, Meiji period (ILLUS.) **$1,500-2,000**

Lacquer, five-case, signed "Kajikawa saku," kinji ground decorated with "Dream of Rosei" (the hero unseen, but in his dream he is carried by carriage in a procession seen among clouds and pines) in takamakie with color, kirigane and nashiji, 3⅞" l., minor chipping **2,000-3,000**

Lacquer, four-case, signed "Kajikawa saku," roiro ground with nashiji, decorated with monkey and his trainer, both beneath willow branches, all in gold and color with gold foil and inlaid aogai, minor losses, 3" l. **1,200-1,800**

Lacquer, four-case, late 18th c. or early 19th c., fundame ground decorated with two samurai fighting, gold togidashi

Japanese Two-case Inro

ground, nashiji interiors, 3¼",
slightly worn **800-1,200**

Lacquer, three-case, 19th c., wide form with
kinji ground and birds on branch in sumi-
e togidashi, red lacquer interiors, worn,
rubbed, 3" l. **700-900**

Wood, three-case, signed "Ichosai," 19th c.,
carved with rectangular panels on both
sides with Benkei and Yoshitsune on the
Uji Bridge, carved pit ojime, ebony
netsuke of insect upon lotus,
inro 4" l..**$1,200-1,800**

PRICE LISTINGS
for Netsuke

Iron, mask of saru, 18th c., the monkey cast
with the himotoshi formed by a looped
bar on the back, 2" l. **$400-600**

Ivory, Ebisu, Osaka School, early 19th c.,
lightly stained, inlaid eyes, 1⅞" l. **400-650**

Ivory, an emaciated Rakan, late 18th or
early 19th c., 2" l. **400-650**

Ivory, Daikoku, signed "Yasumasa," early
20th c., holding mallet, polychrome,
2" l. **1,500-2,500**

Ivory, Hotei hiding inside his treasure sack,
signed "Tomokazu," chipped **200-300**

Ivory, Jurojin holding his staff, post-World
War II, Hong Kong, 2" l. **50-75**

Ivory, Jurojin holding his staff, early 20th c.,
1⅞" l. **250-375**

Ivory, Jurojin holding his staff and attended
by a child, late 19th c., 2" l.........................**550-750**

Ivory, all the animals of the zodiac with
coral inlay, signed "Masatsugu" but the
work of 20th c.,artist Masatoshi
(Color Illus. pg. 204) **5,500-6,500**

Ivory, 19th c., Jurojin and attendant with
basket containing treasure ship, signed
"Hidechika" (ILLUS.) **3,000-4,000**

Ivory, 20th c., Bishamon with polychrome
embellishments (ILLUS.) **200-300**

Ivory, 20th c., four figures in a dragon boat
upon waves, signed "Sosui" (Color Illus.
pg. 204) **3,000-4,000**

Ivory, kagamibuta, 19th c., the ivory bowl
with dark shibuichi plate decorated in
low-relief with tiger and plants,
2¼" d. **1,000-1,500**

Ivory, kagamibuta, late 19th or early 20th c.,
ivory bowl with shibuichi plate inlaid with
Kikujido seated by a stream in gold, silver,
shakudo and shibuichi, 2¼" d., bowl
cracked **800-1,200**

Ivory, kappa, post-World War II,
Hong Kong...**50-100**

Ivory, manju, carved with kappa and elder,
signed "Yasufasa," 1⅞" d. **750-1,000**

Ivory, seated shishi on rectangular platform,
early 19th c., 1¾" l. **650-950**

Ivory study of a recumbent horse, 19th c.,
Kaigyokusai Masatsugu, its head turned to
the right, minor crack (ILLUS.) **10,000-15,000**

Ivory study of rat on fruit and nuts, 18th c.,
rat resting on cluster of nuts and fruit
with the himostoshi naturally formed
by a stalk and foliage, 2¼" l. **450-650**

Ivory Netsuke of a Recumbent Horse

Shishi-form Japanese Netsuke

Boxwood Netsuke of Hankai

Ivory Netsuke of Bishamon

Ivory Netsuke of Jurojin

Porcelain, Hirado ware, in form of Shishi
    with openwork patterns
    (ILLUS.) **1,500-2,000**

Pottery, manju in Kenzan-style, mid-19th
    c., square with canted corners, the center
    with Okame in low-relief, colors and gilt,
    2" l. **1,200-1,800**

Pottery, model of a tortoise, late 19th c.,
    Kyoto ware, undecorated, covered with
    crackle glaze, 2⅛" l. **300-500**

Pottery, Satsuma, kagamibuta, early
    19th c. (Color Illus. page 203) **2,500-3,500**

Pottery, study of Hotei, Kyoto ware, mid-
    19th c., decorated in colors and gilt,
    2" l. **800-1,200**

Pottery, study of a lion dancer,
    Satsuma, late 19th c., gilt and
    colors, 1⅞" l. **900-1,200**

Silver, Meiji period, Daikoku's mallet
    (ILLUS.) **1,500-2,000**

Staghorn manju, Asakusa School, carved
    with bat and fungi, unsigned.....................**500-900**

Wood, boxwood, 18th c., Hankai bursting
    into his Emperor's dining room carrying
    the door, signed "Hidekazu" (ILLUS.) ..**1,800-2,500**

Meiji Period Silver Netsuke

Wood, boxwood, study of puppy, Masano (Ise, Yamada), early 19th c., seated, its head turned to the left, legs drawn under, eyes inlaid, 1⅜" l. **900-1,500**

Wood, boxwood, 19th c., study of quails, two birds resting on a pile of millet heads and foliage, 2⅜" l....................................**800-1,200**

Wood, boxwood, 18th c., Shoki holding Oni, Shoki's sword behind his back, good patina and slightly worn, 3½" l. **3,500-5,500**

Wood, figure of Kappa, early 19th c., standing upright, worn **500-700**

Wood, figure of Ronin, late 18th c., signed "Minkoku," hiding under his straw cape, he waits, sword partially drawn, restored, 2" l. **900-1,500**

Wood, mask of Naminari, the grinning face with short horns, the wood slightly worn, 3" l. **250-350**

Wood, netsuke of a lotus pod with movable seeds, early 20th c.......................................**100-125**

Wood, study of bamboo shoot, Masatsugu, 19th c., three bamboo shoots tied with a rope, the himotoshi formed by the rope, 1⅞"...**650-900**

Wood, study of Mt. Fuji, Seisai, mid-19th c., a dragon curling around Mt. Fuji **1,000-1,500**

Wood, study of a monkey, 18th c., signed "Minko," seated, eating a chestnut, one leg forming the himotoshi, inlay missing from one eye, 1¾" l. **900-1,200**

Wood, study of a rat, Meiji period, 2⅛" l. **300-500**

Wood, study of a reclining boar, late 19th c., 2¼" l. **550-750**

PRICE LISTINGS
for Ojime

Copper, fish in relief, 19th c. **$350-500**

Cloisonné, round, blue ground with pink and white flowers, silver wires, ca. 1900 ....**500-700**

Gold, round with relief design of butterflies, late 19th c. **1,000-1,500**

Ivory, carved with Shishi, Meiji period..........**450-750**

Ivory, carved in relief and pierced work, design of Rakan, 19th c. **500-600**

Ivory, carved with Daikoku and Ebisu, Meiji period, cracked...**250-350**

Ivory, model of a chestnut, 20th c. **150-250**

Ivory with brass collars, carved with dragon chasing flaming pearl, 19th c. (left) **$375-475;** Silver ojime with silver collars, openwork design of clouds, 19th c. (right) (ILLUS.) **300-400**

Japanese Ivory and Silver Ojime

Porcelain, Hirado ware, blue and white
leaves, 19th c. **800-1,200**

Satsuma, round with maples leaves and gilt,
20th c. **200-400**

Shakudo, Daikoku's mallet, late 19th c. **700-900**

Silver, round, pierced with kiku mon,
19th c. **500-750**

Stag antler, carved in peach-form,
19th c. **250-375**

PRICE LISTING
for Smoker's Accessories

Kiseruzutsu, boxwood, late 18th or early
19th c., senryu-zutsu-type, with inlaid
ivory and ivory basket with pierced work,
pipe not original and of a later date,
7¾" l. (Color Illus. pg. 203) **$2,000-3,000**

Kiseruzutsu, boxwood, signed "Hokei,"
19th c., muzo-sutsu-type, carved in relief
on both sides with 12 Zodiac animals,
8¾"....................................**3,000-4,000**

Kiseruzutsu, silver, 19th c., made in two
parts which screw together, each section
with a short tube of wood mounted at
either end in silver, the wood lacquered in

gold hiramakie and the silver engraved
with birds and waves, 11" **450-650**

Kiseruzutsu, stag antler, signed
"Shungyoku," 19th c., otoshi-zutsu-type,
carved with warrior hiding among pine
trees, 8", minor chips.................................**400-600**

**Tabako-ire with Kiseruzutsu and
netsuke,** netsuke signed "Hakuunsai,"
leather pouch and pipe case, ivory
netsuke in form of Rokkasen, slightly
stained.....................................**900-1,200**

Tonkotsu, inlaid wood, 19th c., carved in
the form of a pouch and inlaid with a
snail, fungus on the reverse, minor
losses, 4" **300-450**

Tonkotsu, inlaid wood, signed
"Tokoku,"19th c., inlaid with design of a
sparrow on one side and two sparrows on
the other, the top with chestnuts and
leaves, inlay of horn, ivory and mother-of-
pearl, runners inset with bone, chipped
and losses **500-750**

Tonkotsu, wood, signed "Kokaku," early
19th c., carved in the form of a woven
basket upon which there are turtles, fitted
with large netsuke of a turtle **1,600-2,400**

Chapter 19
SCREENS

●

PRICE LISTINGS

for Oriental Screens

Chinese Coromandel screen, 19th c., black lacquer screen with scenic design of a palace garden, foliate borders, the reverse with flowers and birds, 100" h. x 128" w. (Color Illus. pg. 205) **$5,000-7,500**

Chinese Coromandel screen, black, 19th c., eight panels decorated with fish, a dragon boat, and figures, the reverse with birds and flowers, the borders with birds and flowers, the reverse with flowering branches, 6' h. x 84" w., old repairs **2,000-3,500**

Chinese Coromandel screen, black, early 18th c., twelve panels carved with numerous figures in landscapes with pavilions and gardens, the border with Buddhist emblems the reverse with birds and flowering trees, 110" h. x 220" w................................**15,000-25,000**

Chinese Coromandel screen, late 17th or early 18th c., black, twelve panels, continuous scene of figures in a palace setting, the border with auspicious emblems, 100 antiques and flowers, the reverse with animals, birds and flowers, losses, old restorations, 110" h. x 208" w...............................**12,000-18,000**

Chinese Coromandel screen, 19th c., eight panels, a continuous design of gardens and palace with figures all within floral borders, the reverse with flowers and birds, 102" h. x 136" w.........................**5,500-8,500**

Chinese screen, 19th c., six panels, rosewood, each panel carved with a panel of flowers below a panel of gilt flowers, the largest portion of each panel carved with mountainscapes, 120" h. x 120" w...................................**2,000-3,500**

Chinese wallpaper screen, early 19th c., four panels with wallpaper mounted on hardwood, decorated with a continuous scene of figures walking and seated beside a lake, damages to paper, old repairs with in-painting, possibly cut down, 86" w., 80" h......................................**4,500-7,500**

Japanese two-panel screen, landscape in colors and ink on gold ground, rubbed, early 19th c., 35" x 35"..........................**800-1,200**

Japanese four-panel screen, sumi (black ink) on gold paper, birds and pine trees, good condition, 20th c., 96" w., 47" h.......................................**1,000-1,500**

Japanese four-panel screen, late 19th or early 20th c., "The Tale of Genji," ink and colors on gold paper, 46" x 76", repaired **1,000-1,500**

Japanese four-panel screen, Rimpa School, garden with chrysanthemums on a gold ground, early 19th c., 140" l., 68" h. **5,000-7,500**

Japanese six-panel screen, cranes, pine, and plum blossoms beside a stream, ink, color and gofun on goldleaf ground, each panel, 24" w., 59" h. **6,000-8,500**

Japanese six-panel screen, Kano School, 18th c., ink, colors and goldleaf on paper, cranes standing in various poses, 60" x 140" **15,000-20,000**

Japanese six-panel screen, Rimpa School, 17th c., in color and gofun on goldleaf ground with design of white chrysanthemums and brushwood fences, each panel 22¼" w., 64" h. **10,000-15,000**

Japanese six-panel screen, 19th c., Rimpa-style, ink, color and gofun on paper with autumnal flowering plants, each panel 23½" w., 65 1/4" h., restored **8,000-10,000**

Japanese table screen, bamboo frame with silk painting of three equestrians in the snow, signed "Okyo Maruyama," early 19th c. (ILLUS.) **1,000-1,500**

Korean four-panel screen, 20th c., a continuous hunting scene, colors on paper, 4' w., 4' h. **800-1,200**

Korean six-panel screen, 18th c., each panel mounted with paintings of scholars' articles, colors on cloth, each panel 11⅞" w., 51" h. **15,000-25,000**

Korean six-panel screen, 20th c., black velvet with embroidered flowers and foliage in bright colors, each panel 12" w., 5' h. **250-500**

Korean eight-panel screen, 19th c., each panel with colored embroidery on silk with designs of birds and flowers, mounted on cloth, each panel 12" w., 23" h..**2,000-4,000**

Korean ten-panel screen, 19th c., colors and ink on silk with hunting scenes, each panel 12" w., 37 1/2" h. **7,500-10,500**

Korean ten-panel screen, 19th c., ink and color on paper with continuous battle scene, each panel 11⅝" w., 47" h. **25,000-35,000**

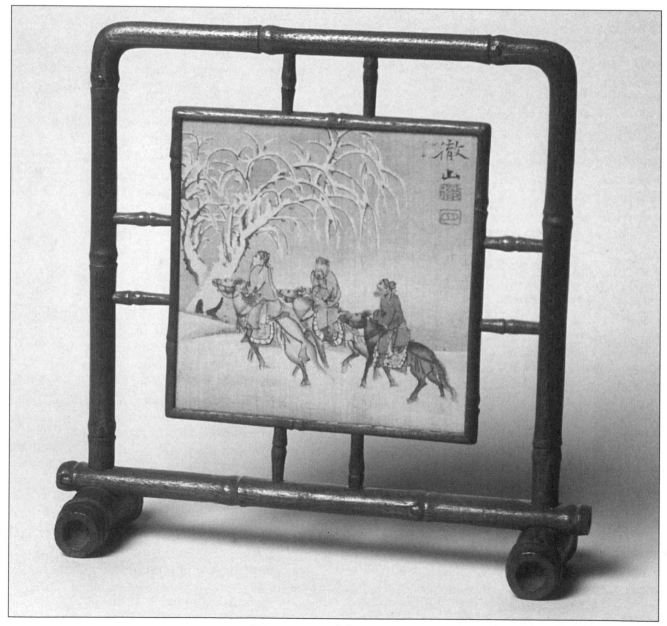

Japanese Table Screen

Chapter 20
SNUFF BOTTLES

Snuff is a derivative of tobacco. Although the Chinese found it unacceptable to smoke tobacco, snuff was considered medicinal. Snuff bottles have been produced for functional and decorative purposes. Both antique and contemporary bottles are highly collectible in today's market.

For Chinese date marks found on inside-painted snuff bottles see Appendix G

PRICE LISTINGS
for Snuff Bottles

Agate, ovoid-form with mask and mock ring handles in low-relief, carved with fish, dark inclusions, 20th c. **$100-200**

Agate, flattened ovoid-form with brown markings, early 20th c. **100-175**

Agate, spade-shaped with butterfly in low-relief, early 20th c. **125-175**

Amber, early 19th c., carved with bird on branch, well hollowed **1,000-1,500**

Amber, with basketweave pattern, well hollowed (Color Illus. pg. 207) **600-900**

Amethyst, fruit-form with relief branch, 20th c. **100-200**

Bamboo root, 19th c., carved in the form of a pea pod **1,000-1,500**

Canton enamel on copper, Famille Rose palette, 19th c., each side painted with a portrait of European lady, four-character Qianlong mark on base, losses **350-550**

Canton enamel on copper, Famille Rose palette, with designs of flowers and insects on a yellow ground, early 19th c. **2,000-3,000**

Canton enamel on copper Famille Rose palette, flask-form, each side with ladies and children, minor chipping, early 19th c. **650-950**

Cloisonné, first half 19th c., decorated with floral sprays on a blue ground between floral borders **500-700**

Cloisonné, late 18th-early 19th c., one side with dragon the other with a phoenix in colors on a blue ground...........................**1,500-2,000**

Coral, carved in relief with flowers and foliage, 20th c. **200-300**

Glass, enameled, Famille Rose palette, Ku Yueh Hsuan (Guyuexuan) on base, design of flowers **400-600**

Glass, enameled, Famille Rose palette, Guyuexuan three-character mark on base in red, decoration of various fruits, post-1949 ....**600-900**

Glass, enameled, Famille Rose palette, marked as above, continuous landscape, ca. 1911 ....**1,500-2,500**

Inside-painted Glass Snuff Bottle

Glass, four-color overlay, decorated with dragons and clouds, 18th c., chipped...**2,000-3,000**

Glass, inside-painted, signed "Chen Zhongsan" and dated "1918," one side painted with figures and horse, the other with grasshopper and foliage **1,200-1800**

Glass, inside-painted, with aquatic designs, carved on the exterior with water plants, by the Ye studio, signed "Ye Zhongsan" (ILLUS.) **2,000-3,000**

Glass, inside-painted, signed "Zhou Leyuan," dated "1890," painted with cranes, pine and rockwork, the reverse with birds in flight..**5,000-7,000**

Glass, inside-painted, continuous landscape and warriors on horseback, ca. 1910..........**275-450**

Glass, inside-painted, flowers on each side, ca. 1920s **100-150**

Glass, red overlay on snowflake ground, flattened pear-shape, carved design of bamboo, 18th c., chipped **500-700**

Glass, ruby red, pear-shaped, carved in relief with archaistic vessels.............................**700-1,200**

Glass simulating agate, 19th c. (ILLUS.) **750-950**

Glass simulating agate, ovoid-form with dragon in low-relief, ca. 1900 ....**100-200**

Glass simulating coral, low-relief carvings of flowers, early 20th c. **500-700**

Glass simulating coral, with design of fish in low-relief, early 20th c. (ILLUS.) **750-950**

Glass, teal blue, the base with incised "Xuantong" mark (ILLUS.) **1,000-1,800**

Glass, 18th c.: left - milk glass with red overlay, **$800-1,200;** right - snowflake glass with red overlay pattern of "100 Antiques" (Color Illus. pg. 207)............**1,000-1,500**

Ivory, late 19th c., carved with a scene of figures on a balcony, polychrome............**800-1,200**

Ivory, late 19th-early 20th c., carved with women and children in a pavilion, polychrome **750-1,200**

Jadeite, emerald and white, rectangular-form with mask and mock ring handles in low-relief, carved with pine, lotus and crane, first half 19th c., well hollowed **4,000-5,000**

Jadeite, green with white mottling, ovoid-form, well hollowed, 19th c. **400-600**

Jadeite, green, lavender and white with mottling, carved with low-relief carp, ca. 1920s **650-950**

Jadeite, green and white mottling, compressed ovoid shape with low-relief carvings of bats and prunus blossoms, early 20th c. **3,000-4,000**

Jadeite, white, eggplant-form, 19th c. **3,000-4,000**

Lac Burgaute, ovoid-form, floral designs, post-World War II **50-75**

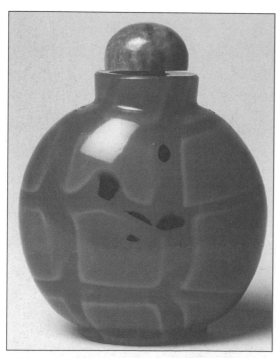

Glass Simulating Agate

Glass Simulating Coral

Lac Burgaute, spade-shaped, crane decoration, ca. 1900................**200-300**

Nephrite, celadon, flattened ovoid-form, post-World War II **100-175**

Nephrite, celadon and brown, rectangular-form with low-relief carving of kylin, early 20th c. **200-300**

Nephrite, gray, rectangular-form, ca. 1900 ..**100-175**

Nephrite, mutton fat, flattened ovoid-form with pine tree in low-relief, 19th c. **300-400**

Nephrite, spinach green, carved with children in very low-relief, late 19th c.......**300-500**

Porcelain, late 19th, underglaze-blue and white with dragons and flames, 3" h. **100-175**

Porcelain, late 19th or early 20th c., underglaze-blue and white, prunus decoration, 2½" h. **100-150**

Porcelain, late 19th c., tapered-form, underglaze-blue and white dragon chasing a flaming pearl above wave patterns, Qianlong mark on base **700-900**

Porcelain, Qianlong mark but ca. 1800, Famille Rose palette with decoration molded in relief, the reverse with figure of a woman (Color Illus. pg. 206)................**900-1,200**

Porcelain, late 19th c., Famille Rose palette, elder holding a basket, the reverse with bats, rubbed, 3" h. **175-200**

Porcelain, Guyuexuan, late Qing Dynasty, Famille Rose palette decoration of flowers and insects, signed on the base "Guyuexuan" (ILLUS.) **3,500-4,500**

Porcelain, late 19th-early 20th c., Famille Rose palette, scene of an elderly woman and her attendants in a garden **300-500**

Porcelain, 19th c., Famille Rose palette molded in relief with 18 Lohans and their attributes, gilt highlights, 2½" h. **375-500**

Porcelain, late 19th c., Famille Rose palette, molded in relief with figures in a boat, spade-shaped, base with Qianlong mark....**600-900**

Porcelain, double snuff bottle, Guangxu mark and period, designs of roosters (Color Illus. pg. 207) **550-750**

Rock crystal, ovoid-form, carving of bat and carp, ca. 1900 ....**150-250**

Silver, Mongolian-style, coral and turquoise stones, ca. 1900, dents...............................**100-150**

Silver, Mongolian-style, the sides with lion head masks, front and back with longevity symbols and bats, early 20th c. **150-200**

Tortoiseshell, ovoid-form, low-relief carving of equestrian, late 19th c. **700-950**

Turquoise, fruit-form with leaf and fruit in low-relief, well hollowed, 19th c. **500-700**

Teal Blue Glass Snuff Bottle

Qing Dynasty Porcelain Snuff Bottle

Chapter 21
SOUTHEAST ASIAN ART

PRICE LISTINGS
for Southeast Asian Metalwares

Laotian bronze bust of Buddha, face with pointed chin, mouth with outlined lips, downcast eyes, hair in rows of spiky curls, wearing a sanghati with long sash in relief on left side, 17th c., 11½" h. **$2,000-3,000**

Nepalese copper plaque of Durga, repoussé in relief with the figure of the goddess stepping to right on an oblong lotus base, her primary hands holding a kapala and karttrka, her remaining ten arms radiating around her and holding various weapons, 16th c., 4½" h. **900-1,200**

Nepalese copper and parcel-gilt Wheel of Life plaque, Yama holding the wheel from behind, his bear-like face with fangs bared, bulging eyes inset with white and blue glass, short curly beard, the wheel profusely decorated with scrolling foliate and vine sprays, and rosettes inset with semiprecious stones, surrounded by a band of flames, a hinged compartment in the center, a Bodhisattva in coral on the cover, opening to reveal a figure of Amitabha Buddha seated within, 19th c., 25" h. **3,500-5,000**

Nepalese gilt-bronze figure of Acala with consort, the kneeling divinity in yab-yum with his consort, brandishing a sword and noose, his sakti holding a karttrka and kapala, four deities trampled beneath them on the circular throne, both figures with foliate crowns, 16th c., 3½" h. **2,500-3,500**

Nepalese gilt-bronze Stupa, the square base supported on lion's paw feet centering scalloped foliage aprons, the top incised with line of Nepalese script, the bell-shaped central section with lotus borders, the bottom with four plaques of Buddha, 17th c., 9¼" h. **1,500-2,500**

Sino-Tibetan silver figure of Amitayus, seated in dhyansana on a beaded lotus base, hands in dhyana mudra and holding a kalasa, hair tied in topknot, gilded, late 18th c., 7" h. **1,500-2,200**

Sino-Tibetan gilt and lacquered bronze figure of Buddha, seated in dhyanasana on a lotus throne, his hands in bhumisparsa and dhyana mudra, wearing long monastic robes with beaded hem, right shoulder bare, face with meditative expression, hair arranged in small pointed curls with spherical cintamani surmounting the usnisa, 18th c., 11" h. **2,500-3,500**

Tibetan bronze figure of Aksobhya Buddha, 17th c., seated in dhyanasana on a lotus throne with a vajra in front, his hands in bhumisparsa and dhyana mudra, wearing a sanghati with incised floral hemline, spherical cintamani surmounting his usnisa, 11" h. (Color Illus. pg. 209) **5,500-7,500**

Tibetan gilt-bronze figure of Mahakala, holding a karttrka and kapala in his primary hands, his remaining four hands holding a damaru, mala of skulls and flayed elephant skin, 18th c., 4" h. **2,000-3,000**

Tibetan gilt-bronze figure of a Lama, seated in dhyanasana with his hands in dharmacakra mudra, wearing a monastic robe with incised foliate hemlines, 17th or 18th c., 9½" h. **2,500-3,500**

PRICE LISTINGS
for Southeast Asian Paintings

Thanka, Eastern Tibetan Mandala of the Dakini Na-ro kha-cho-ma, Karma Gadri style, ca. 17th c., the dakini striding vigorously to her left and trampling two figures, her head arched back and drinking from a blood-filled kapala in her raised left hand, a karttrka in her right hand, a khavtvanga balanced on one shoulder, the goddess within a three-dimensional six-pointed star within a three-storied pagoda inhabited in the upper levels by a large group of lamas and a figure of Vajradhara, six ecstatically dancing celestial attendants at the base of the structure, the pagoda encircled by three concentric bands of lotus petals, a band with seven cemetery scenes interspersed by rivers, and an outer band of flames, the lower corners with the guardian of the north, Vaisravana, seated on his lion at the right, two citapati dancing within a house composed of human bones at the left, the sky filled with attendants, four lamas, and a figure of Cakrasamvara flanked by Simhavaktra and another dakini, approximately 30" x 20" framed (Color Illus. pg. 208) ..**$12,000-18,000**

Thanka, Tibetan, 18th c., 11-headed Lokeshvara, each of the six arms with attributes, standing on lotus base before an aureole, surrounded by four attendants in the corners, framed, framed size 28½" x 22½" (Color Illus. pg, 209) **1,000-2,000**

Thanka, Tibetan, "Scenes from the Life of Buddha," Buddha seated in dhyanasan at center on a lotus blossom, surrounded by a mountainous landscape filled with

vignettes from his life, original embroidered border, 18th c., approximately 40" x 25" **$3,500-5,500**

Thanka, Tibetan, Prajnaparamita seated in dhyanasan with her primary hands in dharmacakra mudra, her secondary hands holding lotus flowers supporting a vajra and pustaka, flanked by two female attendants, surrounded by rectangular polychrome panels containing various forms of seated Buddha, 17th c., approximately 40" x 30" **5,000-7,000**

Thanka, Tibetan, Hayagriva, the ferocious Dharmapla with eight legs, holding attributes, the three heads sharing a mass of flaming hair, Beg-tse in the foreground, Amitabha flanked by Tsong-kha-pa and Padmasambhava above, 19th c., approximately 25" x 15" **3,000-4,000**

Thanka, Tibetan, Vajrapani stepping to right on a lotus base holding a vajra in his raised right-hand, wearing a tiger skin dhoti, a horse head emerging form his mass of fiery hair, surrounded by an aureole of flames with small figure of Garuda at the top, early 19th c., approximately 25" x 16" **1,000-1,500**

PRICE LISTINGS
for Southeast Asian Sculptures

Burmese head of Buddha, white marble, Mandalay, face with eyes slightly downcast, delicate features, 18th c., 3⅝" h. **$300-600**

Indian figure of Ganesha, buff sandstone, the elephant-headed god of wealth with trunk scrolled to left in lively attitude, 12th c., 13" h. **2,500-3,500**

Indian figure of a Jina, white marble, seated in dhyanasana on an incised molded throne, his hands resting on his lap in dhyana mudra, 13th c., 18½" h. **1,000-1,500**

Javanese Lava rock carving of Ganesha, 13th c., 8" h. (ILLUS.) **1,000-1,500**

Pala stele of Padmapani, black stone, eastern India, seated in lalitasana with his hands in varada and vitarka mudras, lotus flower above right shoulder, hair domed and knotted, 7½" h. **750-1,000**

Thai head of Buddha, sandstone, Ayuthia, oval face with small mouth, elongated nose, downcast eyes, hair arranged in rows of small Rouen curls, 17th c., 14" h. **2,000-3,000**

Lava Rock Carving of Ganesha

Chapter 22
TEXTILES AND GARMENTS

●

For additional information on Chinese textile design motifs see Appendix H

PRICE LISTINGS
for Garments

Chinese dragon robe, 19th c., blue silk with couched gold dragons amid blue and green satin stitched clouds, 54" l. **$3,000-5,000**

Chinese informal coat, 19th c., blue silk with applied dragon roundels in couched gold, 40" l. **1,000-1,500**

Chinese insignia badge, 17th c., peacock symbol of civil official 3rd rank, dark blue, sea green, gold and orange satin stitches on couched gold ground, 14" x 14", rare..**8,000-10,000**

Chinese jacket, late 19th c., purple silk worked with baskets of flowers in satin stitch and Peking knot, with couched stitch gauze borders, 37" l. **800-1,200**

Chinese lady's jacket, late 19th c., pink silk woven with lotus and butterflies, applied with wide blue borders embroidered with various flowers, butterflies and long-tailed birds, within blue brocade and black ground bands, the cuffs finely worked on the reverse with couched gold and silver threads depicting phoenix, peony and auspicious objects, 35" l. (Color Illus. page 211) **1,000-1,500**

Chinese lady's robe, late Qing dynasty, eight floral roundels worked in couched stitches above waves, the red silk gauze embroidered in green, yellow, white and pink, 54½" l. **2,500-3,500**

Chinese Mandarin square (rank badge), mid-19th c., blue ground, displaying a paradise flycatcher, civil official 9th rank, worked in Peking knots and gold outlines with the bird in the center amid dense

clouds perched on a rock issuing from waves, the design incorporating the eight Buddhist emblems, within a key scroll band couched in gold beneath peony, framed, framed size 12" x 12" (ILLUS.) **500-650**

Chinese twelve-symbol robe, late 19th c., worked with couched gold dragons, 12 Imperial symbols, all above dense waves and lishui stripe, 56" l...........................**5,500-7,500**

Japanese embroidered silk panel, ca. 1915, design of standing cranes among weeds in satin stitches, shades of gray, silver, muted tones of blue and green, 30" x 26" framed **450-700**

Japanese fukusa, post-World War II, gold and brown with Good Fortune symbol on one side, 26" x 28" **75-125**

Japanese kimono, ca. 1925, cream ground with embroidered roundels filled with foliage, colors and gilt satin stitches, 53" l. **300-400**

Japanese kimono, ca. 1930, black silk with painted decoration of irises at the hemline **300-500**

Japanese kimono, ca. 1920s, gold and red satin stitches forming pattern of trees and cranes, wear to underarm, 50" l................**100-175**

Japanese wedding kimono, 20th c., overall gold and silver birds and cranes..**200-400**

Korean embroidered court official rank apron, 19th c., court official 3rd rank, a panel with two columns of flower-bordered panels enclosing flying cranes, all between chain stitch bands, frayed, stitches missing, staining, framed, frame size 12" w x 16" l. **800-1,200**

Korean embroidered rank badge, late 19th c., made for a civil official of the 1st to 3rd rank, design of cranes grasping a pulloch'o stalk in mouth, above stylized waves and rockwork amid clouds outlined in couching, the design in shades of blue, green, white, red and purple on a blue ground, framed, approximately 9" x 8", (Color Illus. pg. 211) **2,000-3,000**

PRICE LISTINGS
for Textiles

Chinese kesi, 17th c., woven with boys at play in landscape, metallic gold ground, framed, frame size 29"x 15", rare ..**$15,000-20,000**

Chinese kesi, 19th c., woven with a battle scene of warriors on horseback, on fine metallic ground, framed, frame size 37" x 41" **4,500-6,500**

Chinese temple hanging, 19th c., red wool field, with dragon in metallic gold with precious objects, bats, and other elaborate designs, 98" x 120" **5,500-8,500**

Chinese textile for temple, 19th c., red felt ground, decorated with dragon chasing flaming pearl, surrounded by bats (wufu) and precious objects in satin stitches and Peking knots with borders of immortals, all amid predominately blue clouds, 120" x 90" (Color Illus. pg. 211)..**10,000-15,000**

Japanese embroidery on silk, Edo Period, design in mon form with metallic gold and silver thread in satin stitch and couching, 15" x 15" (Color Illus. pg. 210) **1,500-2,000**

Japanese silk embroidered panel, ca. 1900, large cockerel perched on a drum flanked by dragons, in colors and gilt in satin stitch on a silk ground covered with blossoms, frayed and minor water stains, approximately 48" x 72" **1,000-1,500**

Japanese silk embroidered panel, early Meiji period, metallic and silk satin stitch design of paulownia on a floral ground, repaired and stained, framed, approximate size 36" x 48" **450-650**

Chinese Mandarin Square—Paradise Flycatcher

Chapter 23
WOODCARVINGS, BASKETS AND SHOP SIGNS

●

PRICE LISTINGS
for Woodcarvings, Baskets, and Shop Signs

Chinese bamboo brush pot, 17th c., tree trunk-shape, slightly bent, carved with pine, 5" h. **$3,500-4,500**

Chinese bamboo wrist rest, 19th c., carved on one side with calligraphy, 11" l. **600-800**

Chinese boxwood figure of a seated lohan, 18th c., one arm resting upon one knee, open robe revealing chest and belly, the face with beard and mustache, 2¼" h. **5,500-7,000**

Chinese boxwood figure of Guanyin (Kuan Yin), 19th c., long flowing robes with folds, long prayer beads hanging over the front of the garment, one hand holding a scroll, a chignon and diadem beneath a cowl, seated upon a lotus petal plinth, restored, 14" h. **6,000-8,000**

Chinese boxwood ruyi scepter, 18th c., long narrow shaft terminating in a ruyi fungus head, 12¾" l. **7,500-9,500**

Chinese rosewood carving of Budai, ca. 1925, sack and staff, large protruding stomach, bone eyes and teeth, 10" h. **85-125**

Chinese rosewood carving of an Immortal, ca. 1920, he holds beads, bone eyes and teeth, 12½" h. **85-125**

Chinese rootwood carving of Li Bai, 17th c., the poet is sitting with one hand leaning slightly to one side, in other hand he holds a cup, his face with mustache and beard, 9½" h. **5,500-9,500**

Chinese Wood Carving

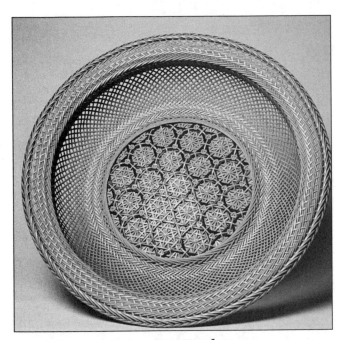

Japanese Basket

Chinese wood carving of two boys holding a large basket and lifting cover, 3" h. (ILLUS.) 1,500-2,500

Chinese zitan brush pot, 18th c., tree trunk-form carved with knots, 4" h. 2,000-3,000

Japanese basket, woven smoked bamboo, Meiji period, 11" h. 500-700

Japanese basket, woven, shaped ovoid body, interwoven bamboo strips on exterior, 20th c., 12½" h. 375-550

Japanese basket, woven, natural wood frame, ovoid irregular shape, 20th c., 15" h. 700-900

Japanese basket, ca. 1950s, artist-signed, 16" d. (ILLUS.) 300-500

Japanese rootwood carving of melon, late Meiji period, 6½" h. 300-400

Japanese shop sign (Kamban), Abacus, late 19th c., 40" x 12" 200-300

Japanese shop sign (Kamban), gourd-form, Pawn Shop, late 19th c., 40" h. 800-1,200

Japanese shop sign (Kamban), Meiji period, money changer, 12" d. (ILLUS.) 500-775

Japanese shop sign (Kamban), Ladies' Pharmacy, reverse-painting on glass in lacquer frame, late Meiji period, 32" h. 4,000-5,000

Japanese shop sign (Kamban), Pharmacist, late Meiji period, deteriorated, 25" w., 15" h. 200-275

Japanese Kanban Shop Sign

Japanese shop sign (Kamban), wood with traces of polychrome, "Kimono Shop," late Edo period, 38" x 21" (ILLUS.)............700-900

Japanese wood carving, itobori-style, of woman wearing painted kimono with floral design, Taisho or early Showa period, 14½" h. 150-200

Japanese wood carving of a standing man holding a mask of Okina, signed, mask removable, Taisho or early Showa period 10" h. (ILLUS.)......................................2,000-2,500

Japanese wood carving of Fukusukesan, some chipping, traces of pigment, late 19th c., 12½" h. 600-800

Japanese wood carving of Hotei with staff and sack, Meiji period, 12" h. (Color Illus. pg. 212) 1,200-1,800

Japanese wood carving of nobleman, arms and legs missing, Momoyama period, 28" h. 1,500-2,500

Japanese wood carving of Shayamuni, mid- to late-18th c., the Buddha stands upon a graduated lotus base , face is meditative, eyes inlaid with mother-of-pearl, rock crystal on the forehead denoting byakugo (third eye), hair curled and toped by usnisa, cracks and minor restoration to both levels of the base, 38" h. (Color Illus. pg. 212)..............10,000-15,000

Japanese wood carving of standing figure of Buddha, loosely draped robes, face in a downcast pose, traces of pigment, early 19th c., 9" h. **500-700**

Japanese wood chaire (tea caddy), natural wood, ca.1955, 4" h. (ILLUS.) **100-125**

Korean wood animal-form candlestand, late 18th or early 19th c., in the form of a mythological lion in recumbent position, the wood with some color intact, losses to upper portion which would hold candle, cracked and chipped, 20" w. **6,000-8,000**

Korean wood brush pot, 19th c., cylindrical, flat base, the body carved with four roundels filled with auspicious characters, cracked, 6" h.......................**2,000-3,000**

Japanese Carving of Man Holding Mask

Japanese Kimono Shop Sign

Japanese Wood Chaire

Chapter 24
WOODBLOCK PRINTS
(UKIYO-E)

Japanese woodblock prints (ukiyo-e) were developed in the last half of the 17th century. The prints were produced with an artist's rendering which an engraver transferred in outline form onto the woodblocks. Both sides of the block were used. There was a keyblock with additional blocks for each color change. The woodblocks had a negative image of the design in relief. The printer (painter), following the designated colors (indicated by the artist), charged each block with color using brushes. Each block had a kento (right angle)cut into the corner. Dampened papers were aligned with the kento and laid down, in turn, on each block then hand-rubbed with a baren (pad). The blocks were recharged with color after each impression was made. Many modern print artists, working after World War II, carved their own blocks and printed and published their own prints.

Subjects include: aizuri-e (prints with blue shading); bijin-ga (beautiful women); egoyomi (calendar prints); ehon (books); kacho-e (flowers and birds); musha-e (warriors); okubi-e (bust portraits); shunga (erotica); sumo-e (wrestlers); uchiwa-e (fan prints).

Sizes in inches are: aiban (13 x 9"); chuban (10 x 7"); hashira-e (28 x 4½"); hosoban (13 x 5"); kakemono (30 x 9"); large oban (22 x 12½"); oban (15 x 10"); tanzaku (15 x 5"). Tate-e have a vertical format while yoko-e have a horizontal format. Prints sizes can vary slightly.

PRICE LISTINGS
for Prints by Various Artists

EISEN (1790-1848)

Kakemono-e, full-length portrait of a man wearing checked robes and holding a fan, signed "Keisai Eisen ga," published by Tsutaya Kichizo, good impression, faded, torn, rubbed **$1,000-1,500**

Oban tate-e, Nihonbashi nishi gashi (The west bank of the Sumida River by Nihonbashi), a woman in purple kimono holding an umbrella, signed "Keisai Eisen ga," published by Tsutaya Juzaburo, good impression, color, wormage, binding holes, rubbed and slightly soiled **2,500-3,500**

EIZAN (1787-1867)

Kakemono-e, full-length portrait of a woman in aubergine kimono and green checked obi, blind printing, signed "Eizan hitsu," published by Wakasay Yoichi, good impression, color and condition **6,000-8,000**

Kakemono-e, full-length portrait of a woman wearing an orange kimono with red inner robe, gray sash, signed "Kikugawa Eizan hitsu," fine impression, very good color, small hole on lower right, slightly soiled **4,000-5,000**

GOYO (1880-1921)

Dai oban yoko-e, "Mt. Ibuki in Snow," signed "Goyo ga," dated Taisho 9 (1920), published by Watanabe, from an edition of 100, very good impression, color and condition **3,000-4,000**

Oban yoko-e, Mandarin ducks swimming in a lotus pond, signed "Goyo ga," dated Taisho 9 (1920), very good impression, color and condition, margins slightly trimmed **3,000-4,000**

HARUNOBU (CA. 1724-1770)

Chuban tate-e, two women in an interior, one sleeping under a mosquito net, the other reads a love letter, signed "Harunobu ga," moderate impression, faded, toned, soiled, water stain **3,500-5,500**

Chuban tate-e, children performing as shishimai dancers, signed "Suzuki Harunobu ga," good impression, faded, rubbed, creased, tears repaired **2,000-4,000**

HIROSHIGE I (1797-1858)

Chu-tanzaku, a Mejiro white eye on a persimmon branch, with poem above by Jintei, signed "Hiroshige hitsu," sealed Ichiryusai, good impression, faded, bad edges on right and left side **3,000-4,000**

O-tanzaku, Kacho-e, two swallows, flowering peach branches and full moon with poem above, signed "Hiroshige hitsu," moderate impression, faded, torn, wormage, toned **900-1,500**

Oban tate-e, Mutsu, Matsyushima fukei (View of Matsushima, Mutsu Province), from the series Rokujuyoshu meisho zue (Pictures of Famous Places in the Sixty Odd Provinces), signed "Hiroshige hitsu,"

Hiroshige—"Suijin Grove and Masaki on the Sumida River"

published by Koshimuraya Heisuke, good impression and color, binding holes, margins trimmed **1,500-2,000**

Oban tate-e, Ise futamigaure (The Wedded Rocks in Futami Bay in Ise Province), from the series Fuji sunjurokkei (The Thirty-Six Views of Mt. Fuji), signed "Hiroshige ga," published by Tsutaya Kichizo, good impression and color, wormage restored, slightly toned **800-1,200**

Oban tate-e, Sumidagawa Suijin nomori Masaki "Suijin Grove and Masaki on the Sumida River" from the series Meisho Edo hyakkei "One View of Famous Places in Edo", signed Hiroshige ga, published by Yoya Eikichi, good impression, color, faded, small holes, corner restored, soiled, (ILLUS.)..**900-1,200**

Oban yoko-e, Hodogaya Shimmachibashi (The Shimmachi Bridge, Hodogaya) from the series Tokaido gojusan tsugi no uchi (The Fifty-Three Stations of the Tokaido), signed "Hiroshige ga," published by Koeido/Senkakudo, good impression, color, left margin trimmed, soiled **3,000-5,000**

Oban yoko-e, Hara, asa no Fuji (Fuji in the Morning), from the series "Fifty-Three Stations of the Tokaido," signed "Hiroshige ga," published by Hoeido/Senkakudo, good impression, color, and condition ..**5,000-7000**

Oban yoko-e, Shono hakuu (White rain, Shono), from the series "Fifty Three Stations of the Tokaido," signed "Hiroshige ga," published by Hoeido/Senkakudo, very good impression, color, center fold, stained, margin on left trimmed............**2,500-3500**

As above, fine impression, color, left and right margins trimmed, in-painted **4,000-6,000**

Oban yoko-e, Shono haku-u (White rain, Shono) from the series Tokaido gojusan tsugi no uchi (The Fifty-Three Stations of the Tokaido), signed Hiroshige ga, published by Hoeido/Senkakudo, good impression and color, margins trimmed, toned and rubbed, stained (Color Illus. pg. 213) **6,000-9,000**

Oban yoko-e, Kambara yoru no yuki "Night Snow, Kambara," from the series Tokaido gojusan tsugi no uch "The Fifty-three Stations of the Tokaido," signed Hiroshige ga, published by Hoeido/Senkakudo, very good impression and color, margins trimmed (ILLUS.)..................................**4,000-5,000**

Hiroshige—"Night Snow, Kambara,"

Oban yoko-e, Kameyama yukibare (Clear weather after snow, Kameyama), from the series Tōkaidō gojusan tsugi no uchi (The Fifty-Three Stations of the Tokaido), signed "Hiroshige ga," published by Hoeido/Senkakudo, good impression and color, margins trimmed, soiled, minor wormage **2,000-3,000**

Oban yoko-e, Kameyama yukibare (as above), fine impression and color, margins soiled **10,000-15,000**

Oban yoko-e, Fukushima, station 38 from the series Kisokaido rokujukyutsugi no uch (The Sixty-Nine Stations of the Kisokaido), signed "Hiroshige ga," published by Iseya Rihei, good impression and color, minor tears restored, left margin slightly trimmed **1,000-1,500**

HIROSHIGE II (1829-1869)

Bikunibashi setchu (In the midst of snow at Bikuni Bridge), from the series Meisho Edo hyakkei (One Hundred Views of Famous Places in Edo), oban tate-e, signed "Hiroshige ga," published by Yoya Eikichi, very good impression, some in-painting, trimmed, tape on verso **1,800-2,700**

Kazusa, Kasamori ji, Iwa tsukuri Kannon (Rock Kannon, Kasamori Temple, Kazusa Province) from the series Shokoku meisho hyakkei (One Hundred Views of Famous Places of all the Provinces), oban tate-e, signed "Hiroshige ga," published by Yoya Eikichi, good impression, color, slightly toned **2,000-3,000**

Shinshu, Suwako yatsune unagi akazaka nao toru (Eel and red fish fishing at Lake Suwa, Shinshu Province), from the series "One Hundred Views of Famous Places in all the Provinces," signed "Hiroshige ga," published by Yoya Eikichi, good impression, color and condition **2,000-3,000**

Suo Iwakuni no Kintaibashi (Kintai Bridge), series as above, signed "Hiroshige ga," published by Yoya Eikichi, good impression, slightly faded, surface dirt **1,500-2,500**

HOKUSAI (1760-1849)

Oban yoko-e, Kanagawa okinami ura "The Great Wave" (Hollow of the wave off Kanagawa), from the series Fugaku sanjurokkei "The Thirty-six Views of Mt. Fuji", signed Hokusai aratame Itsu hitsu, published by Eijudo (Nishimuraya Yohachi), blue outline, good impression, faded, center fold, wormage, stained, restorations (ILLUS.) **30,000-40,000**

Oban yoko-e, Kanagawa oki nami ura (In the well of the great wave off Kanagawa) from the series Fugaku sanjurokkei (The Thirty-six Views of Mt. Fuji), signed "Hokusai aratame Iitsuhitsu," published by Eijudo (Nishimuraya Yohachi), blue outlines, good impression, faded, foxed, restored, tape on verso **25,000-35,000**

Oban yoko-e, as above, a Meiji period reproduction **300-500**

Oban yoko-e, a view of farmers working in a field, and thatched roofs of a village, the poem of Dainagon Tsunenobu, from the series Hyakunin isshu uba ga etoki (The One Hundred Poems As Told By The Nurse), signed "Zen Hokusai," published by Nishimuray Yohachi, good impression, faded, creased, toned, wormage, backed **1,000-1,500**

Oban yoko-e, Tokaido Okazaki Yahagi no hashi (Yahagi Bridge at Okazaki on the Tokaido) from the series "Wondrous Views of Famous Bridges In All The Provinces," signed "Zen Hokusai Iitsu hitsu," published by Nishimuraya Yohachi (Eijudo), fair impression, toned and faded, rubbed, backed **1,000-1,500**

HOSHI JOICHI (1913-1979)

Autumn Light (Shuko), signed "J. Hoshi" and sealed, dated "'78," framed, (condition unknown) **700-900**

Summer Day, signed "Joichi Hoshi" and sealed, dated "'77," framed (condition unknown) **700-900**

Hokusai—"The Great Wave"

Yellow Forest, dai oban yoko-e, signed and dated "Joichi Hoshi 75," tape on verso, tape on edges, toned **1,000-1,800**

White Tree, Soshun (Early Spring), signed in pencil and dated "'74," framed and glazed **600-800**

ITO SHINSUI (1898-1972)

A Dressing Beauty (Kesho Bijin), dai oban tate-e, signed and sealed, from a limited edition of 250, published by Katsumura, 1935, good impression, good color, slightly toned, slightly trimmed **1,500-1,800**

After the Bath (Yoku-go) dai oban tate-e, from the series "The Collection of Modern Beauties, No. 1," signed "Shinsui" and sealed, published by Watanabe, dated Showa 5 (1939), good impression, faded, the verso browned, trimmed...............**1,000-1,500**

Gifu Lantern (Gifu Chochin), from the series "The Collection of Modern Beauties No. 1," dai oban tate-e, a woman hanging a lantern, signed and sealed "Shinsui ga," published by Watanabe, dated "Summer 1930," good impression, good color, slightly trimmed, tape on verso, minor foxing....................................**2,000-3,000**

Scent of hot spring water (Yu no kaori), from the series "The Collection of Modern Beauties, No. 1," dai oban tate-e, a woman standing on rock drying her feet after a bath, signed and sealed "Shinsui ga," published by Watanabe, dated Showa 5 (1930), good impression, slightly toned and faded, tape stains on verso **1,200-1,800**

Snowy Morning (Asa No Yuki), dai oban tate-e, signed and sealed, published by Watanabe, 1939, good impression, good color, good condition **1,200-1,800**

KABURAGI KIYOKATA (1878-1973)

Oban tate-e, a beauty kneeling and holding blue cloth, signed "Kiyokata," dated Taisho 12 (1923), good impression and color, laid down on board, slightly foxed..............**1,500-1,800**

Dai oban tate-e, a portrait of a woman standing before a fence and morning glories, a view of two ships at anchor in the background, signed and sealed, good impression and color, foxing, creased **1,000-1,800**

KASAMATSU SHIRO (1898-1992)

Oban tate-e, "Autumn in the Musashi Fields," signed "Shiro," dated Showa 32 (1957), very good impression, color and condition **800-1,200**

Oban tate-e, "Snow at Red Gate Entrance," signed and sealed, dated 1935, published by Watanbe, very good impression, color and condition....................................**1,500-1,800**

Oban tate-e, "Bodhisatva," 1960, from an edition of 100, good impression, color and condition, margins toned, tape on corners of verso **400-600**

Oban tate-e, "Temple in Snow," dated Showa 8 (1933), blue outlines, fine impression, color and condition, signed and sealed Kasamatsu Shiro, published by Watanabe (Color Illus. pg. 214)............**1,500-2,000**

Oban yoko-e, "Great Lantern at Asakusa Temple," signed and sealed, dated 1934, published by Watanabe, very good impression, color and condition **1,200-1,800**

Oban yoko-e, as above but posthumous **200-300**

Oban yoko-e, "Misty Evening at Shinobazu Pond," signed and sealed, dated 1932, published by Watanabe, framed, faded, mat burn **100-200**

Oban yoko-e, as above, good impression, color and condition................................**800-1,200**

KAWASE HASUI (1883-1957)

Ginkaku-ji, "Temple in the Snow, Kyoto," oban tate-e, signed "Hasui" and sealed, published by S. Watanabe, dated 1951, very good impression, very good color, very good condition **1,200-1,800**

As above, mounted on board, faded **200-300**

Inokashira no yuki "Snow at Inokashira" (Benten Shrine), dai oban tate-e, signed "Hasui" and sealed, published by Watanabe Shozaburo, dated Showa 3 (1928), good impression and color, tape residue on edges, rubbed and creased, stained along top and bottom....**900-1,200**

Kintai-Baishi, "Bridge in Spring Evening," Yamaguchi, oban tate-e, signed "Hasui" and sealed, published by S. Watanabe, dated 1947, very good impression, very good color, very good condition **1,800-2,200**

Oban tate-e, "Evening At Tago No Ura," dated Showa 15 (1940), signed and sealed Hasui (Kawase), published by Watanabe, fine impression, color and condition (Color Illus. pg. 214) **1,500-2,000**

Oban tate-e, "Terajima Village in a Snowy Twilight," Mukojima, Tokyo, signed and sealed Hasui (Kawase), fine impression and color, margins trimmed, dated 1920 (Color Illus. pg. 215) **2,500-3,500**

"Nightfall in Snow at Terajima Village" (Yuki no kururu Terajimamura), from the series "Twelve Views of Tokyo" (Tokyo junikei), oban tate-e, signed "Hasui" and dated on the image Taisho 9 (1920), published by Watanabe, very good impression, color and condition **6,500-8,500**

"Nightfall in Snow at Terajima Village," as above, good impression, color, margins trimmed to image **1,500-2,000**

Shiobara arayu no aki "Fall at Arayu hot spring in Shiobara," from the series Tabi miyage dai isshu (Souvenirs of my travels—first series), oban yoko-e, signed "Hasui" and sealed, dated Taisho 9 (1920), published by Watanabe Shozaburo, good impression and condition, toned margins into image, faded, tape on verso, otherwise good condition **550-900**

As above, very good impression and color, margins trimmed, tape residue on verso..**1,200-1,800**

As above, fine condition, fine impression, very good color **6,000-8,000**

Tsuruoka Hachimangu "Tsuruoka Hachiman Shrine," dai oban tate-e, signed "Hasui" and sealed, published by S. Watanabe, dated Showa 6, (1931), good impression, good color, soiled and trimmed margins, tape stains at top **800-1,200**

KIYOSHI SAITO (b. 1907)

Dai oban tate-e, "Maiko, Kyoto," series L, 196, signed in white ink, very good impression, color and condition **3,500-4,500**

Dai oban tate-e, "Iyacko-in Kyoto," 1966 from an edition of 50, signed and sealed, good impression, color and condition ..**1,500-2,500**

Oban yoko-e, "White Horse," unlimited edition, signed an sealed, good impression, color and condition...................................**300-500**

Oban yoko-e, "Snow in Aizu," signed and sealed, good impression, color and condition, light paper backing **600-900**

Oban yoko-e, "Teahouse," unlimited, signed and sealed, good impression, color and condition **300-500**

KOBAYASHI KIYOCHIKA (1847-1915)

"Evening View of Toranomono" (Toranomon yukei), oban yoko-e, signed Kobayashi Kiyochika, published by Fukuda Kumanjiro, dated Meiji 13 (1880), very good impression, color, right margin trimmed, dirt spots................................**2,000-3,000**

"Fireflies At Ochanomizu" (Ochanomizu hotaru), signed and published by Matsuki Heikichi, very good impression and color, slightly trimmed....................................**1,800-2,500**

"Moon and Sea at Kawasaki" (Kawasaki gekkai), oban yoko-e, signed "Kobayashi Kiyochika hitsu" and published by Fukuda Kumanjiro, dated Meiji 10 (1877), good impression, color and condition **1,500-2,500**

"Night at the Sumida River" (Sumidagawa yoru), oban yoko-e, two figures in silhouette on the riverbank, signed "Kobayashi Kiyochika" and published by Fukuda Kumanjiro, dated Meiji 10 (1877), very good impression and color, margins trimmed, dirt spots........**1,500-2,500**

"Night Festival," oban yoko-e, signed Kiyochika hitsu, published by Fukuda Kumanjiro, dated Meiji 10 (1877), very good impression, color and condition (Color Illus. pg. 213) **3,500-4,500**

"View of Flourishing Horidome" (Horidome hanka no zu), oban yoko-e, signed "Kobayashi Kiyochika hitsu," published by Fukuda Kumajiro, dated Meiji 10 (1877), very good impression, color and condition **4,000-7,000**

KUNICHIKA (1835-1900):

Oban tate-e, "Beauty and Sho (musical instrument)," dated Dec. 1878, fine impression, color and condition (Color Illus. pg. 218) **1,000-1,500**

Okubi-e of Kawarazaki Gonnosuke (Ichikawa Danjuro IX) in the role of Daroku, from the play Nani oboshi kanagaki fude, Meiji 2 (5/1869), signed "Kunichika hitsu," published by Gusokuya Kahei, very fine impression, color and condition **3,000-5,000**

Triptych showing the actor Ichikawa Sadanji I in the role of the otkodate Danjuro Bozu Sankichi, from the series Haiyu otokodate den (Actors as Chivalrous Men), signed "Toyohara Kunichika hitsu," published by Akiyama

Buemon, dated Meiji 27 (1894), very good impression, color, trimmed, binding holes, backed **800-1,300**

Triptych of Ichikawa Danjuro IX in the role of Komatsu Shigemori, from the series Shijuhachijo kenja koseki (48 Wise Men), signed "Oju Toyohara Kunichika hitsu," published by Sasaki Toyokichi, dated Meiji 23 (1890), very good impression, color, backed, slightly trimmed, foxing **700-1,200**

Triptych from "Tales of Genji," Prince Genji with objects floating in a bowl for good luck, oban, signed "Kunichika ga," published by Kiya Sojiro, dated 1862, good impression, color and condition ..**1,200-1,800**

Triptych, oban, Ichikawa Danjuro as Uesugi Kenshin and Nakamura Shikan as Wada Masayuki from the series "A Famous Mirror of Modern Times" (Tosei komei kagami), signed, published by Kurata Tasuke, dated Meiji 15 (1882), good impression, water stains (red pigment blurred and smeared overall), otherwise good condition **200-300**

KUNISADA I (1786-1865)
(changed his name to Toyokuni III in 1844)

Aiban uchiwa-e, from the series Furyu yami no kaori (Elegant Perfume of the Dark), signed "Konomi ni oji Toyokuni ga," published by Kojimaya Jihei, good impression, toned, soiled, wormage, trimmed **300-500**

Kakemono, "Japanese Woman Walking in the Snow," signed "Kochoro Kunisada ga," published by Sanoya Kihei, very good impression, faded, toned, trimmed, backed, minor holes on lower left........**2,000-3,000**

Oban tate-e, triptych, "A View of the Interior of a Brothel" (Shoka nairan shuken zu), signed "Kunisada ga, " published by Tsuruya Kinsuke, very good impression and color, wormage restored, trimmed, toned from old mat and framing **800-1,200**

Oban tate-e, "A Hero with Tatoos," from the series Kinsei Suikoden (Modern Sukoden), signed "Toyokuni ga," published by Ise-, ane, good impression, soiled, stained, wormage, creased, backed **150-225**

Oban tate-e, "Choryo on a Dragon," from the series "Battle Tales of the Han and

Chu," signed "Oju Gototei Kunisada ga," published by Nishimuraya Yohachi, good impression and color, trimmed, backed, and toned into image from old mat **300-550**

Oban yoko-e, okubi-e, the actor Sawamura Sojuro IV from the series Yakusha hanjimono (Actor Puzzles), signed "Gototei Kunisada ga," published by Nishimuraya Yohachi, good impression and color, wormage restored, rubbed and soiled................**3,500-5,500**

Oban yoko-e, "Beauties at the Gate to a Villa in the Snow," signed "Gototei Kunisada ga," good impression, faded, center crease, binding holes, minor wormage **300-500**

Oban yoko-e, two women and Ariwara no Narihira walking on a bridge in a garden of irises, signed "Kochoro Kunisada ga," published by Yamaguchiya Tobei, good impression, faded, creases, torn corners restored, soiled, trimmed..........**200-275**

KUNIYOSHI (1798-1861)

Oban tate-e, Omi Shimidzu no Kwanja Yoshitaka and the rat, from the series "The Sixty Odd Provinces of Japan," signed, published by Yawata-ya Sakujiro, ca. 1845, good impression, color and condition **800-1,200**

Oban tate-e, Kokusempu Riki destroying the gate to the Hakuryojin Temple with an ax, from the series Tsuzoku Suikoden goketsu hyakuhachinin no hitori (The Hundred and Eight Heroes of the Popular Suikoden), signed "Ichiyusai Kuniyoshi ga," published by Kagaya Kichiemon, good impression and color, wormage restored, backed with heavy paper..........**800-1,200**

Oban tate-e, Shin-Ohashi kyoka no chobo (The View Beneath the Shin Ohashi Bridge), form the series Toto fujimi sanjurokkei (Thirty-Six Views of Mt. Fuji from the Eastern Capital), signed "Ichiyusai Kuniyoshi ga," published by Marataya Jirobei, good impression, center crease, margins trimmed into seal, wormage, backed................**3,000-4,000**

Oban yoko-e, "The Heavenly Weaver," from the series Nijushiko doji kagami (A Mirror for Children of the Twenty Four Paragons of Filial Piety), signed "Ichiyusai Kuniyoshi ga," published by Wakasaya Yoichi, good impression, faded, wormage, binding holes, top margin trimmed **800-1,200**

Oban yoko-e, "Saijun attacked by Robbers," from the series Morokoshi nijushiko (The Twenty-Four Chinese Paragons of Filial Piety), signed "Ichiyusai Kuniyoshi ga," published by Izumiya Ichibei, good impression and color, margins trimmed, wormage **800-1,200**

Migata Toshihide (1863-1925)

Oban tate-e, from the series Bijin Junishi (Beautiful Women for the 12 Months), 9th month, a woman gazing at the falling maple leaves, signed "Toshihide," published Akiyama Buemon, dated Meiji 34 (1901),very good impression, color and condition **1,000-1,500**

Oban tate-e, from the series Sanshogo Sugata, dated Meiji 26 (1894), signed and sealed Toshihide (Migata), fine impression, color, very good condition (Color Illus. pg. 218)................**900-1,200**

Okubi-e, Ichikawa Danjuro IX in the role of Benkei, from Danjuro juchaiban, oban tate-e, published by Sasaki Toyo, dated Meiji 26 (1885), very good impression, color and condition **600-900**

Triptych, Ichikawa Danjuro VIII as Kato no Kiyomasa, from the series Taiko gunki Chosen no maki (Military Exploits of Hideyoshi), signed and sealed, published by Sasaki Toyokichi, dated Meiji 24 (1891), good impression, color, right sheet trimmed, some toning, foxing........**800-1,200**

Mori Yoshitoshi (1898-1992)

Akazaya, signed "Y. Mori," and sealed, dated "'77," good condition......................**275-475**

Yoichi No Ninoya, signed "Yoshitoshi Mori" and sealed, dated "'71," good condition **300-500**

Munakata Shiko (1903-1975)

"Becoming Buddha," sumizuri-e (black and white) and color, signed and sealed, good condition **3,000-4,000**

"Fireflies on a Summer Evening," sumizuri-e and color, a woman wearing a yukata passing on a stone bridge along a bamboo fence, a poem about fireflies above, from the series Utautaban gasaku no uci, Hotaru-zoe, signed in pencil and sealed, dated 1956, laid down, framed, toned **3,000-4,000**

"Fish, Flower, Buddha," signed in pencil and sealed, dated 1957, sumizuri-e (black and white), tape on verso, foxing, toned, trimmed, 17" x 12⅞" **2,000-3,000**

"On the Beach," sumizuri-e (black and white), from the series "The Story of the Cormorant," signed and sealed, 13" x 16", trimmed, slightly toned, foxed, tape on verso....................................**2,500-3,500**

Natori Shunsen (1886-1960)

Okubi-e, Bando Hikosaburo as Matsuo in the play Sugawa wearing a white kimono decorated with pine, sealed Natori, signed "Shunsen," published by S. Watanabe, good condition **500-700**

Okubi-e, Ichikawa Uzaemon XI, oban tate-e, mica ground, signed and sealed, published by Watanabe, ca. 1920s, good condition **700-900**

Okubi-e, Nakamura Tomijuro IV as a dancing kamuro, oban tate-e, dated Showa 27 (1952), good condition, slightly toned **450-600**

Ogata Gekko (1859-1920)

"Plum Blossom Garden at Koshikawa" (Koishikawa baien), from the series "Modern Images of Elegant Women" (Fujin fuzoku ga), oban tate-e, signed "gekko," published by Matsuki Heikichi, dates Meiji 31 (1898), good impression and color, backed (from an album) **350-550**

Oban tate-e, from the series "Customs and Manners of Ladies," a woman watches fireworks from her balcony, signed and sealed, published by Sasaki Ugen, dated Meiji 24 (1891), fine impression, color and condition............................**300-500**

Oban tate-e, from the series "A Selection of Elegant Ladies," two women looking at a snow-covered garden, signed and sealed, published by Sasaki Ugen, dated Meiji 24 (1891), fine impression, color and condition **300-500**

Ohara Shoson (1877-1945)
(also used the name Koson)

Geese among water reeds on a black ground, oban tate-e, signed "Shoson," published by Watanabe, dated 1928, from an edition of 300, good impression, color and condition....................**800-1,200**

"**Goose Landing in the Water,**" hosoban, signed Koson and sealed, fine impression, color and condition **700-900**

"**Two White Herons Flying Past Bamboo,**" oban tate-e, signed and sealed "Shoson," published by Watanabe, good impression, color and condition **800-1,200**

PAUL JACOULET (1902-1960)

Christmas Cards:

"**Le Bonze Errant, Coree,**" in original folder with yellow design on cover, good condition **200-300**

"**Les Jades: Mandchoukuo,**" in original folder with red design on cover, excellent condition **300-500**

As above, toned and faded image **50-100**

"**Longevite,**" original folder with red design on cover, very good condition **200-300**

"**Pelerinages (Japon),**" original folder, toned and browned with mat burn **45-90**

"**Vieil Aino Hokkaido,**" original folder with green design on cover, very good condition **300-500**

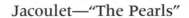

Jacoulet—"The Pearls"

Dai Oban tate-e:

"**Fumes De Santal,**" Mandchuoukuo (Sandalwood Smoke), signed in pencil, Mitsu-Tomoe seal, carved by Kentaro Maeda and printed by Shunosuke Fujii, published 1948, from an edition of 350, dedicated to King George VI of England, slight toning on reverse, mat adhered to front margins **2,500-3,500**

"**La Balance Chinois,**" (The Scale), signed in pencil lower right above Tea Jar seal. seals of the carver, Kentaro Maeda and printer Fusakichi Ogawa in lower right margin, from an edition of 350. Published 5 February 1939. Very good impression, color, slightly toned (Color Illus. pg. 218) **850-1,000**

"**La Chenille Verte. Coree**" (**The Green Caterpillar**), signed in pencil, Daikoku Mallet seal, carved by Kentaro Maeda, printed by Matashiro Uchikawa, published 1936, edition of 350, good condition, mica rubbed **800-1,200**

"**La Geisha Kiyoka, Tokyo**" (The Geisha, Kiyoka), signed in pencil lower left, Mandarin duck seal, carved by Kentaro Maeda, printed by Matashiro Uchikawa, published May 1935, series of 350, fine condition, slight browning on the back **2,000-3,500**

"**La Peche Miraculeuse. Isu, Japon**" (**The Miraculous Catch. Izu, Japan**), signed in pencil, Boat seal, carved by Maeda, printed by Onodera, published 1939, very good condition **2,500-3,500**

"**Le Peche Miraculeuse. Isu, Japon,**" as above but first printing, printer Uchikawa Honda, published 1939, from an edition of 100, very good condition..................**3,500-5,000**

"**La Bonze Errant. Coree**" (**The Wandering Buddhist Priest, Korea**), signed in pencil, Peach seal, carved by Kentaro Maeda and printed by Tetsunosuke Honda, published 1948, from an edition of 250, toned and faded, some foxing.....................................**300-600**

"**Le Marie. Seoul, Coree**" (**The Bridegroom, Seoul, Korea**), signed in pencil, Owl seal, carved by Maeda, printed by Uchikawa, from an edition of 100, published 1950.....................................**1,800-2,500**

"**Le Marie. Seoul, Coree,**" as above, laid down on board and framed **275-400**

"Les Jades. Chinoise" (Jade Lady), signed in pencil, Boat Seal, carved by Kentaro Maeda and printed by Shunosuke Fujii, published 1940, edition of 350, very good condition **2,500-3,500**

"Les Perles," Mandchoukuo, "The Pearls," signed in pencil lower left, seals of the carver, Kentaro Maeda, and printer, Tetsunosuke Honda, December 1950, fine color and impression, toned margins, reverse toned, (ILLUS.)...........................**800-1,200**

"Retour D'Un Banquet. Coree Seoul" (After the Banquet. Seoul, Korea), signed in pencil, Owl seal, carved by Maeda, printed by Onodera Honda, edition of 350, very fine condition **2,500-3,500**

"Retour D'Un Banquet. Coree Seoul," as above, laid down on board, trimmed **500-700**

"Vieillard Au Chapelet Kawadzu" (The Old Man in the Chapel, Mr. Kawada), signed in pencil, Butterfly seal, carved by Kentaro Maeda, printed by Fusakichi Ogawa, published 1940, edition of 300, good color, laid down on board.................**300-500**

Kotondo—"Rain"

SASAJIMA KIHEI (b. 1906)

"White Road," embossed, signed in pencil, from an edition of 50............................**1,200-1,600**

TAJIMA HIROYUKI (1911-1984)

"Altar," dai oban tate-e, 1972, 9/50........**1,000-1,500**

"An Exile (C)," dai oban yoko-e, 1970, 1/50 ....**1,000-1,500**

"Wild Grape (A)," dai oban tate-e, 1968, 1/100 ....**1,000-1,500**

TORII KOTONDO (1900-1976)

"Morning Hair (Asa negami)," dai oban tate-e, a portrait of beauty resting her chin on a pillow, mosquito netting serving as the background, signed and sealed, from a series of 100, very good impression, color and condition....................................**15,000-18,000**

As previous, faded, foxing, verso browned, tape residue on verso...........................**1,500-1,800**

"Rain" (Ame), dai oban tate-e, 1929, published by Sakai and Kawaguchi from an edition of 200, fine impression, color, condition (ILLUS.) **5,500-7,500**

"Rain" (Ame), dai oban tate-e, signed "Kotondo ga," published by Sakai and Kawaguchi of Tokyo, dated 1929, good impression, good color and condition **1,500-2,000**

As above, very good impression, very good color, very fine condition **4,000-6,000**

TOYOKUNI I (1769-1825)

Aiban tate-e, double portrait of actors Ichikawa Yaozo and Segawa Kikunojo, signed "Toyokuni ga," published by Nishimuraya Yohachi, good impression, trimmed, wormage, faded **1,200-1,800**

Oban tate-e, a single sheet from a triptych, three women on a verandah looking out at a garden, signed "Toyokuni ga," published by Izumiya Ichibei, good impression and color, backed, restored at top corners **500-700**

Oban yoko-e, Furyu uki-e Megurosan no zu (Fashionable Perspective View of Mt. Meguro), signed "Utagawa Toyokuni," published by Izumiya Ichibei, good impression and color, binding holes, minor wormage **1,000-1,500**

TOYOKUNI II (1777-1835)

Oban yoko-e, Kamakura bansho (Evening Bell, Kamakura) from the series Meisho hakkei (Eight Views of Famous Places), signed "Toyokuni hitsu," sealed Utagawa, published by Iseya Riehi, good impression, faded and toned, foxing, soiled, center crease, scotch tape residue on verso........**800-1,200**

TSUCHIYA KOITSU (1870-1949)

Oban tate-e, "Two Beauties at Yosuya," dated 1936, signed and sealed, published by Doi, very good impression, color and condition **650-950**

Oban yoko-e, "Spring Snow in Maruyama Park," posthumous, very good impression, ca. 1963 ....**200-300**

Oban yoko-e, "View of Mt. Fuji," dated 1933, signed and sealed, very good impression, color and condition **600-900**

Oban yoko-e, "Fishing with Cormorants," dated Showa 15 (1940), signed and sealed Koitsu, published by Watanabe, fine impression, color and condition (Color Illus. pg. 215) **750-950**

Oban yoko-e, as above, a posthumous print **200-300**

TSUKIOKA KOGYO (1869-1927)

Kami (Spirit), from the series Nogaku hyakuban (One Hundred No-plays), oban tate-e, an actor in the role of the spirit of a deceased person, fine impression, color and condition................................**300-500**

"Two Actors," from the series Nogaku hyakuan (One Hundred No-plays), oban tate-e, set on a yellow background, signed and sealed Kogyo, dated 1900, fine impression, color and condition **300-500**

"The Spider Monster" (No play Tsuchigumo), from the series Nogaku hyakuban (One Hundred No-plays), oban tate-e, signed and sealed "Kogyo," published by Matsuki Keikichi, dated 1899, fine impression, color, condition **300-450**

YOSHIDA HIROSHI (1876-1950)

Dai oban yoko-e, "Mt. Rainier," signed in brush Yoshida and in pencil Hiroshi Yoshida, jizuri seal, dated Taisho 14 (1925), good impression, color, toned from mat and frame, some soiling, laid down (ILLUS.) **400-600**

Dai oban yoko-e, "Sea of Cloud," signed Yoshida and Hiroshi Yoshida in pencil, jizuri seal, dated Showa 3 (1928), very good impression, good color, minor toning in margins, creases..............................**4,000-6,000**

Oban tate-e, Toshogu Shrine, Showa 2 (1927), jizuri seal, signed in pencil "Hiroshi Yoshida," very good impression, color and condition. When this print was new it retailed for $15. (Color Illus. pg. 214) **1,000-1,500**

Oban tate-e, "Study of a Nude," signed in pencil "Hiroshi Yoshida," jizuri seal, dated Showa 2 (1927), good impression, color and condition **1,000-1,500**

Oban tate-e, "Himeji Castle, Evening," dated 1926, jizuri seal, good impression, toned, browning on verso **400-700**

Oban tate-e, "Singapore," jizuri seal, dated 1931, very good impression, good color, good condition **800-1,200**

TSUKIOKA YOSHITOSHI (1839-1892)

Chuban, from the series Yoshitoshi ryakuga (Sketched by Yoshitoshi), Empress Jingu fishing for a cat, signed and sealed Yoshitoshi, published by Funazu, dated 10/5/1882, very good impression, color and condition with blind printing **400-600**

Chuban, same series as above, Kaika no Daruma, the zen priest Daruma as the client of a courtesan, signed Yoshitoshi, seal Taiso, published by Funazu, dated 15/5/1882, very good impression, color and condition...**500-700**

Oban tate-e, "The Moon of the Oban Festival," from the series "100 Aspects of the Moon," dancing women in the moonlight, signed "Yoshitotshi," sealed Taiso, published by Akiyama Buemon, dated 1886, good impression, color and condition **800-1,200**

Oban tate-e, as above, water stains, blurred pigments..**100-200**

Oban tate-e, Saimyoji Tokiyori Nyudo standing in the snow, holding his hat, from the series "A Mirror of Famous Japanese Generals," signed and sealed, published by Shojiro Runazu, dated 1878, good, impression, color and condition **600-900**

Yoshida Hiroshi—"Mt. Rainier"

Oban tate-e, Okigatsukiso Meiji nenkan saikunno guzoku, from the series "Thirty-two Aspects of Women," a woman opening a lit paper lantern, signed Yoshitoshi, published by Tsunashima Kamekichi, good impression, color and condition **800-1,000**

Oban tate-e, a No actor holding a long staff, from the series "One Hundred Aspects of the Moon," signed "Yohsitoshi," published by Akiyama Buemon, dated Meiji 20 (1887), good impression, color and condition **800-1,200**

Oban tate-e, "Faith in the Third Day Moon, Yukimori," from the series "One Hundred Aspects of the Moon," 1886, signed "Yoshitoshi," seal Taiso, published by Akiyama, good impression, color and condition **650-850**

Oban tate-e, "A Poem by Mizuki Tatsunosuke" from the series "The 100 Aspects of the Moon," dated Meiji 24 (1891), 6th month (June), signed Yoshitoshi, seal Taiso, published by Akiyama Buemon, carved by Chokuzan, fine impression, color and condition (Color Illus. pg. 218)..............................**800-1,200**

Oban tate-e, Chinzei Hachiro Tametomo and Oniyasha from the series "A Mirror of Famous Japanese Generals," dated Meiji 12 (1879), signed "Oju Yoshitoshi," seal Taiso, published by Chujiro Funazu, fine impression, color, and very good condition (Color Illus. pg. 218) **750-950**

Oban tate-e, "Moon at Ogurusu in Yamashitro. The Ambush of Akechi

Mitsuhide by Moonlight," from the series "The 100 Aspects of the Moon," signed "Yoshitoshi," seal Taiso, published by Akiyama, carver Enkatsu, dated Meiji 19 (1886), fine impression, color and condition (Color Illus. pg. 218) **900-1,200**

Oban tate-e, "The Moon of Sumiyoshi" from the series "The 100 Aspects of the Moon," dated Meiji 20 (1887), 6th month 23rd day (June 23), signed "Yoshitoshi," seal Taiso, published by Akiyama Buemon, carver Yamamoto, fine impression, color and condition (Color Illus. pg. 218) **800-1,200**

UTAGAWA YOSHITORA (ACTIVE 1850-1880)

Oban tate-e, from the series Edo ga no kei (Views of Scenes in Edo), a teahouse beauty holding a sake cup, next to her a telephone pole and gaslight, signed, dated Meiji 12 (1880), very good impression, color and condition **2,000-3,000**

UTAMARO (1750-1806)

Oban tate-e, Nakadaya (The Nakadaya Teahouse), signed "Utamaro hitsu," published by Yamaguchiya Chusuke, good impression, toned, soiled, restored along edges and corners **1,000-1,500**

Oban tate-e, a bijin holding a bucket, signed "Utamaro hitsu," dated 1805, publisher Iwai-ya, good impression, faded, backed, soiled **1,000-1,500**

Oban tate-e, "Feeding the Silk Worms," from the set Joshoku kaiko tewaza-kusa (Silkworm Culture—Handiwork of Women), signed "Utamaro hitsu," published by Tsuruya Kinsuke, good impression, faded, stained, soiled, backed **1,000-1,500**

Oban tate-e, single sheet from a triptych, courtesan dancing, titled "Seven Drunken Shojo," signed "Utamaro suichu hitsu," good impression, faded, soiled, stained, holes...**400-600**

Oban tate-e, a bust portrait of Okita of the Naniwaya holding a hand towel in her teeth, signed "Utamaro hitsu," published by Yamaguchiya Chusuke, good impression, faded, laid down **3,500-5,500**

Illustrated right
   Japanese kagamibuta (netsuke),
   Satsuma ware, early 19th c.
                    $2,500-3,500

———————————●———————————

Illustrated below
   Japanese boxwood Kiseruzutsu,
   late 18th or early 19th c., senryu-
   zutsu-type, with inlaid ivory
   and ivory basket with pierced
   work, pipe not original and of a
   later date, 7¾" l.

                    $2,000-3,000

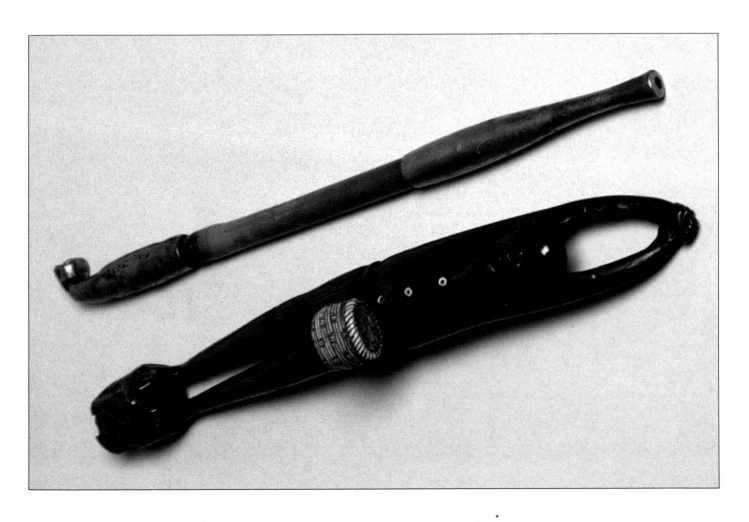

Illustrated Top Right:
Japanese netsuke, ivory, all the animals of the zodiac with coral inlay, signed "Masatsugu" but the work of 20th c. artist Masatoshi.
$5,500-6,500

Illustrated Above:
Chinese Coromandel screen, 19th c., black lacquer screen with scenic design of a palace garden, foliate borders, the reverse with flowers and birds, 100"·h. x 128" w.
$5,000-7,500

Illustrated Bottom Right:
Japanese netsuke, ivory, 20th c., four figures in a dragon boat upon waves, signed "Sosui."
$3,000-4,000

Illustrated left:
Chinese porcelain snuff bottle, Qianlong mark but ca. 1800, Famille Rose palette with decoration molded in relief, the reverse with figure of a woman.

$900-1,200

Illustrated top right:
Chinese porcelain double snuff bottle, Guangxu mark and period, designs of roosters.

$550-750

Illustrated bottom right:
Chinese glass snuff bottles, 18th c.: left - milk glass with red overlay, $800-1,200; right - snowflake glass with red overlay pattern of "100 Antiques."

$1,000-1,500

Illustrated left:
Chinese Snuff Bottle, amber with basketweave pattern, well hollowed.

$600-900

IIllustrated left:

Eastern Tibetan Mandala Thanka of the Dakini Na-ro kha-cho-ma, Karma Gadri style, ca. 17th c., the dakini striding vigorously to her left and trampling two figures, her head arched back and drinking from a blood-filled kapala in her raised left hand, a karttrka in her right hand, a khavtvanga balanced on one shoulder, the goddess within a three-dimensional six-pointed star within a three-storied pagoda inhabited in the upper levels by a large group of lamas and a figure of Vajradhara, six ecstatically dancing celestial attendants at the base of the structure, the pagoda encircled by three concentric bands of lotus petals, a band with seven cemetery scenes interspersed by rivers, and an outer band of flames, the lower corners with the guardian of the north, Vaisravana, seated on his lion at the right, two citapati dancing within a house composed of human bones at the left, the sky filled with attendants, four lamas, and a figure of Cakrasamvara flanked by Simhavaktra and another dakini, approximately 30" x 20" framed.

$12,000-18,000

IIllustrated above:

Tibetan Thanka, 18th c., 11-headed Lokeshvara, each of the six arms with attributes, standing on lotus base before an aureole, surrounded by four attendants in the corners, framed, framed size 28½" x 22½".

$1,000-2,000

———————————●———————————

IIllustrated left:

A Tibetan bronze figure of Aksobhya Buddha, 17th c., seated in dhyanasana on a lotus throne with a vajra in front, his hands in bhumisparsa and dhyana mudra, wearing a sanghati with incised floral hemline, spherical cintamani surmounting his usnisa, 11" h.

$5,500-7,500

IIlustrated above:
Japanese embroidery on silk, Edo Period, design in mon form with metallic gold and silver thread in satin stitch and couching, 15" x 15".

$1,500-2,000

Illustrated top right:

Korean embroidered rank badge, late 19th c., made for a civil official of the 1st to 3rd rank, design of cranes grasping a pulloch'o stalk in mouth, above stylized waves and rockwork amid clouds outlined in couching, the design in shades of blue, green, white, red and purple on a blue ground, framed, approximately 9" x 8".

$2,000-3,000

———————●———————

Illustrated bottom right:

Chinese textile for temple, 19th c., red felt ground, decorated with dragon chasing flaming pearl, surrounded by bats (wufu) and precious objects in satin stitches and Peking knots with borders of immortals, all amid predominately blue clouds, 120" x 90".

$10,000-15,000

———————●———————

Illustrated below:

Chinese lady's jacket, late 19th c., pink silk woven with lotus and butterflies, applied with wide blue borders embroidered with various flowers, butterflies and long-tailed birds, within blue brocade and black ground bands, the cuffs finely worked on the reverse with couched gold and silver threads depicting phoenix, peony and auspicious objects, 35" long.

$1,000-1,500

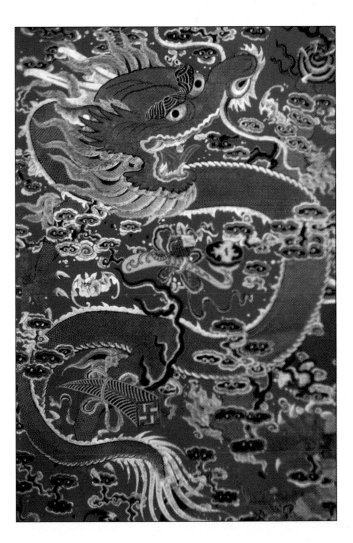

Illustrated left:
Japanese wood carving of Shayamuni, mid- to late-18th c., the Buddha stands upon a graduated lotus base, face is meditative, eyes inlaid with mother-of-pearl, rock crystal on the forehead denoting byakugo (third eye), hair curled and toped by usnisa, cracks and minor restoration to both levels of the base, 38" h.

$10,000-15,000

Illustrated below:
Japanese wood carving of Hotei with staff and sack, Meiji period, 12" h.

$1,200-1,800

Illustrated above:

Hiroshige: oban yoko-e, Shono haku-u (White rain, Shono) from the series Tokaido gojusan tsugi no uchi (The fifty-three stations of the Tokaido), signed Hiroshige ga, published by Hoeido/Senkakudo, good impression and color, margins trimmed, toned and rubbed, stained.

$6,000-9,000

———————————————●———————————————

Illustrated right:

Woodblock print: Kiyochika, oban yoko-e; "Night Festival," signed Kiyochika hitsu, published by Fukuda Kumanjiro, dated Meiji 10 (1877), very good impression, color and condition.

$3,500-4,500

Illustrated top left
Woodblock print: Yoshida, oban tate-e; Toshogu Shrine, Showa 2 (1927), jizuri seal, signed in pencil "Hiroshi Yoshida," very good impression, color and condition. (When this print was new it retailed for $15.)

$1,000-1,500.

Illustrated bottom left
Woodblock print: Hasui, oban tate-e; "Evening At Tago No Ura," dated Showa 15 (1940), signed and sealed Hasui (Kawase), published by Watanabe, fine impression, color and condition.

$1,500-2,000

Illustrated bottom right
Woodblock print: Kasamatsu Shiro, oban tate-e; "Temple in Snow," dated Showa 8 (1933), blue outlines, fine impression, color and condition, signed and sealed Kasamatsu Shiro, published by Watanabe.

$1,500-2,000

Illustrated right:
Woodblock print: Koitsu, oban yoko-e; "Fishing with Cormorants," dated Showa 15 (1940), signed and sealed Koitsu, published by Watanabe, fine impression, color and condition.

$750-950

Illustrated below:
Woodblock print: Hasui, oban tate-e, "Terajima Village in a Snowy Twilight," Mukojima, Tokyo, signed and sealed Hasui (Kawase), fine impression and color, margins trimmed, dated 1920.

$2,500-3,500

Gold Medallion China

LONG before the Orient opened its doors to Western trading, Gold Medallion China — "The aristocrat of the chinaware world"—was the pride of the American house-wife.

❧ Then as now it represented all that was best in chinaware and fortunate, indeed, was the woman who could point to a limited collection of it.

❧ The Gold Medallion China imported by us is manufactured in exactly the same manner as that brought home by the Far Eastern traders of early Colonial days, and its exquisite colorings and artistic designs are more popular to-day than ever.

❧ For the hostess who seeks Chinaware of distinctiveness and individuality, there is nothing that can compare with Gold Medallion, and being an "open pattern," you may buy an entire set or only a few pieces and add to these from time to time until your set is complete.

❧ Because of its artistic decorative appearance and serviceability it is particularly appropriate for wedding gifts, and as our stock always includes a large supply of all pieces, the recipient is afforded the pleasure of collecting additional pieces from time to time, as needed.

For complete price list of Gold Medallion China, see page 48.

Author's note:

These advertisements are reproduced from a catalogue issued by A.A. Vantine & Co., Inc., Fifth Ave. & 39th Street, New York, in 1914. Although the name of the dinner service is Gold Medallion China it is in fact Rose Medallion. The service for both the Medallion and Canton have the same shapes, sizes, and functions as sets made earlier. For the most part, pieces sold by Vantine's were not marked

Canton China

EVERYBODY knows Canton China—the always popular "willow" pattern—with its pagodas, bridges, streams, boats, little figures of men and women, and the love birds. A quaint legend has it that the story depicted on the china tells how a mandarin had an only daughter, Li-Chi, who fell in love with her father's secretary, Chang.

The mandarin forbade the match, so the lovers eloped, hiding for a time in a gardener's cottage, until at last they attempted to make their escape to an island which was Chang's home. The mandarin pursued them, whip in hand and would have killed them had not the gods come to the rescue and changed the two into a pair of turtle doves.

In the design will be seen the mandarin's house with a fence round it, the gardener's cottage, a bridge over which the mandarin ran after his daughter, who, with a staff in hand, was accompanied by Chang. Above are the turtle doves, and beyond is a boat crossing to the island. At the time of the elopement the willow was shedding its leaves, hence the name of the design.

For over half a century Vantine's has been the headquarters in this country for Canton China, and in no other establishment in the United States may be found such a complete assortment as we always carry in stock.

For complete price list of Canton China, see page 48.

with country of origin. Stickers and/or markings on shipping crates were sufficient indicators for country of origin. What is interesting to note is the last line of each page which says, "For over half a century Vantine's has been the headquarters in this country for Canton China, ..." The price list reproduced in Appendix L on page 247 also tells us about the variety of pieces which were produced and their correct names and uses.

Illustrated first row, left:
Woodblock print: Toshihide, oban tate-e; from the series Sanshogo Sugata, dated Meiji 26 (1894), signed and sealed Toshihide (Migata), fine impression, color, very good condition.
$900-1,200

Illustrated first row, right:
Woodblock print: Paul Jacoulet, dai oban tate-e, "La Balance Chinois", (The Scale), signed in pencil lower right above Tea Jar seal. seals of the carver, Kentaro Maeda and printer Fusakichi Ogawa in lower right margin, from an edition of 350. Published 5 February 1939. Very good impression, color, slightly toned.
$850-1,000

Illustrated second row, left:
Woodblock print: Kunichika, oban tate-e, "Beauty and Sho (musical instrument)," dated Dec. 1878, fine impression, color and condition.
$1,000-1,500

Illustrated second row, right:
Woodblock print: Yoshitoshi, oban tate-e; Chinzei Hachiro Tametomo and Oniyasha from the series "A Mirror of Famous Japanese Generals," dated Meiji 12 (1879), signed "Oju Yoshitoshi," seal Taiso, published by Chujiro Funazu, fine impression, color, and very good condition.
$750-950

Illustrated third row, left:
Woodblock print, Yoshitoshi, oban tate-e, "Moon at Ogurusu in Yamashitro. The Ambush of Akechi Mitsuhide by Moonlight," from the series "The 100 Aspects of the Moon," signed "Yoshitoshi," seal Taiso, published by Akiyama, carver Enkatsu, dated Meiji 19 (1886), fine impression, color and condition.
$900-1,200

Illustrated third row, right:
Woodblock print: Yoshitoshi, oban tate-e; "A Poem by Mizuki Tatsunosuke" from the series "The 100 Aspects of the Moon," dated Meiji 24 (1891), 6th month (June), signed Yoshitoshi, seal Taiso, published by Akiyama Buemon, carved by Chokuzan, fine impression, color and condition.
$800-1,200

Illustrated fourth row:
Woodblock print: Yoshitoshi, oban tate-e; "The Moon of Sumiyoshi" from the series "The 100 Aspects of the Moon," dated Meiji 20 (1887), 6th month 23rd day (June 23), signed "Yoshitoshi," seal Taiso, published by Akiyama Buemon, carver Yamamoto, fine impression, color and condition.
$800-1,200

APPENDIX A
CARE, KEEPING AND RESTORATION OF ORIENTAL WORKS OF ART

●

FURNITURE

Light woods, such as kiri, should be cleaned with a solution of 1/3 turpentine, 1/3 vinegar and 1/3 tepid water. Always test the solution on an inconspicuous area. If the solution cleans that area safely, apply it overall. The finest grade steel wood pad will take off old wax and dirt. A shoe polish or hard wax, same color as the finish, should be applied after cleaning. Approximately 12 to 15 layers will be needed for a fine finish. The last layer should be buffed with a soft cloth.

IVORY AND IVORY SUBSTANCES

It is best to use a soft brush for cleaning ivory and ivory substances, although mild soap and warm water can be used to remove surface dirt (provided the object is in perfect condition). To prevent warping and cracking, dry the ivory immediately.

HARDSTONES

Hardstones such as jadeite and nephrite can be washed with mild soap and warm water. Be sure to rinse thoroughly and use a soft cloth for drying. It is important to remember that hardstones, such as lapis lazuli, jadeite, etc., which have been dyed, may lose their color if left soaking for too long.

LACQUER

The best way to clean lacquer wares is by wiping the object with a soft lint-free cloth. Application of a small amount of lemon oil is permissible. Lacquer wares need to be stored in a room with a humidifier. They also need to be rotated from time to time, and must be kept away from dry heat.

METALWARES

The only metalwares which should be cleaned are gold and/or silver. A fine quality polish should be used. Never clean other metals because cleaning will remove the natural patina which is highly prized. Never use abrasive cleaners on metalwares.

POTTERY AND PORCELAIN

Never put pottery or porcelain in the dishwasher! Pottery: A dampened cloth is the best cleaning implement together with dusting. Porcelain: Mild soap and warm water can be used to clean porcelain.

PAINTINGS, SCREEN, AND KAKEMONO (SCROLLS)

Silk and/or paper paintings, screens, and hanging scrolls should be displayed for short periods of time. Never display them in direct sunlight, which causes fading. Storage of painting, screens and scrolls requires keeping them away from sunlight, heat and dampness. Always place acid-free paper in layers between panels or on paintings before rolling them up.

PRINTS

Like scrolls prints should be stored between sheets of acid-free paper. If framed, mats should be acid free. Never hang prints in direct sunlight for it will cause fading.

RESTORATION

Antiques and collectible objects such as, ceramics, ivory, lacquer, metal, paper, etc., are not always found in perfect condition. Objects, including paper, can be professionally restored, whether the restoration is hidden, or in the case of ceramics, mended with gold lacquer and/or silver lacquer. Two restorers recommended by the author are Mike Kaye and Grady Stewart. Mike Kaye does work with various metals, lacquer, wood and ivory. Grady Stewart works with pottery and porcelain. There are restorers who work with paper, paintings, textiles and other forms of art.

Mike Kaye	Grady Stewart
P.O. Box 381	2019 Sansom St.
Oceanside NY 11572	Philadelphia, PA 19103

The author suggests you check locally as well. Don't forget to ask for references as well as looking at completed works.

APPENDIX B
RESEARCH SOURCES

———————————●———————————

MUSEUMS AND ORGANIZATIONS

MUSEUMS:

The Art Institute of Chicago
Michigan Ave. and Adams St.
Chicago, IL 60603

The Boston Museum of Fine Arts
465 Hunt Ave.
Boston, MA 02115

The Brooklyn Museum
188 Eastern Pkwy.
Brooklyn, NY 11238

The Cincinnati Art Museum
Eden Park
Cincinnati, OH 45202

The Cleveland Museum of Art
11150 East Blvd.
Cleveland, OH 44106

The Denver Art Museum
100 W 14 Pkwy.
Denver, CO 80204

The M.H. De Young Memorial Museum
Golden Gate Park
San Francisco, CA 94118

The Freer Gallery of Art (The Sackler)
Washington, DC

Los Angeles County Museum Of Art
5905 Wilshire Blvd.
Los Angeles, CA 90036

The Metropolitan Museum of Art
5th Ave. at 82nd St.
New York, NY 10028

The Minneapolis Institute of Arts
2400 3rd Ave.
Minneapolis, MN 55404

William Rockhill Nelson Gallery of Art
Mary Atkins Museum of Fine Art
4525 Oak St.
Kansas City, MO 64111

The Portland Art Museum
Portland, OR

Royal Ontario Museum
100 Queen's Park
Toronto, Ontario Canada M5S 2C6

Seattle Art Museum
Volunteer Park
Seattle, WA 98112

The Walters Art Gallery
222 State St.
Springfield, MA 01103

Yale University Art Gallery
New Haven, CT 06520

ORGANIZATIONS:

Asia Society
725 Park Ave.,
New York, NY 10021

Society for Japanese Arts
Mr. Pankenstraat 12
5571 CP Bergeyk
The Netherlands

Japan House
33 E. 47 St.
New York, NY 10017

Netsuke Kenkyukai Society
Box 11248
Torrance, CA 90510

The Ukyio-e Society of America
Box 665, F.D.R. Station
New York, NY 10150

The Japanese Sword Society
of the United States, Inc.
P. O. Box 712
Breckenridge, TX 76424

PUBLICATIONS:

Edited and published by Sandra Andacht, The Orientalia Journal is issued four times a year for collectors, dealers, and appraisers. Each issue contains special features and illustrations on such topics as prints, cloisonné, hardstones, pottery, porcelain, netsuke, rugs, paintings, and all other aspects of Orientalia. A question/answer column provides reader responses. The Orientalia Journal costs $21/yr.; $38/2 yrs.(in the US). Its foreign rate is $38 payable in US funds. A single copy and index of articles, $7.50. Payment should be made direct to The Orientalia Journal, P.O. Box 94, Little Neck, New York 11363.

BIBLIOGRAPHY

The author suggests that a good reference library, consisting of both general references as well as specific areas of interest, is essential for collectors and dealers. Suggested titles include:

Andacht, Sandra. *The Orientalia Journal Annual of Articles*. Little Neck, New York: Sandra Andacht Publishing. 1982

Beurdeley, M., *Chinese Furniture*, New York; Kodansha International USA, Ltd., 1979

Bushel, Raymond. *Collector's Netsuke*, Salem, Mass.; John Weatherhill, Inc.,

Chung, Young. *Art of Oriental Embroidery*, New York; Charles Scribner's Sons, 1979

Cox, Warren. *Pottery and Porcelain*, New York, Crown Pub. Co.

Hobson, R.L. *Chinese Pottery and Porcelain*, New York; Dover Publications, Inca. 1976

Jenys, S. *Later Chinese Porcelain*, New York, 1965

Lane, Richard. *Images From The Floating World*, Tabard Press, New York, 1978

Macintosh, Duncan. *Chinese Blue and White*. North Pomfret, Vermont: David and Charles Inc., 1977

Morse, Edward. *Japanese Homes and Their Surroundings*, New York; Dover Publications, Inc. 1961

National Palace Museum. *Chinese Cultural Art Treasures*. National Palace Museum Series, Taipei, 1969

Teng Shu P'ing. *One Hundred Jades From The Lantien Shanfang Collection*, Chinese and English text, Taipei, 1995

Wang Shixiang, *Classic Chinese Furniture*, Chicago, 1991

APPENDIX C
CHRONOLOGICAL TABLE

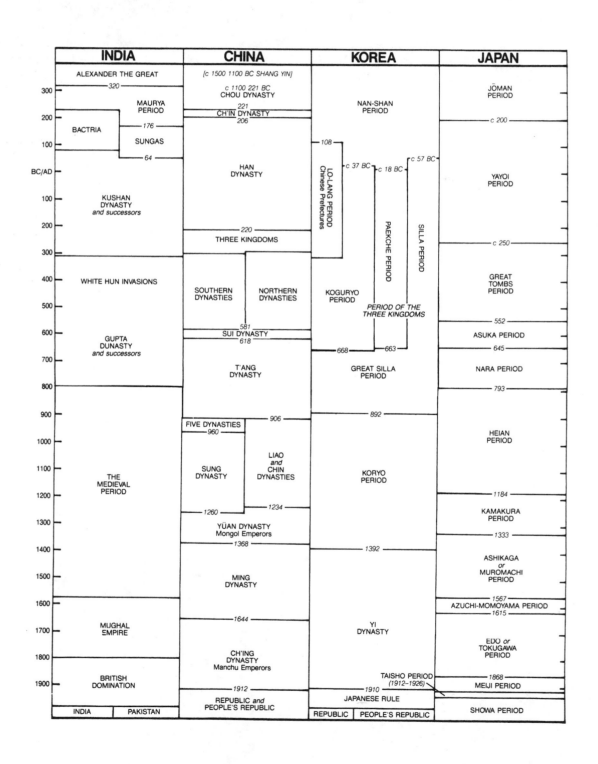

	INDIA	CHINA	KOREA	JAPAN
300	ALEXANDER THE GREAT — 320 —	*[c 1500 1100 BC SHANG YIN]* *c 1100 221 BC* CHOU DYNASTY		JŌMON PERIOD
200	MAURYA PERIOD	221 CH'IN DYNASTY 206	NAN-SHAN PERIOD	*c 200*
100	BACTRIA — 176 — SUNGAS	HAN DYNASTY	108	
BC/AD	— 64 —		*c 37 BC* *c 18 BC* *c 57 BC*	YAYOI PERIOD
100	KUSHAN DYNASTY *and successors*		LO-LANG PERIOD Chinese Prefectures PAEKCHE PERIOD SILLA PERIOD	
200		220		
300	WHITE HUN INVASIONS	THREE KINGDOMS		*c 250*
400		SOUTHERN DYNASTIES NORTHERN DYNASTIES	KOGURYO PERIOD	GREAT TOMBS PERIOD
500			*PERIOD OF THE THREE KINGDOMS*	
600	GUPTA DUNASTY *and successors*	581 SUI DYNASTY 618	668 663	552 ASUKA PERIOD 645
700		T'ANG DYNASTY	GREAT SILLA PERIOD	NARA PERIOD
800				793
900	THE MEDIEVAL PERIOD	906 FIVE DYNASTIES 960	892	HEIAN PERIOD
1000				
1100		SUNG DYNASTY LIAO *and* CHIN DYNASTIES	KORYO PERIOD	
1200				1184
1300		1260 1234 YÜAN DYNASTY Mongol Emperors		KAMAKURA PERIOD 1333
1400		1368	1392	ASHIKAGA *or* MUROMACHI PERIOD
1500		MING DYNASTY		
1600	MUGHAL EMPIRE	1644	YI DYNASTY	1567 AZUCHI-MOMOYAMA PERIOD 1615 EDO *or* TOKUGAWA PERIOD
1700				
1800	BRITISH DOMINATION	CH'ING DYNASTY Manchu Emperors	TAISHO PERIOD *(1912–1926)*	1868
1900		1912	1910	MEIJI PERIOD
	INDIA PAKISTAN	REPUBLIC *and* PEOPLE'S REPUBLIC	JAPANESE RULE REPUBLIC PEOPLE'S REPUBLIC	SHOWA PERIOD

APPENDIX D
CHINESE DYNASTIC
CHRONOLOGICAL TABLE

———————————●———————————

Neolithic . . . . .10th-early 1st millenium BC
Shang Dynasty . . . . .16th Century-c.1050 BC
Zhou Dynasty . . . . .c.1050-221 BC
Qin Dynasty .221-206 BC
Han Dynasty . . . . .206 BC-AD 220
Three Kingdoms . . . . .AD 220-265
Jin Dynasty . . . . .AD 265-420
Southern and Northern Dynasties . . . . .AD 420-589
Sui Dynasty . . . . .AD 581-618
Tang Dynasty . . . . .AD 618-907
Five Dynasties . . . . .AD 907-960
Liao Dynasty . . . . .AD 907-1125
Song Dynasty . . . . .AD 960-1279
  Northern Song . . . . .AD 960-1127
  Southern Song . . . . .AD 1127-1279
Xixia Dynasty . . . . .AD 1038-1227
Jin Dynasty . . . . .AD 1115-1234
Yuan Dynasty . . . . .AD 1279-1368
Ming Dynasty . . . . .AD 1368-1644
  Hongwu . . . . .AD 1368-1398
  Jianwen . . . . .AD 1399-1402
  Yongle . . . . .AD 1403-1424
  Hongxi .AD 1425
  Xuande . . . . .AD 1426-1435

Zhengtong . . . . .AD 1435-1449
Jingtai .AD 1450-1456
Tianshun . . . . .AD 1457-1464
Chenhua . . . . .AD 1465-1487
Hongzhi . . . . .AD 1488-1505
Zhengde . . . . .AD 1506-1521
Jiajing .AD 1522-1566
Longqing . . . . .AD 1567-1572
Wanli .AD 1573-1619
Taichang .AD 1620
Tianqi .AD 1621-1627
Chongzhen . . . . .AD 1628-1644
Qing Dynasty . . . . .AD 1644-1911
Shunzhi . . . . .AD 1644-1661
Kangxi . . . . .AD 1662-1722
Yongzheng . . . . .AD 1723-1735
Qianlong . . . . .AD 1736-1795
Jiaqing . . . . .AD 1796-1820
Daoguang . . . . .AD 1821-1850
Xianfeng . . . . .AD 1851-1861
Tongzhi . . . . .AD 1862-1874
Guangxu AD1875-1908
Xuantong . . . . .AD 1909-1911

APPENDIX E
SPELLING AND PRONUNCIATION OF TERMS

●——————————————

CHINESE

The letters in the left-hand columns below are from the Pinyin system currently being used to romanize the Chinese language. The letters in the right hand columns are from the standard Wade-Giles system. For a summary of common terms as they appear in each system, see the more extensive table which follows the spelling key.

Note that collectors tend to use whichever system suits them best. Both are acceptable; both have been used in this guide.

SPELLING KEY

Initial		Termination	
Pinyin	**Wade-Giles**	**Pinyin**	**Wade-Giles**
b	p	an	en
p	p′	e	o
d	t′	i	ih
g	k	i (si)	u (ssu)
k	k′	ie	ieh
zh	ch	ong	ung
j	ch	uo	o
ch	ch′	ui	uei
c	ts′, tz′	yi	i
r	j	you	yu
x	hs		

WADE-GILES/PINYIN COMPARISON CHART

DYNASTIES

Pinyin	Wade-Giles	
Shangyin	Shang Yin	B.C. 1600-1027
Zhou	Chou	1027-475
Qin	Ch'in	221-206
Han	Han	206-220 A.D.
Sui	Sui	581-618
Tang	T'ang	618-906
Liao	Liao	916-1125
Song	Sung	960-1279
Jin	Chin	1115-1234
Yuan	Yuan	1279-1368

REIGNS

Pinyin	Wade-Giles	
Ming		
Hongwu	Hung Wu	1368-1398
Yongle	Yung Lo	1402-1423
Xuande	Hsüan Te	1426-1435
Chenghua	Ch'eng Hua	1465-1487
Hongzhi	Hung Chih	1488-1505
Zhengde	Cheng Te	1506-1521
Jaijing	Chia Ching	1522-1566
Longqing	Lung Ch'ing	1567-1572
Wandi	Wan Li	1573-1619
Tianqi	T'ien Ch'i	1621-1627
Chongzheng	Ch'ung Cheng	1628-1643
Qing		
Shunzhi	Shun Chih	1644-1661
Kangxi	K'ang Hsi	1662-1723
Yongzheng	Yung Cheng	1723-1736
Qianlong	Ch'ien Lung	1736-1796
Jiaqing	Chia Ch'ing	1796-1820
Daoguang	Tao Kuang	1821-1850
Xianfeng	Hsien Feng	1851-1861
Tongzhi	T'ung Chih	1862-1874
Guangxu	Kuang Hsü	1875-1908
Xuantong	Hsüan T'ung	1909-1912
Hongxian	Hung Hsien	1916

BRONZES

	Pinyin	Wade-Giles
Vessels:	Ding	Ting
	Li	Li
	Gui	Kuei
	Dou	Tou
	Jue	Chüeh
	Jiao	Chiao
	Jia	Chia
	Gu	Ku
	Zun	Tsun
	Fangyi	Fang-i
	Hu	Hu
	Lei	Lei
Dagger Axe:	Ge	Ko
Thunder pattern:	Leiwen	Lei-wen
Dragon:	Kui	K'uei
Monster mask:	Taotie	T'ao-t'ieh

JADE

	Pinyin	Wade-Giles
Jade:	Yu	Yü
Kingfisher:	Feicuiyu	Fei-ts'ui-yü
Disc:	Di	Pi
Disc:	Huan	Huan
Disc:	Yuan	Yüan
Tube:	Cong	Ts'ung
Sceptre:	Gui	Kuei
Disc:	Xuanji	Hsüan-chi
Grain pattern:	Guwen	Ku-wen
Belt hook:	Daigou	Tai-kou
Sceptre:	Ruyi	Ji-i

CERAMICS

Pinyin	Wade-Giles
Yue	Yüeh
Xing	Hsing
Ding	Ting
Ru	Ju
Guan	Kuan
Longchuan	Lung-ch'uan
Ge	Ko
Cizhou	Tz'u-chou
Jian	Chien
Jizhou	Chi-chou
Jingdezhen	Ching-te-chen
Dehua	Te-hua
Yixing	I-hsing
Yingqing	Ying-ch'ing
Qingbai	Ch'ing-pai
Jihong	Chihung
Sancai	San-ts'ai
Wucai	Wu-ts'ai
Doucai	Tou-ts'ai
Anhua	An-hua
Fahua	Fa-hua
Nianzhi	Nien-chih
Nianzao	Nien-tsao
Yuzhi	Yu-chih
Guyeuxuan	Ku Yüen Hsüen
Guangdong	Kuang-tung

APPENDIX F
CHINESE DYNASTIC MARKINGS

The McKinley Tariff Act of 1891 was instituted in order to provide consumers with the knowledge of what they were buying and where the item was produced. In the original McKinley Tariff Act it was specified that all articles of foreign manufacture would be plainly marked, stamped, branded or labeled in legible English words so as to indicate the country of origin. From 1891 to March 21, 1921, the word Nippon was acceptable as proper marking for country of origin for goods manufactured in Japan, and exported to the United States. Later, Treasury Decision #36989 used the words "gummed label" and "rubber stamp" for the first time. It was always assumed that the use of an affixed sticker on Japanese export wares (Chinese and Korean to a lesser degree) was not initiated until this decision of 1917. However, the word "labeled" in the 1891 Act also indicated an affixed sticker. Therefore, we find that the use of labels has been acceptable as markings for "country of origin" since March 1, 1891. Many wares which are unmarked or marked with Oriental characters, without country of origin (written in English), are not necessarily objects produced prior to 1891.

CHINESE MARKS

Chinese marks can be six-character reign marks written in three vertical rows, or six-character reign marks written in two horizontal rows (see marks). Chinese marks can also be found having four-character markings (the first two characters being omitted (see marks). Chinese marks were generally written in standard script. Seal marks were generally written with a brush. Incised and stamped marks were also used. Although underglaze-blue was generally used for markings, it is not uncommon to find marks in other colors such as gold, orange, reddish orange, etc. In addition to reign marks, hall marks, maker's marks, place marks, commendation marks and symbols were also used.

The reign marks which were copied most often in later periods, and on 20th century reproductions,

include: Yongle (Yung Lo), Xuande (Hsuan Te), Chenghua (Cheng Hua), Wanli (Wan Li), Kangxi (K'ang Hsi), Yongzheng (Yung Cheng), Qianlong (Ch'ien Lung), and Daoguang (Tao Kuang).

MING DYNASTY:

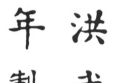

Hung Wu
Hongwu
(1368-1398)

Hung Wu (seal form)
Hongwu
(1368-1398)

Yung Lo
Yongle
(1403-1424)

Yung Lo (archaic form)
Yongle
(1403-1424)

Hsuan Te
Xuande
(1426-1435)

Hsuan Te (seal form)
Xuande
(1426-1435)

大明成化年製
Ch'eng Hua
Chenghua
(1465-1487)

成化 (seal form)
Ch'eng Hua (seal form)
Chenghua
(1465-1487)

CH'ING DYNASTY:

大清順治年製
Shun Chih
Shunzhi
(1644-1661)

Shun Chih (seal form)
Shunzhi
(1644-1661)

大明弘治年製
Hung Chih
Hongzhi
(1488-1505)

大明正德年製
Ch'eng Te
Zhengde
(1506-1521)

大清康熙年製
K'ang Hsi
Kangxi
(1662-1722)

K'ang Hsi (seal form)
Kangxi
(1644-1722)

大明嘉靖年製
Chia Ching
Jiajing
(1522-1566)

大明隆慶年製
Lung Ch'ing
Longqing
(1567-1572)

大清雍正年製
Yung Cheng
Yongzheng
(1723-1735)

Yung Cheng (seal form)
Yongzheng
(1723-1735)

大明萬曆年製
Wan Li
Wanli
(1573-1619)

曆 (archaic form)
Wan Li (archaic form)
Wanli
(1573-1619)

大清乾隆年製
Ch'ien Lung
Qianlong
(1736-1795)

Ch'ien Lung (seal form)
Qianlong
(1736-1795)

大明天啟年製
T'ien Ch'i
Tainqi
(1621-1627)

崇禎年製
Ch'ung Chen
Chongzhen
(1628-1644)

年製 嘉慶

Chia Ch'ing
Jiaqing
(1796-1820)

Chia Ch'ing (seal form)
Jiaqing
(1796-1820)

治年製 大清同

T'ung Chih
Tongzhi
(1862-1874)

T'ung Chih (seal form)
Tongzhi
(1862-1874)

光年製 大清道

Tao Kuang
Daoguang
(1821-1850)

Tao Kuang (seal form)
Daoguang
(1821-1850)

緒年製 大清光

Kuang Hsü
Guangxu
(1874-1908)

Kuang Hsü (seal form)
Guangxu
(1874-1908)

豐年製 大清咸

Hsien Feng
Xianfeng
(1851-1861)

Hsien Feng (seal form)
Xianfeng
(1851-1861)

統年製 大清宣

Hsuan T'ung
Xuantong
(1909-1911)

年製 洪憲

Hsuan T'ung
Xuantong
(1909-1911)

APPENDIX G
CHINESE DATE MARKS FOUND ON INSIDE-PAINTED SNUFF BOTTLES

甲子	乙丑	丙寅	丁卯	戊辰	己巳	庚午
1744, 1804	1745, 1805	1746, 1806	1747, 1807	1748, 1808	1749, 1809	1750, 1810
1864, 1924	1865, 1925	1866, 1926	1867, 1927	1868, 1928	1869, 1929	1870, 1930
辛未	壬申	癸酉	甲戌	乙亥	丙子	丁丑
1751, 1811	1752, 1812	1753, 1813	1754, 1814	1755, 1815	1756, 1816	1757, 1817
1871, 1931	1872, 1932	1873, 1933	1874, 1934	1875, 1935	1876, 1936	1877, 1937
戊寅	己卯	庚辰	辛巳	壬午	癸未	甲申
1758, 1818	1759, 1819	1760, 1820	1761, 1821	1762, 1822	1763, 1823	1764, 1824
1878, 1938	1879, 1939	1880, 1940	1881, 1941	1882, 1942	1883, 1943	1884, 1944
乙酉	丙戌	丁亥	戊子	己丑	庚寅	辛卯
1765, 1825	1766, 1826	1767, 1827	1768, 1828	1769, 1829	1770, 1830	1771. 1831
1885, 1945	1886, 1946	1887, 1947	1888, 1948	1889, 1949	1890, 1950	1891, 1951
壬辰	癸巳	甲午	乙未	丙申	丁酉	戊戌
1772, 1832	1773, 1833	1774, 1834	1775, 1835	1776, 1836	1777, 1837	1778, 1838
1892, 1952	1893, 1953	1894, 1954	1895, 1955	1896, 1956	1897, 1957	1898, 1958
己亥	庚子	辛丑	壬寅	癸卯	甲辰	乙巳
1779, 1839	1780, 1840	1781, 1841	1782, 1842	1783, 1843	1784, 1844	1785, 1845
1899, 1959	1900, 1960	1901, 1961	1902, 1962	1903, 1963	1904, 1964	1905, 1965
丙午	丁未	戊申	己酉	庚戌	辛亥	壬子
1786, 1846	1787, 1847	1788, 1848	1789, 1849	1790, 1850	1791, 1851	1792, 1852
1906, 1966	1907, 1967	1908, 1968	1909, 1969	1910, 1970	1911, 1971	1912, 1972
癸丑	甲寅	乙卯	丙辰	丁巳	戊午	己未
1793, 1853	1794, 1854	1795, 1855	1796, 1856	1797, 1857	1798, 1858	1799, 1859
1913, 1973	1914, 1974	1915, 1975	1916, 1976	1917, 1977	1918, 1978	1919, 1979
庚申	辛酉	壬戌	癸亥			
1800, 1860	1801, 1861	1802, 1862	1803, 1863			
1920, 1980	1921, 1981	1922, 1982	1923, 1983			

Appendix H
Designs Used in
Chinese Decorative Arts

Insignia of Nobles, 1759-1912

For Emperor and Twelve Ranks

Emperor:

Large pearl on Hat-spike, or Hat-knob.

Dragon Robe: usually bright, or clear, yellow; some all blue known; at least one red one. Four front-facing five-clawed dragons on upper part and five profile ones on lower part. The "Twleve Symbols." Five-coloured clouds. The Eight Buddhist Symbols on border.

Coat: purple-black, with four medallions, each with a front-facing five-clawed gold dragon. Sun and Moon on shoulder medallions. Shou character on breast and back medallions.

Heir Apparent:

Ruby on Hat-spike, ruby* or coral on Hat-knob.

Dragon Robe: Same as his father's but "apricot yellow" and without the "Twelve Symbols."

Coat (p'u-fu): Like his father's but without the symbols or shou.

Princes:

All wore Ruby on Hat-spike, ruby* or coral on Hat-knob, and Dragon Medallions on their coats.

1st Degree

Dragon Robe: same as Heir Apparent's but "gold yellow," and without the five-coloured clouds.

P'u-fu: Four Medallions; two with front-facing five-clawed dragons, front and back. Two with profile ones, on shoulders.

2nd Degree

Dragon Robe: same as above.

P'u-fu: Four Medallions; all with profile five-clawed dragons.

3rd Degree

Dragon Robe: same, but "Indigo Blue."

P'u-fu: Two Medallions; with front facing four-clawed dragons (mang), front and back.

4th Degree

Dragon Robe: same as above.

P'u-fu: Two Medallions; with profile four-clawed dragons (mang), front and back.†

Imperial Dukes, Marquises, Earls, and Sons-in-law of 1st Degree Princes:

All wore Ruby on Hat-spike, and ruby* or coral on Hat-knob. Squares, not Medallions, front and back on their coats, with the front-facing four-clawed dragon.

A square with a five-clawed dragon is that of a Duke with an extra claw added by favour of the Emperor.

Nobles of 9th, 10th, 11th, and 12th Degrees:

Wore mandarin squares like those for the four highest military officials, with the unicorn (ch'i-lin), lion, leopard, and tiger, respectively.

---

*This ruby was often just clear red glass.

†Cammann: "The Development of the Mandarin Square," *HFAS*, Vol. 8, p. 92.

INSIGNIA OF OFFICIALS*

Classes of Officials	Round Hat Knob Worn with the Dragon Robe and a small jewel on the brim at front of hat	Insignia of the "Mandarin Squares"	
		Civil Officers, birds	Military officers, animals
1st Degree	Ruby or transparent red stone (in theory); in practice usually coral, plain. And a brilliant pearl.	Manchurin Crane	Unicorn (Ch'i-lin)
2nd Degree	Red coral, or opaque red stone, engraved. And a small red stone.	Golden Pheasant	Lion
3rd Degree	Sapphire or transparent blue stone. And a small red stone.	Malay Peacock	Leopard
4th Degree	Lapis lazuli or opaque blue stone. And a small blue stone.	Wild Goose	Tiger
5th Degree	Crystal or transparent white stone. And a small blue stone.	Silver Pheasant	Black Bear
6th Degree	White opaque stone. And a small blue stone.	Lesser Egret	Tiger Cat (Panther)?
7th Degree	Crystal or transparent white stone but smaller than Degree 5. For simple ceremonies a plain gold knob,	Mandarin Duck	Tiger Cat (Panther)?
8th Degree	Gold, chased wtih flowers in relief.	Quail	Seal, lit: "Sea Horse"
9th Degree	Silver, engraved. But for ceremonies of the ordinary kind he would wear a gold hat-knob, either plain or engraved.	Paradise Flycatcher	Rhinocerous

* From Le P. Guy Boulais: *Manuel du Code Chinois*, Ts. of Kuang Hsü Ed. 1890, pp. 380-391 (Variétés Sinologiques, No. 55, Shanghi, 1924); Thos. Taylor Meadow: *Desultory Notes on Gov. and People of China*, 1847; and Cammann, *HFAS*, Vol. 8, pp. 104-106.

THE EIGHT BUDDHIST SYMBOLS OF HAPPY AUGURY
(OF INDIAN ORIGIN)

1. The Canopy, Symbol of a Monarch; Shelters all Living Beings.

2. A Lotus Flower, Symbol of Purity; rising unsullied through muddy water.

3. The State Umbrella, Symbol of an incorruptible Official.

4. The Sacred Vase, which holds the Amrita, or Water of Life. Rebus: P'ing (vase) for P'ing (peace).

5. A Conch Shell, Symbolizing the Voice of Buddha calling to Worship.

6. A Pair of Fish, Symbol of Domestic Felicity, and of Fertility.

7. The Wheel of the Law, or Kharma; the ever-turning wheel of Transportation.

8. The Endless Knot; "Intestines," a Symbol of Longevity.

CHARACTERS USED AS ORNAMENTAL DESIGNS

Various Forms of the Character Shou, "Longevity." In some cases other auspicious characters seem incorporated in the design, such as wan, "10,000," hsi, "joy, " and chi, "luck."

The Shuang-Hsi character, or "Double Joy," a favourite Wedding Symbol.

FLOWERS OF THE FOUR SEASONS

Prunus—Winter   Tree Peony—Spring   Lotus—Summer   Chrysanthemum—Autumn

ATTRIBUTES OF THE EIGHT TAOIST IMMORTALS

1. Sword of Lü Tung-pin

2. The Double Gourd & Crutch of Li T'ieh-kuai

3. The Lotus Pod of Ho Hsien Ku

4. The Flute of Han Hsiang-tzu

5. The Bamboo Tube & Rods of Chang Kuo Lao

6. The Fan of Chung-li Chüan

7. The Castanets of Ts'ao Kuo-ch'iu

8. The Basket of Peaches (or Flowers) of Lan Ts'ai-ho

MISCELLANEOUS SYMBOLS AND DESIGNS

1. The Ling-chih Fungus, Symbol of Longevity, because when dried it keeps a long time.

2. A Sceptre called ju-i, "as you wish," with a head like the Longevity Fungus. The swastika stands for wan, "10,000." Rebus: "May you have everything you wish."

3. A Scroll Motive in the shape of a ju-i Sceptre Head, and conveying the same meaning, "good wishes for a Long Life as you desire."

4. Butterfly, tieh, stands for tieh, "70 years old;" also a Symbol of Conjugal Felicity.

5. The Swastika-Fret. The Swastika is a mystic Symbol of Buddha's Heart.

6. Crane, Symbol of Long Life, usual attendant of Shou Lao, the God of Longevity.

7. A Bat (fu) for Happiness (fu), with a Swastika, wan "10,000." Rebus: "May you have the greatest joy."

8. An Ingot, ting, of silver, tied with ribbon, stands for ting, to fix. Rebus: "May it be fixed (as you desire)."

9. A Bat (fu) for Happiness (fu), with the peaches of Longevity. Rebus: "May you live long and be happy."

10. Orchid, much worn by the Empress Dowager, who had been called "The Orchid."

11. Narcissus, Flower of the New Year.

12. A Buddha-hand Citron, Symbol of Good Luck.

SIX OF THE EIGHT PRECIOUS THINGS OF ANCIENT LORE

Two Lozenges

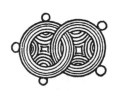

Two "Cash"

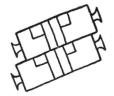

A Pair of Books

A Jewel

A Musical Stone of Jade

A Pair of Rhinocerous Horn Cups

The Painting and the Artesmia Leaf, which complete the Eight; are rarely depicted on Chinese robes.

TWELVE SYMBOLS OF THE OFFICIAL ROBE

1. Sun

2. Moon

3. Constellation

4. Mountain

5. Dragon

6. Flowery Bird

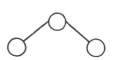

7. Temple Cups

8. Water Weed

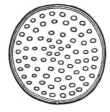

9. Millet

10. Fire

11. Axe

12. Symbol of Distinction (Fu)

CLOUD FORMS ON THE MANCHU ROBES

1. K'ang Hsi

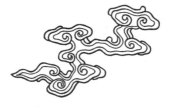

2. Ch'ien Lung

3. Ch'ien Lung (and later)

4. Tao Kuang

5. Hsien Fêng

6. Kuang Hsü

APPENDIX I
JAPANESE DYNASTIC MARKINGS

●

JAPANESE MARKS

The Japanese marks and seals can be maker's names, date marks, place marks, etc. They too were copied, forged, bartered, etc. In addition, Chinese reign marks can be found on Japanese wares including Imari.

The characters for "Great Japan" were not incorporated into Japanese marks until the Meiji period.

GLOSSARY

Bijin—Beautiful girl.

Cha no yu—Tea ceremony.

Cha wan—Tea bowl.

Chaire—Tea caddy.

Conventional—Traditional-style of design.

Diaper—Repetitive pattern.

Fundame—A matte gold lacquer ground.

Gofun—Powdered oyster shell.

Hiramakie—Lacquer designs in low relief.

Kakemono—Hanging scroll.

Karako—Chinese children depicted in Japanese art.

Kiku—Chrysanthemum.

Kogo—Box for incense.

Koro—Incense burner.

Namban—Items with European influence.

Rakan (Lohan)—Buddhist disciples.

Ruyi—Scepter or staff.

Shibayama—Decorative inlay work.

Takamakie—Raised lacquer sprinkled with metallic powder to form high relief designs.

Zogan—Inlay as applied to decorative designs on metalwork.

JAPANESE PRONUNCIATION

a as in father
e as in hay
i as in meet
o as in no
u and in flue
g as in go
j as in gin
Example: Netsuke is pronounced *Net Skay* (When u precedes k or g, it becomes practically silent.)

YEAR PERIODS (NENGO)

Characters		Name of Period	Commenced A.D.
永	應	O-ei	1394
長	正	Shocho	1428
享	永	Eikio	1429
吉	嘉	Kakitsu	1441
安	文	Bun-an	1444
德	宝	Hotoku	1449
德	享	Kotoku	1452

Characters	Name of Period	Commenced A.D.	Characters	Name of Period	Commenced A.D.
正康 正禄 正 正 仁 明 享 德 應 龜 正 永 禄 文 治 禄	長 寬 文 應 文 長 延 明 文 永 大 享 天 弘 永	Kosho	Genki	1570
	Choroku	1457		Tensho	1573
	Kwansho	1460		Bunroku	1592
	Bunsho	1466		Keicho	1596
	Onin	1467		Genna	1615
	Bunmei	1469		Kwanei	1624
	Choko	1487		Shoho	1644
	Entoku	1489		Keian	1648
	Meio	1492		Jo-o	1652
	Bunki	1501		Meireki	1655
	Eisho	1504		Manji	1658
	Daiei	1521		Kwambun	1661
	Koroku	1528		Empo	1673
	Tembun	1532		Tenna	1681
	Koji	1555		Jokio	1684
	Eirko	1558		Genroku	1688

Characters	Name of Period	Commenced A.D.
永 宝 德 正 保 享 文 元 保 寛 享 延 延 寛 曆 宝 和 明 永 安 明 天 政 宝 和 享	Hoei	1704
	Shotoku	1711
	Kioho	1716
	Gembun	1736
	Kwampo	1741
	Enkio	1744
	Kwanen	1748
	Horeki	1751
	Meiwa	1764
	Anei	1772
	Temmei	1781
	Kwansei	1789
	Kiowa	1801

Characters	Name of Period	Commenced A.D.
化 文 政 文 保 天 化 弘 永 嘉 政 安 延 萬 父 文 治 元 應 慶 治 明 大 正 昭 和	Bunkwa	1804
	Bunsei	1818
	Tempo	1830
	Kokwa	1844
	Kaei	1848
	Ansei	1854
	Manen	1860
	Bunkiu	1861
	Genji	1864
	Keio	1865
	Meiji	1868
	Taisho	1912
	Showa	1926

APPENDIX J
JAPANESE POTTERY AND PORCELAIN MARKS

●

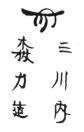     

Zoshuntei maker   Hichozan Shimpo maker   Kutani (place name)   Mikawaji maker (maker and place)   Kutani/Kayo (place name)

Mori Chikara, Mikawachi (maker and place)   Shimodo maker   Hirado   Found on Hirado wares   Yamaka maker

Zoshuntei maker   Happiness   Banko (impressed mark)   Banko (impressed mark)   Yusetsu maker (Banko)

Gozan maker   Siekozan maker   Kozan (Makuzu) maker   Denka maker   Myakawa Kozan maker

Fuyeki maker
(Banko)

Banko (impressed marks)

Banko—
Tekizan maker

Ganto—Sanzin maker

Kutani
(place name)

The Yofu factory

Banko ware

Kutani (place name)

Fuyeki maker

Kutani (place name)

Fukagawa maker

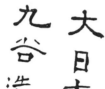

Kiokuzan maker

Yuzan maker

Fukagawa maker

Kochoken maker

Koko maker

Tsuji/Tokyo, Japan
(maker and place mark)

Kinko factory maker

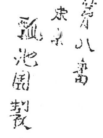
Hiocheyen
Tokyo maker

Gosaburo maker

Makuzu Kozan maker

Meizan maker

Kenya maker

Ryozan maker

Kitei maker

Inuoe Ryosai

Inuoe Ryosai

Inuoe Ryosai

Iwazo maker

Zoroku maker

Hichibeye maker

Sahei maker

Scifu maker

Raku

Eiraku maker

Eiraku maker

Kanzan Denshichi maker

Makuzu Kozan maker

Shuzan maker

Kinunken maker

Taizan maker

Taizan maker

Taizan maker

Bizan maker

Seikozan maker

Shuhei maker

Kai maker

Kawamoto Hansuke maker

Hozan maker

Awata (place mark)

Ryozan

Kinkozan

Gyokuzan maker

Kenzan

Tozan maker

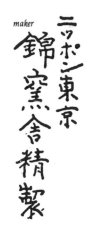
maker
ニッポン東京
錦窯舎精製

Kinsho Company,
Tokyo (maker and
place mark)

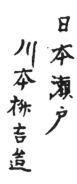
日本瀬戸
川本栗吉造

Kinkozan

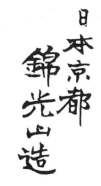
日本京都
錦光山造

Kawamoto Masukichi Rokubeye maker
Maker/Seto, Japan

大日本

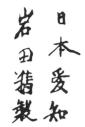
日本愛知
岩田舊製

Iwata, Aichi, Japan

Toyosuke maker

Eizan maker

尾張

Owari (place mark)

北半製 奇陶軒

Hokuhan maker

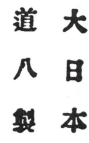
大日本
道八製

Dohachi

七寶會社

Nagoya (place mark)

大日本
幹山製

Kanzan maker

不破素堂筆画

Fuwa Sodo maker

Nakajima maker

嵐山

Ide maker

川本
枡吉

Kawamoto
Masukichi maker

薩摩

Satsuma
(place mark)

Satsuma
(place mark)

Hoju maker

Hohei maker

Hoyei maker

APPENDIX K
MARKS, SEALS, AND SIGNATURES ON WOOD BLOCK PRINTS

PUBLISHERS' MARKS

PUBLISHER

1. Katoya	41. Urokogataya
2. Ezakiya Kichibei	42. Tsujiokaya Bunsuke
3. Mikawaya Kihei	43. Nishimuraya Yohachi
4. Maruya Kusaemon	44. Moriya Jihei
5. Mikawaya Rihei	45. Iseya Magobei
6. Sugiya Kihei	46. Sanoya Kihei
7. Tsuruya Kiemon	47. Yamamotoya Heikichi
8. Tsuruya Kiemon	48. Shimizuya
9. Tsuruya Kiemon	49. Maruya Jinpachi
10. Tsuruya Kinsuke	50. Takeuchi Magohachi
11. Tsuruya Kichizo	51. Etsuke
12. Tsuruya Juzaburo	52. Itoya Yohei
13. Maruya Kiyojiro	53. Iseya Tetsukiro
14. Yamadaya Shojiro	54. Iseya Chubei
15. Fujiokaya Hikotaro	55. Ibaya Sensaburo
16. Echigoya Keisuke	56. Gusokuya Kahei
17. Iseya Sanjiro	57. Daikokuya
18. Nishimuraya Yohachi	58. Wakabayashiya Kiyobei
19. Iwatoya Kisaburo	59. Okuroya Kinnosuke
20. Takatsuya Itsuke	60. Hiranoya Heisuke
21. Ningyoya Takichi	61. Ogawa Heisuke
22. Kagaya Yasubei	62. Sumiyoshiya Masagoro
23. Enshuya Hikobei	63. Wakasaya Yoichi
24. Soshuya Yohei	64. Maritaya Shigezo
25. Enshuya Matabei	65. Joshuya Shigezo
26. Kagaya Yoshibei	66. Yamaguchiya Tobei
27. Murataya Jirobei	67. Kawaguchiya Uhei
28. Kawachiya Chozo	68. Kagiya Hanjiro
29. Eirakuya Bunsuke	69. Aito
30. Izumiya Ichibei	70. Enshuya Yasubei
31. Kikuya Kozaburo	71. Owariya Kiyoshichi
32. Emiya Kichiemon	72. Tamaya Sosuke
33. Izuymiya Ichibei	73. Mokuya Sojiro
34. Iwatoya Genpachi	74. Tsujiya Yasubei
35. Ebiya Rinnosuke	75. Uwoya Eikichi
36. Kikuya Ichibei	76. Sagamiya
37. Soneya Ginjiro	77. Hirookaya Kosuke
38. Kazusaya	78. Tenki
39. Ezakiya Tatsuzo	79. Minatoya Kohei
40. Nishimuraya Yohachi	80. Morimoto Junzaburo

DATE AND CENSOR SEALS

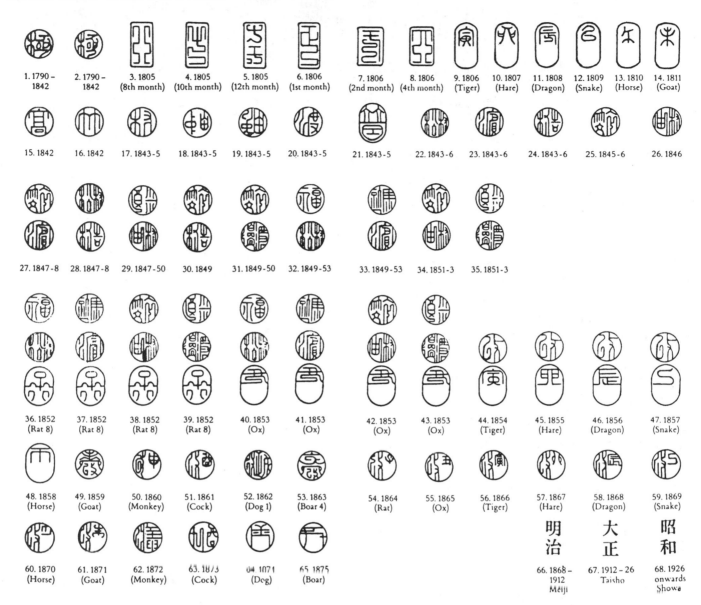

Censor seals and date seals often help to date the prints. The kiwame seal (1,2) was introduced in the ninth month of 1790 and occurs on most prints until 1842. In 1805 additional seals showing the number of the month of publication appear and continue until the fourth month of 1806 (3-8). From the fifth month of 1806 until 1811 the year is designated by its zodiacal symbol with a numeral for the month (9-14, numerals omitted to avoid confusion). Between 1811-14 various gyoji seals appear (not illustrated). From the seventh month of 1842 to the end of 1846 single nanushi censor seals appear (15-26) and from early 1847-1852 these occur in pairs (27-35). From the sec-

ond month of 1852 to the eleventh month of 1853 an added date seal gives the year and month (35-43). From the last month of 1853 to the end of 1857 the aratame seal replaces the nanushi seals (44-47). In 1858 the date seal appears alone (48). From 1859-71 a single seal combining aratame, the zodiacal year symbol and a number denoting the month (mostly omitted from the table) occurs (49-62). Between 1872 and 1875 a simple year-month date seal is found (63-65). From 1876 formal censorship ceased but dates are often given by reference to the years of the Emperor's reign (66-68).

Wood Block Artists' Signatures (Ukiyo-e)

芦廣 *Ashihiro*	万里 *Banri*	英泉 *Eisen*	寄志 *Enshi*	春信 *Harunobu*	久信 *Hisanobu*	北洲 *Hokushu*
芦清 *Ashikiyo*	文調 *Buncho*	英山 *Eizan*	房種 *Fusatane*	春重 *Harushige*	北溪 *Hokkei*	北翠 *Hokutsui*
芦国 *Ashikuni*	大浪 *Bunro*	栄之 *Eishi*	岳亭 *Gakutei*	春次 *Haruji*	北馬 *Hokuba*	北英 *Hokuei*
芦麿 *Ashimaro*	長喜 *Choki*	栄昌 *Eisho*	五柳 *Gokyo*	秀麿 *Hidemaro*	北我 *Hokuga*	廣重 *Keisai (Eisen)*
芦幸 *Ashiyuki*	榮壽 *Eiju*	栄水 *Eisui*	五 *Goshichi*	廣景 *Hirokage*	北鵞 *Hoku-I*	菊久麿 *Kikumaru*
萬亀 *Banki*	栄里 *Eiri*				北寿 *Hokuju*	
兜器 *Banki II*	水理 *Eiri* *(Rekisentei)*	艶鏡 *Enkyo*	崋山 *Hanzan*	廣重 *Hiroshige*	北斎 *Hokusai*	清廣 *Kiyohiro*

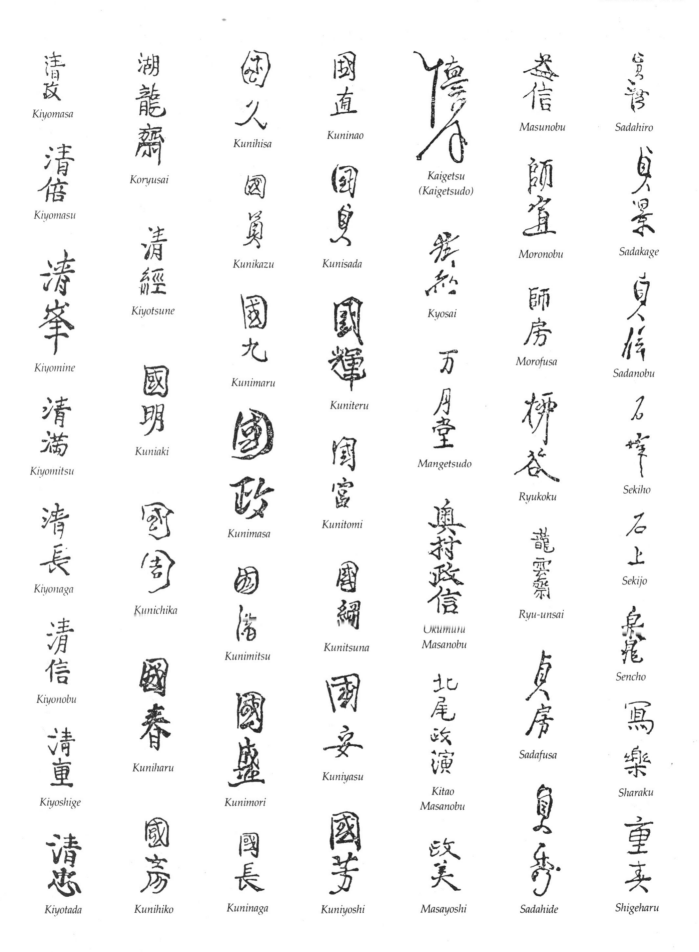

清政
Kiyomasa

清倍
Kiyomasu

清峯
Kiyomine

清満
Kiyomitsu

清長
Kiyonaga

清信
Kiyonobu

清重
Kiyoshige

清忠
Kiyotada

湖龍齋
Koryusai

清經
Kiyotsune

國明
Kuniaki

國周
Kunichika

國春
Kuniharu

國芳
Kunihiko

國久
Kunihisa

國員
Kunikazu

國九
Kunimaru

國政
Kunimasa

國光
Kunimitsu

國盛
Kunimori

國長
Kuninaga

國直
Kuninao

國貞
Kunisada

國輝
Kuniteru

國富
Kunitomi

國綱
Kunitsuna

國安
Kuniyasu

國芳
Kuniyoshi

懷月堂
Kaigetsu
(Kaigetsudo)

暁齋
Kyosai

万月堂
Mangetsudo

奥村政信
Okumura
Masanobu

北尾政演
Kitao
Masanobu

政美
Masayoshi

益信
Masunobu

師宣
Moronobu

師房
Morofusa

柳谷
Ryukoku

龍雲齋
Ryu-unsai

貞房
Sadafusa

貞秀
Sadahide

貞廣
Sadahiro

貞景
Sadakage

貞信
Sadanobu

石樵
Sekiho

石上
Sekijo

象麗
Sencho

寫樂
Sharaku

重春
Shigeharu

Shigemasa

Shinsai

Shunro
(later Hokusai)

Sori (Hokusai)

Toyoharu

Toyomasa

Yoshikazu

Shigenaga

Shucho

Shunsen
(Katsukawa)

Sugakudo

Toyohide

Toyonobu

Yoshikuni

Shigenobu

Shuncho

Shunsen
(Kashosai)

Sukenobu

Toyohiro

Toyoshige

Yoshimaru

Shigenobu
(Yanagawa)

Shundo

Shunsho

Taito
(Hokusai)

Toyohisa

Tsukimaro

Yoshinobu

Shigenobu
(Hiroshige II)

Shunjo

Shuntei

Terushige

Toyokuni
(also used by
Toyokuni II
(Toyoshige)
and
Toyokuni III
(Kunisada))

Utamaro

Shikimaro

Shunko

Shunei

Tominobu

Yoshichika

Yoshitora

Shiko

Shunkyo

Shunzan

Toshinobu

Toyomaru

Yoshiharu

Yoshitoshi

Shunman

APPENDIX L
PRICE LIST FOR 1914 VANTINE CATALOG COLOR PAGES

Price List

All prices quoted are f. o. b. New York

Gold Medallion China

Illustrated on Page 24

	Dozen
Plates, flat, 9½ inch	$15.00
Plates, flat, 8½ inch	14.00
Plates, flat, 8 inch	13.50
Plates, flat, 6½ inch	10.50
Plates, deep, 9½ inch	15.00
Plates, deep, 8½ inch	14.00
Plates, deep, 8 inch	13.50
Plates, deep, 6½ inch	10.50
	Each
Meat Dishes, oblong, 10½ inch	2.00
Meat Dishes, oblong, 11½ inch	2.50
Meat Dishes, oblong, 12½ inch	3.00
Meat Dishes, oblong, 14 inch	4.00
Meat Dishes, oblong, 15 inch	5.25
Meat Dishes, oblong, 16½ inch	6.50
Meat Dishes, oblong, 18½ inch	8.00
Gravy Dishes, with Well, 15½ inch	7.50
Soup Tureen, with Stand, L. S.	13.50
Soup Tureen, with Stand, S. S.	10.00
Covered Dish, oval, 10½ inch	4.00
Covered Dish, square, 9½ inch	4.00
Sauce Tureen with Stand	3.00
Sauce Boat with Stand	4.00
Salad Bowl	4.00
Bakers, oblong, 9 inch	2.00
Bakers, oblong, 10 inch	2.25
Bakers, oblong, 11 inch	2.50
Pickles, Leaf, S. S	.75
Pickles, Leaf, M. S	1.00
Pickles, Leaf, L. S	1.25
Fruit Baskets, with Stand, 8½ inch	4.00
Fruit Baskets, with Stand, 9½ inch	5.00
Fruit Baskets, with Stand, 11 inch	5.25
Nappies, Scalloped, 8½ inch	2.00
Nappies, Scalloped, 9½ inch	2.50
Nappies, Scalloped, 10 inch	3.00
Creamers	1.50
Pitchers, pint	1.75
Mugs, pint	.75
Pitcher, 1½ pint	2.50
Odd Dishes, 4 styles, each	2.50
	Dozen
Coffee Cups and Saucers, low	18.00
Coffee Cups and Saucers, after-dinner	12.00
Tea Cups and Saucers, low	15.00
Tea Cups and Saucers, low	15.00
This quality Hexagon, Fluted and Plain Shapes	
	Each
Tea Pot, straight, L. S	3.50
Tea Pot, straight, S. S	2.50
Bowls, 5 inch	1.00
Bowls, 6 inch	1.50
Bowls, 7 inch	2.25
Sugar, L. S	3.50
Sugar, with handles, S. S	2.00
Punch Bowl, 10 inch	7.50
Punch Bowl, 12 inch	9.00
Punch Bowl, 13½ inch	10.50
Punch Bowl, 15 inch	12.50
Punch Bowl, 16 inch	15.00
Cuspidors, low	3.50
Cuspidors, high, 14 inch	5.00
Cuspidors, high, 15½ inch	7.50

Blue Canton China

Illustrated on page 25

	Dozen
Plates, flat, 10 inch	6.50
Plates, flat, 9 inch	5.00
Plates, flat, 7½ inch	3.25
Plates, flat, 6 inch	2.50
Plates, deep, 10 inch	6.50
Plates, deep, 9 inch	5.00
Plates, deep, 7½ inch	3.25
Plates, deep, 6 inch	2.50
Fine Plates, flat and deep, 6 inch	5.00
Fine Plates, flat and deep, 7½ inch	7.50
Fine Plates, flat and deep, 8½ inch	8.00
Fine Plates, flat and deep, 9½ inch	10.00
Hot Water Plates, uncovered	1.25
Hot Water Plates, covered	1.75
	Each
Meat Dishes, oblong, 10 inch	.90
Meat Dishes, oblong, 11 inch	1.00

Blue Canton China

Continued

	Each
Meat Dishes, oblong, 12 inch	1.25
Meat Dishes, oblong 13 inch	1.50
Meat Dishes, oblong, 14 inch	2.25
Meat Dishes, oblong, 14½ inch	2.50
Meat Dishes, oblong, 15½ inch	3.00
Meat Dishes, oblong, 16 inch	3.75
Meat Dishes, oblong, 17 inch	4.50
Meat Dishes, oblong, 18 inch	6.00
Gravy Dishes, with Well, 14½ inch	4.00
Gravy Dishes, with Well, 15½ inch	5.00
Soup Tureen, with Stand, L. S.	5.00
Soup Tureen, with Stand, S. S.	4.00
Covered Dish, square, 11¼ inch	3.00
Covered Dish, square, 9½ inch	2.00
Covered Dish, square, 8½ inch	1.50
Covered Dish, square, 8 inch	1.50
Covered Dish, oval, 11 inch	3.00
Covered Dish, oval, 10½ inch	2.25
Covered Dish, oval, 9½ inch	1.50
Covered Dish, oval, 9 inch	1.50
Covered Dish, oval, 8 inch	1.25
Sauce Tureen with Stand	1.50
Sauce Boat with Stand, low	1.00
Sauce Boat with Stand, high	1.50
Salad Bowl	2.00
Bakers, oblong, 9 inch	1.00
Bakers, oblong, 10 inch	1.25
Bakers, oblong, 11 inch	1.50
Scallops, round, 9 inch	.90
Scallops, round, 9½ inch	1.25
Scallops, round 10¼ inch	1.50
Bakers, round, 8 inch	1.00
Bakers, round, 9¼ inch	1.25
Bakers, round, 11 inch	1.50
Pickles, leaf, S. S	.40
Pickles, leaf, M. S	.50
Pickles, leaf, L. S	.60
Fruit Baskets, with Stand, 8¾ inch	2.75
Fruit Baskets, with Stand, 9¾ inch	3.25
Fruit Baskets, with Stand, 10¾ inch	3.25
Pitchers, 4 inch	.75
Pitchers, 5 inch	1.00
Pitchers, 1 quart	1.50
Pitchers, 2 quart	2.00
Pitchers, 4 quart	2.50
Odd Dishes, 5 styles	1.50
	Dozen
Individual Butters, 2¼ inch	1.20
Individual Butters, 3 inch	1.50
Individual Butters, 3¾ inch	1.75
	Each
Mugs, 4 inch	.75
Creamers	.75
Bowls, 5 inch	.25
Bowls, 6 inch	.45
Bowls, 7 inch	.75
Bowls, 8 inch	1.00
Bowls, 9 inch	1.25
	Dozen
Coffee Cups and Saucers, extra handled, high 4¼ inch	7.50
Coffee Cups and Saucers, handled, low, 4¼ inch	7.50
Coffee Cups and Saucers, unhandled, 4¼ inch	5.00
Tea Cups and Saucers, extra handled, high, 3¾ inch	7.50
Tea Cups and Saucers, extra handled, high, 3¼ inch	6.50
Tea Cups and Saucers, handled, low, 3¾ inch	7.50
Tea Cups and Saucers, handled, low, 3¼ inch	6.50
Tea Cups and Saucers, unhandled, 3¾ inch	3.50
After Dinnder Coffees, handled, large size, 3 inch	5.00
After Dinner Coffees, handled, small size, 2¼ inch	4.00
	Each
Coffee Pot, L. S	3.00
Coffee Pot, M. S	2.50
Coffee Pot, S. S	2.00
Chocolate Pot, S. S	1.00
Chocolate Pot, M. S	1.25
Chocolate Pot, L. S	1.50
Sugars, handled, S. S	1.00
Sugars, handled, L. S	1.50
Teapot, straight, without Stand, L. S.	1.50
Teapot, straight, without Stand, M. S.	1.25
	Dozen
Fruit Saucers, small size, 4¾ inch	3.60
Fruit Saucers, large size, 5¾ inch	4.20
	Each
Covered Butter, large size	2.00

·A·A·VANTINE·&·CO·Inc·

APPENDIX M
ABOUT THE AUTHOR

Sandra Andacht

Sandra Andacht is the Editor and Publisher of The Orientalia Journal. Her column, "East Meets West," is a regular feature of The Antique Trader Weekly. Her "Orientalia Journal" column appears in many publications including the NEAA News and the NADA Newsletter.

Ms. Andacht has authored several books on Oriental decorative arts as well as numerous articles which have appeared in many publications including: *Interior Design Magazine, Andon, Antique Monthly, The Antique Trader Weekly, Orientalia Journal, etc.*

Sandra Andacht is on the Board of Directors of NADA (National Assoc. of Dealers in Antiques); a Trustee on the Board of The Institute of Appraisal Arts and Sciences; a member of National Association of Personal Property Appraisers (Div. of NADA); a member of NEAA (the New England Appraisers Assoc.)

She is also a faculty member of the Appraisal Studies Programs at New York University, George Washington University (DC), C.W. Post College, Long Island U. Brookville Campus, New York Institute of Technology.

She has lectured at the University of Arkansas in Jonesboro, C.W. Post College, New York University, George Washington University, Yeshiva University (NYC). She has also lectured to the Ukiyo-e Society, the New York Print Club, the Glass Collectors Society of Toledo, the Greater New York Bead Society, etc.

INDEX